Applications of Cognitive Psychology: Problem Solving, Education, and Computing

APPLICATIONS OF COGNITIVE PSYCHOLOGY:
Problem Solving, Education, and Computing

Edited by

DALE E. BERGER
KATHY PEZDEK
The Claremont Graduate School
WILLIAM P. BANKS
Pomona College and The Claremont Graduate School

LAWRENCE ERLBAUM ASSOCIATES, PUBLISHERS
1987   Hillsdale, New Jersey   London

Lawrence Erlbaum Associates, Inc., Publishers
365 Broadway
Hillsdale, New Jersey 07642

Library of Congress Cataloging in Publication Data

Applications of cognitive psychology.

   Includes bibliographies and indexes.
   1. Problem solving.   2. Human information processing.
3. Education—Data processing.   4. Man-machine systems.
5. Computer assisted instruction.   I. Berger, Dale E.
II. Pezdek, Kathy.   III. Banks, William P.
BF441.A63   1986   153.4'3   86-19667
ISBN 0-89859-710-2

Printed in the United States of America
10   9   8   7   6   5   4   3   2

Contents

Preface

In 1981, The Claremont Graduate School held what was to be the first of many annual conferences entitled, "The Claremont Conference on Applied Cognitive Psychology." The purpose of this series of conferences has been to bring together cognitive psychologists from the academic, private, and government sectors who share an interest in applications of cognitive theory and research. It was our hope that these conferences would serve as a vehicle for initiating and maintaining an exchange between researchers in academic and applied settings. Closer to home, we intended these conferences to motivate a greater interest in applied research in cognitive psychology, as well as complement the focus of the Applied Cognitive Psychology Program at The Claremont Graduate School.

The purpose of this volume is to extend our goal and present this work to a larger audience. This volume includes 15 chapters on cognitive psychology applied to topics of problem solving, education, and computing. It is not new for experimental psychologists to study these topics. For example, much of William James' 1890 text, *The Principles of Psychology,* addresses psychological principles relevant to education and learning processes. However, the approach taken in the chapters in this volume is novel in that current theories and methodologies in cognitive psychology have been utilized to study interesting aspects of these real-world behaviors.

The decision to focus this volume on problem solving, education, and computing in no way implies that the range of applications of cognitive psychology is limited to these areas. This choice simply reflects our view that these are domains in which our input as cognitive psychologists is especially relevant. With the proliferation of the computer revolution in schools, in industry, and in the home, the opportunities for cognitive psychologists to study information processing components of this new technology are limitless. On the other hand, in parallel with the success of the computer revolution, students' failure to develop basic problem solving and critical thinking abilities is being recognized as a major educational impediment. This problem has been the focus of national attention.

In this volume, cognitive psychologists present their research and perspectives on these applied topics, and further, they suggest implementations of their findings in applied settings. These research programs are offered as examples of applied cognitive psychology, in which cognitive theory contributes to solving applied problems and the applied problems contribute to the course of development of cognitive theory. We hope that these examples serve to motivate an interest in applied cognitive psychology and promote new areas of application.

the editors

To Peggy, Ed, and Arlene

Applications of Cognitive Psychology: Problem Solving, Education, and Computing

A RANGE OF EDUCATIONAL APPLICATIONS

The first section of the book includes five chapters that highlight a range of educational applications that are of interest to cognitive psychologists. In the first chapter, Kathy Pezdek presents her research on "Television Comprehension as an Example of Applied Research in Cognitive Psychology." She stresses that with children and adults in this country spending more time with television than with any other leisure time activity, it is important to study how we comprehend television and what information we retain from television. Her finding that children's ability to comprehend information presented on television is uncorrelated with reading ability has important implications for presenting educational content, especially to poor readers.

Interest in media processing is also the topic of Patricia Greenfield's chapter, "Electronic Technologies, Education, and Cognitive Development." According to her view, the educational system has developed an overreliance on text as the dominant medium through which education occurs. Her findings support numerous educational advantages for utilizing a broader range of media including television and computer games. For example, she presents support for her view that television viewing develops visual/spatial skills, and that practice with computer games improves problem-solving ability.

The next chapter also focuses on the use of a nontraditional form of media in the classroom, the computer. One specific educational use of computers is the learning of computer programming languages. In their chapter, "Learning Programming Languages: Research and Applications," Richard Mayer, Piraye Bayman, and Jennifer Dyck report some of the findings from their program of research investigating how novices learn computer programming. In particular, they report that novice programmers often have ineffective mental models for how a program operates, they fail to transfer their programming knowledge beyond what is taught and they lack certain cognitive skills that are prerequisite to learning computer programming. Like Greenfield, Mayer and his colleagues have found that some cognitive skills are learned as a byproduct of working with computers. However, they suggest that learning computer programming enhances a specific set of cognitive skills such as procedure comprehension and problem translation. Greenfield claims that computer experience and processing various other forms of media stimulate cognitive development more generally.

As more and more school systems purchase computers for classroom use and incorporate this new educational medium into the curriculum, many questions have arisen regarding how best to utilize these computers. One of these questions has been addressed by David Trowbridge in his chapter, "An Investigation of Groups Working at the Computer." In this chapter, Trowbridge presents his research examining the social and cognitive advantages of having students work on computers individually versus in various sized groups. He reports that there is no need for a computer for each individual student. In fact, there are numerous educational advantages of utilizing task-focused small groups for computer activities.

In the final chapter in this section, we return to a more traditional educational medium, text and the process of reading. In his chapter, "Applying Cognitive Development Theory to the Acquisition of Literacy," George Marsh traces the historical development of numerous approaches to the reading process. These include projects conducted by academic as well as applied researchers. He concludes by describing his work utilizing an information processing approach to study reading, and argues for the advantages of this approach.

Together, the chapters in this section promote a broader view of "education" than is traditionally encountered. These researchers have generally focused on learning skills rather than on the acquisition of declarative knowledge, and have not restricted their interest to the print medium. Productive exchange between research and application is one of the benefits of applied cognitive psychology, in this case leading to findings that have implications for shaping significant aspects of the educational system.

1 Television Comprehension as an Example of Applied Research in Cognitive Psychology

Kathy Pezdek
The Claremont Graduate School

ABSTRACT

This chapter provides a framework for approaching and conducting cognitive psychology research from an applied perspective. Definitions are offered to differentiate *basic* versus *applied research,* and *cognitive applied psychology* versus *applied cognitive psychology.* The development of my own research program examining comprehension and memory for information presented on television is offered as an example that incorporates both the advantages and disadvantages of these various research approaches. By elaborating an alternative to basic research, this chapter aims to encourage cognitive psychologists to step back from their theories and their familiar methodologies and think in practical ways about the behaviors that they are interested in understanding. I assert that there is room in our field to shift the focus in the direction of addressing more interesting applied behaviors without abandoning empirical rigor or theoretical progress.

INTRODUCTION

The goal of this chapter is to provide a framework for approaching and conducting cognitive psychology research from an applied perspective. The development of my own research program examining comprehension and memory for information presented on television is offered as an example of such an approach. This research program, with all of its ups and downs, illustrates the costs and benefits of several different approaches to applied research in cognitive psychol-

3

ogy. I hope that this chapter will consequently motivate a greater interest in and appreciation for the contributions of applied research in cognitive psychology.

COGNITIVE PSYCHOLOGY RESEARCH

Research in the area of cognitive psychology (and other disciplines as well) has traditionally been divided into two categories: (a) basic research and (b) applied research. Simply put, the goal of basic research is to inductively or deductively contribute to the growth of theoretical knowledge in a discipline. The goal of applied research is to come to better understand some interesting real-world behavior. But the real difference between applied and basic research in cognitive psychology is greater than this. As Baddeley (1979) described it, "For many years applied psychology seems to have been regarded either as an occupational net, providing work for those who were not good enough to reach the ethereal heights of 'pure' psychology, or at best as a pardonable perversion practiced among a few eccentric groups of experimental psychologists" (p. 367).

Since the formal origin of the field of cognitive psychology with Broadbent's (1958) classic text, *Perception and Communication,* the large majority of the published research in the field has been basic research. This makes sense in a new field. During the infancy of a field, it is important to develop good theories to provide a structure for the knowledge that is acquired. A theoretical structure successfully provides a firm foundation upon which the field can develop and it also helps to define the parameters of the field. However, the path of development of theory in cognitive psychology is not without criticism, and because cognitive psychology is still such a new field, it is important to consider these critiques and what might be done to respond to them.

The major criticism relevant to the point of this chapter is that despite the proliferation of researchers and research in cognitive psychology over the last few decades, knowledge is not accumulating into an integrated theoretical base in the field. This view has been expressed by Tulving (1979) in his claim that "ours is not yet a cumulative science, . . . we have not yet succeeded in constructing a stable foundation of knowledge and understanding of memory. . . . The progress we have made in the past, therefore, must be regarded as rather modest" (p. 27). A similar position has been taken by Newell (1973), who doubts whether another 30 years of research on isolated phenomena will really advance our understanding of cognitive psychology.

What is the evidence that research in cognitive psychology is not developing a cumulative theoretical knowledge base? Tulving's evidence for his own opinion is largely based on two points of criticism: first, that cognitive psychologists, with their heightened concern for methodological precision, often do experiments on experiments rather than experiments on ideas; and second, that theoretical models have been developed to account for data sets that are too small, in some cases single experiments. Together, these points contribute to segregating rather than integrating the research in cognitive psychology.

Another very convincing line of evidence that the knowledge base in cognitive psychology, and memory in particular, is quite diverse and unfocused has been offered by White (1983). If a field is developing a cumulative knowledge base, then it would be expected that a relatively large and stable source of references would be frequently cited in the literature in that field. White selected the eight most popular textbooks on human memory. The total number of different references (books as well as journal articles) in these eight textbooks was just over 3,500. Of these 3,500 individual references, only .3% (i.e., 10 references) were cited in all eight books!

Similarly disappointing findings were reported by Garfield (1978a, 1978b, 1979). He found that among the approximately 3,000 potentially citable books and articles published in cognitive psychology between 1969 and 1977, only 21 received more than 20 citations a year. Along with these authors, I take the view that if research in cognitive psychology were becoming focused and integrated around a firm theoretical structure in the field, this theoretical structure would be reliably identified in terms of a significant core of frequently cited references, and this apparently is not the case. White refers to this as the "publish-*and*-perish" phenomenon.

What can be done to facilitate the development of a cumulative theoretical knowledge base in cognitive psychology? Several suggestions have been offered by Tulving (1979), Newell (1973), and others in line with utilizing the "strong inferences" notions of Platt (1964) and the principles of a paradigmatic science articulated by Kuhn (1962). These suggestions essentially remind us to follow the method of inductive inference that we all learned in our first research methodology class. This method involves systematically (a) generating alternative hypotheses, (b) devising a critical experiment that excludes one or more of the hypotheses, (c) carrying out the critical experiment, and (d) recycling this procedure making subhypotheses or refining the hypotheses that remain. These reasonable suggestions would have important implications for cognitive psychology. However, this chapter offers an alternative solution to the above problem.

This chapter takes the firm position that theory *is* of central importance to the development of a discipline. Nothing said in this chapter should be misconstrued as promoting an atheoretical approach to cognitive psychology. However, the course of the theoretical development in cognitive psychology has not been encouraging. A number of principals in the field have argued that the plethora of research findings in cognitive psychology is not becoming more integrated or focused around useful theories. We are acquiring more "trees" without acquiring more or better "forests." Given that the large majority of these research findings are from the basic research mold, this chapter suggests that the time has come to encourage a different research mold, specifically that of applied research.

APPLIED RESEARCH IN COGNITIVE PSYCHOLOGY

Applied researchers in cognitive psychology begin by selecting some interesting real-world behavior and try to understand the cognitive processes involved in this behavior. The hope is always that in studying the interesting real-world behavior, sound theoretical advances will be made. But, rather than *beginning* with the theory, as basic researchers do, applied researchers *begin* with an applied problem and either (a) draw on relevant theory or (b) let the theory follow from understanding the applied problem.

Stated differently, if asked, "How would you convince members of Congress to fund your research through the National Science Foundation?" basic and applied researchers would respond differently. A basic researcher would say that if we only better understood theoretically a particular class of cognitive processes, then we would be better able to use this theoretical knowledge to understand a particular relevant real-world behavior. An applied researcher would argue that the particular real-world behavior is an important one to understand cognitively, and that once we better understand the behavior we will (a) be more likely to remediate it and (b) have a better understanding of the underlying theoretical principles. In both cases, advances in theory are valued, and understanding real-world behaviors is valued, but it is a difference in emphasis, and what leads and what follows.

So, what might be gained by encouraging cognitive psychologists to adopt the applied research mold rather than the basic research mold? As Baddeley (1979) put it, "The argument that an understanding of man will inevitably be of great value is a powerful one, but only if you are convinced that what you are doing is making a significant advance in our understanding" (p. 368). Since, with basic research, practical knowledge follows from the theoretical advances, it becomes hard to justify basic research when neither theoretical nor consequently practical advances are developing. If, on the other hand, you start with an interesting real-world behavior and programmatically study it, you will likely obtain answers to the practical questions that motivated the work, and advances in the underlying theoretical notions are consequently encouraged. This is the major reason for promoting applied cognitive psychology research in this chapter; because it is good for the field!

Just as research in the field of cognitive psychology can be classified as basic or applied, applied research can be further dichotomized. Baddeley (1979) differentiates between *cognitive applied psychology* and *applied cognitive psychology*. With cognitive applied psychology, the emphasis is on answering an applied question, but the content of the question and the methodology utilized are from cognitive psychology. With applied cognitive psychology, the researcher still starts with an applied question, but directs the research program by asking, what theoretical notions can we borrow from cognitive psychology to better understand this applied question? These are two quite different models for conducting applied research in cognitive psychology. Table 1.1 graphically differentiates between these two types of research as compared with basic research.

Because practicality so often leads over principles, the real difference between applied cognitive psychology and cognitive applied psychology is often who employs the researcher. An advertising agency may want to know, does memory for a television commercial differ as a function of presenting it at normal speed in 30 seconds versus at compressed speed in 20 seconds? Or a researcher for a computer company may want to know, what are the critical perceptual features of fingerprints so that they can be classified and filed by computer? In both cases, the research program is terminated as ''successful'' when an answer to the question is obtained. These are examples of cognitive applied psychology. In an academic setting, or an applied setting that has a greater emphasis on research and development, the researcher would be presented the applied problem but be encouraged to (a) draw from the most relevant theoretical notions available in the discipline, and (b) relate the findings back to the development of theory in the discipline. The work would thus be classified as applied cognitive psychology. But in both cases, the jumping-off point is with an interesting real-world behavior or an applied question, and thus the research differs from basic research.

In this chapter, I trace the course of my own research examining the issue: What are the principal cognitive processes involved in memory and comprehension of information presented on television.   My interest in television stems from my work on semantic integration of information presented in verbal and pictorial modalities (cf. Pezdek, 1977; Pezdek, 1980; Pezdek & Miceli, 1982). This early work can unequivocally be classified as basic research. However, from this mode of research I switched to an applied cognitive psychology approach, and more recently to a cognitive applied psychology approach. I offer my research as an example, but certainly not as a model, of applied research. Again, the purpose of tracing the course of development of my work through these transitions is to expand the readers' view of the range of research approaches available and to encourage a greater interest in and appreciation for the contributions of applied research in cognitive psychology.

TABLE 1.1
Classification of Various Approaches to
Research in Cognitive Psychology

	Applied Question Leads	Theory Leads
Theory is Heavily Drawn upon	Applied Cognitive Psychology	Basic Research
Theory is not Heavily Drawn upon	Cognitive Applied Psychology	

AN EXAMPLE OF APPLIED RESEARCH:
COMPREHENSION AND MEMORY FOR INFORMATION
PRESENTED ON TELEVISION

In 1977 (Pezdek, 1977) I published a study probing how we remember information about a subject when some of the information is presented verbally in a sentence, and some is presented visually in a picture. The question was, is the verbal and pictorial information integrated into a common memory based on the semantic relatedness of the information, or are the two sources of information stored separately in memory based on modality differences in the presented material? The results were that the verbally and pictorially presented information was semantically integrated into a common memory. I termed this *cross-modality semantic integration*.

This study was a test of the *dual-coding hypothesis* (cf. Paivio & Csapo, 1969). This theory posits that there are two separate coding systems for representing information in memory, a verbal system and an imaginal system. The results of this study reject the dual-coding hypothesis in favor of a unitary semantically based memory system. The Pezdek (1977) study is clearly an example of basic research because the purpose of the study was to test the theoretical notion of the dual-coding hypothesis.

In a subsequent study (Pezdek, 1980), I tested life-span developmental differences in cross-modality semantic integration. In other words, are young children and older adults less likely (than older children and younger adults) to integrate in memory semantically related information that is presented at different points in time in different modalities? The results were yes. The young children and older adults were more likely to remember the information in the form in which it was presented rather than integrating the information on the basis of semantic relatedness.

In a third study (Pezdek & Miceli, 1982), we found that we could encourage semantic integration in the younger children and older adults by presenting the to-be-integrated items at a slower rate (15 seconds per item as compared with 8 seconds per item in the previous studies). In other words, young children and older adults *can* integrate related visual and verbal information, but they must be provided more time for this to occur. The interpretation of this result was that the slower presentation rate was necessary for these subjects to actively rehearse different items together, and that this rehearsal strategy was necessary for integration of information in memory.

I believed the results of this line of research, and I think that these results contributed in interesting ways to theoretical notions in both cognitive psychology and cognitive developmental psychology. But I got stuck when I tried to think of what interesting real-world behavior these results might be relevant to.

My first thought was that these results ought to be relevant to processing of information presented on television. After all, television is a stimulus that consists of simultaneously presented verbal and pictorial information that must be processed together in order to make sense out of what is happening. But if children have difficulty relating verbal and pictorial information presented serially unless it is presented quite slowly, how well are they able to integrate the fast-paced verbal and pictorial information that is simultaneously presented on television? This became an especially compelling question for me when I discovered that children in this country watch an *average* of 27.6 hours of television a week (Lyle & Hoffman, 1972). Are children really comprehending so little from television, yet spending 20% of their waking hours watching it?

This line of inquiry marked the transition in my program of research in this area from a basic research program to an applied one. Rather than letting the theoretical issues lead, I decided (albeit not consciously at that point) to let the behavior of comprehending television lead the line of investigation. At this point, the focus of my research became, what are the principal cognitive processes involved in memory and comprehension of information presented on television? But although I had let the applied behavior lead, I was truly unfamiliar with this approach and found myself quickly looking for theories and experimental findings that would help focus the research question. The work at this stage in the development of this program of research can thus be classified as applied cognitive psychology.

Quite honestly, I found television processing difficult to study. Television is a dynamic stimulus with a great deal of interactive information being presented simultaneously. How do you study this complex dynamic stimulus? My first step was to approach the complex stimulus and try to decide what dimension of television was the most salient in directing memory and comprehension of what is presented on television? If I knew this, it would tell me where to focus attention in subsequent research. The most obvious dimensions of television to be considered were the auditory/verbal features and the visual features. Drawing heavily on the notion of the *visual superiority effect* (cf. Posner, Nissen, & Klein, 1976), I predicted that the visually presented information would dominate over the nonvisual information in memory and comprehension for information presented on television. This notion was tested in a study by Pezdek and Stevens (1984).

One way to test for relative memorability of visually versus auditorily presented information on television is to present a segment on television, present test questions on the visually presented information, present test questions on the auditorily presented information, and then compare performance on these two sets of questions. Although this method has been utilized by other researchers (cf. Hayes & Birnbaum, 1980), it confounds modality differences with question differences. That is, any differences between performance on the visual versus auditory questions could be due to differences in question difficulty rather than differences in processing difficulty. The Pezdek and Stevens (1984) study utilized an alternative design to avoid this artifact.

In this study, 5-year-old children viewed a videotaped segment of "Sesame Street" followed by a comprehension test. Equal numbers of subjects viewed a segment in which (a) the audio and video tracks were from the same segment (A/V match condition), (b) the audio and video tracks included the same characters but were not from the same segment (A/V mismatch), (c) the video track was presented alone, or (d) the audio track was presented alone. The comprehension test included questions that probed visually presented information or auditorily presented information. Responses were scored on a 0 (incorrect or no response) to 2 (correct response without probe) scale. A summary of the results is presented in Table 1.2.

The first question of interest was, how do children allocate their processing to the audio versus video channels on television in the A/V mismatch condition? The results suggest that when children have to choose one channel or the other, processing the audio information suffers more than does processing the video information. Visual attention in the A/V mismatch condition (83.8%) was not significantly less than in the A/V match condition (91.6%). However, comprehension was reduced in the A/V mismatch condition compared to the A/V match condition for both audio information (0.85 vs. 1.51) and video information (1.13 vs 1.61). Comprehension of auditorily presented information in the A/V mismatch condition (0.85) was not significantly better than chance (0.57). Comprehension of visually presented information in the A/V mismatch condition (1.13) was relatively more accurate and significantly better than chance (0.51).

The second question of interest in this study was how comprehension of visually presented information compared in the A/V match versus video-only conditions and how comprehension of auditorily presented information compared in the A/V match versus audio-only conditions. As can be seen in Table 1.2, comprehension of visually presented information was actually better in the A/V match condition (1.61) than in the video-only condition (1.28). Similarly, comprehension of auditorily presented information was better in the A/V match condition (1.51) than in the audio-only condition (1.20). These results, together with the results of the comparison of the A/V match with A/V mismatch conditions, suggest that although the visual information is more salient and memorable than the audio information on television, these two modality channels appear to

TABLE 1.2
Performance on Each Measure in Each Condition in Pezdek and Stevens (1984)

Condition	Percentage of Visual Attention	Visual Comprehension (0-2 Range)	Audio Comprehension (0-2 Range)
A/V match	91.6	1.61	1.51
A/V mismatch	83.8	1.13	0.85
Video only	74.0	1.28	0.57
Audio only	28.4	0.51	1.20

be processed together synergistically. The presence of the audio track actually improves comprehension of visually presented information, and the presence of the visual track improves comprehension of auditorily presented information. The more precise nature of the synergistic relationship between attention and comprehension of auditory versus visual information was specifically probed in studies by Pezdek and Hartman (1983) and Anderson and Levin (1976).

The results of the Pezdek and Stevens (1984) study were certainly consistent with the visual superiority or visual-dominance effect (cf. Posner et al., 1976). However, the theory did not really provide useful insights regarding television comprehension, beyond suggesting that the visually presented information is probably more salient than the verbal auditorily presented information. Because the majority of the research on the visual-dominance effect utilized less complex perceptual and memory tasks than are involved in processing television, the knowledge that can be abstracted from this literature to the study of television comprehension is limited.

Although I remained interested in the issue (what are the principal cognitive processes involved in memory and comprehension of information presented on television?), I seemed at a roadblock in terms of continuing to utilize available theories to either (a) shape useful hypotheses or (b) direct the course of the investigation. The major limitation with the applied cognitive psychology approach at this point was that the available cognitive theories dealt with behaviors and stimuli that were too simple to apply to television comprehension.

I decided to try another tack. Cognitive psychologists know a great deal about the process of text comprehension. It seemed that if we knew the relationship between the ability to comprehend text and the ability to comprehend television, then relevant portions of available reading models could be adapted to the development of a model of television comprehension. This was the purpose of the study by Pezdek, Lehrer, and Simon (1984). This line of inquiry marked a second transition in my program of research in this area: the departure from attempting to let theory lead the direction of the research. The transition is thus one from applied cognitive psychology to cognitive applied psychology.

In the study by Pezdek et al. (1984), the correlation between the ability to comprehend television and the ability to comprehend text was assessed. Several segments were edited to create two matched versions of each—(a) a text version with pictures, and (b) a television version. Third- and sixth-graders read one segment and were presented the television version of another segment, counterbalanced for segment and order of presentation. This study utilized both narrative (story-like) and expository (instructional) media segments. A battery of memory and comprehension tests was administered following both the reading and the television condition.

The principal result was that across a range of tasks, performance in the television condition and performance in the reading condition were not significantly correlated. This pattern of results was similar for both narrative and expository materials. The finding was corroborated with the additional result that standardized reading test scores were not significantly correlated with television comprehension performance. Thus, although comprehending television and comprehending text appear a priori similar in many ways, at least with 8- and 11-year-old children, the ability to comprehend these two forms of media are not correlated. There are apparently sufficient differences between the cognitive processes involved in reading and comprehending television that reading ability does not discriminate good from poor television comprehension.

Because the purpose of the Pezdek et al. (1984) study was to *draw parallels* between the cognitive processes involved in television comprehension and those involved in text comprehension, the results were quite a surprise. Certainly, there are many similarities between comprehension of text and of television. Both involve top-down schema-driven processing. Both involve constructive processes such as integration and drawing of inferences. The apparent similarities are numerous. However, the Pezdek et al. (1984) finding of no correlation between the ability to comprehend television and the ability to comprehend text suggests that salient processing *differences* exist. The purpose of the next study (Pezdek, Simon, MacKenzie, & MacBride, 1985) was to articulate the locus of the cognitive processing differences between memory and comprehension for television versus text.

Pezdek et al. (1985) utilized the individual differences approach to explore the cognitive abilities that underlie good television comprehension, specifically those cognitive abilities that are not also predictive of reading ability. Sixth-graders were tested in this study. The individual differences approach involved testing a group of subjects by (a) measuring television comprehension ability (using the tasks utilized by Pezdek et al., 1984), (b) measuring reading comprehension ability (using the standardized reading achievement cluster of Woodcock & Johnson, 1977), and then (c) administering a set of cognitive and psychometric tests that assess individual differences predicted to underlie television comprehension. A multiple regression analysis was then performed. The question tested in the analysis was, with the variance due to differences in reading ability removed first, are there any individual differences factors that significantly predict television comprehension?

The individual differences tests that were predicted to involve cognitive processes that underlie television comprehension included (a) a test of recognition memory for visual material, (b) several tests of visual/spatial manipulation, and (c) several tests of visual/verbal integration. In the final multiple regression analysis, with the variance in television comprehension due to reading ability removed first, and all other variables entered in a step-wise fashion, one factor significantly predicted television comprehension. This significant factor was performance on a picture-sorting test (F (1,46) = 12.73, $p < .01$). No other tasks were significant. However, the simple correlations revealed that the other tasks were significantly correlated with performance on the reading test.

In the picture-sorting test, subjects were presented a stack of 32 pictures on cards. Each picture presented a drawing of an object or a person. The task of the subject was to classify each card into one of four categories as a function of whether the pictured object was living or nonliving, and larger or smaller than the subject. The time to classify all 32 cards was measured. This task assesses speed to semantically access information presented visually in pictures. Thus, a unique aspect of cognitive processing of television, that does not predict reading ability, is the ability to quickly access the semantic content of visual material.

To summarize, Pezdek et al. (1984) reported that children's ability to comprehend television and their ability to comprehend text were not correlated. The results of Pezdek et al. (1985) suggest that one cognitive processing ability that significantly correlates with television comprehension but not with reading comprehension is the ability to quickly access the semantic content of visual material. This finding, together with the results of Pezdek and Stevens (1984), suggests that the visually presented information on television is especially salient and important to the extent that speedy semantic processing of visual information is predictive of television comprehension, whereas reading ability is not.

CONCLUSIONS

The purpose of this program of research has been to address the question, what are the principal cognitive processes involved in memory and comprehension for information presented on television? The results to date from this work tell us more about where to look for answers than what we will find. Although this has seemed to me like a slow course of investigation, I now see that this slow course, and the transitions through several different research approaches, may have been necessary given the complex nature of the target task. The *basic research* approach was not useful because theories are not available to shed light on the cognitive processes that underlie comprehension of the complex auditory/verbal-plus-visual stimulus known as television. The tradition in cognitive psychology is to study complex behaviors by stripping them down into their simpler component parts. This did not seem like a fruitful approach to the study of television. We know that, for example, the auditory/verbal information on television is synergistically processed with the visual information. To study cognitive processing of these components of television separately would be to miss perhaps the most interesting aspect of this behavior.

The basic research approach was abandoned for the applied cognitive psychology approach. At this first transition, the applied question regarding comprehension of television led the research, but theoretical issues regarding the visual-dominance effect were heavily drawn upon. This approach stimulated several studies. But again, a roadblock was reached because the available cognitive theories dealt with behaviors and stimuli that were too simple to apply to television comprehension.

The cognitive applied psychology approach has been utilized in the most recent and current studies in this program of research. By utilizing this approach, I am confessing that I can find no cognitive theories that direct an interesting course for investigating television comprehension. As such, it would be premature to try to force a theory to fit my study or to force my study to fit a theory. Rather, I need to spend some time putting the behavior of comprehending television under the microscope to see what is there; by seeing what other tasks it seems similar to and different from; by seeing what individual differences factors predict television comprehension; by seeing what types of information people comprehend with facility and with difficulty on television. In these ways we will get a better sense of the behavior of television comprehension, and I hope that out of this knowledge will come the basis for generating good theories regarding cognitive processing of television.

The principal point of this chapter, and indeed of this book, is to remind us that there are many research approaches available to cognitive psychologists. The majority approach, via basic research, has both strengths and weaknesses that need to be considered. I hope that this chapter motivates researchers to step back from their theories and their familiar methodologies and think in practical ways about the behaviors that they are interested in understanding. This does not mean that we will abandon either our empirical rigor or our theoretical progress. I am simply suggesting that there is room in our field to shift the focus in the direction of addressing *more interesting applied behaviors.* We do not need to abandon this focus when the support from theory is not obvious.

It is important in our field to develop good theories, but sometimes good theories lead the empirical work and sometimes they follow from it. On the other hand, it is *critical* to our field to study interesting behaviors. Without this focus, cognitive psychology has no validity. Applied research in cognitive psychology offers hope for preserving our validity.

REFERENCES

Anderson, D. R., & Levin, S. R. (1976). Young children's attention to "Sesame Street." *Child Development, 47,* 806–811.

Baddeley, A. (1979). Applied cognitive and cognitive applied psychology: The case of face recognition. In L-G. Nilsson (Ed.), *Perspectives on memory research* (pp. 367–388). New York: Halsted Press, Wiley.

Broadbent, D. E. (1958). *Perception and communication.* London: Pergamon.

Garfield, E. (1978a, August 7). The 100 articles most cited by social scientists, 1969–1977. *Current Contents,* 5–14.

Garfield, E. (1978b, September 11). The 100 books most cited by social scientists, 1969–1977. *Current Contents,* 5–16.

Garfield, E. (1979). *Citation indexing.* New York: Wiley.

Hayes, D. S., & Birnbaum, D. W. (1980). Preschoolers' retention of televised events: Is a picture worth a thousand words? *Developmental Psychology, 16*, 410–416.

Kuhn, T. S. (1962). *The structure of scientific revolutions.* Chicago, IL: University of Chicago Press.

Lyle, J. L., & Hoffman, H. R. (1972). Children's use of television and other media. In E. A. Rubinstein, G. A. Comstock, & J. P. Murray (Eds.), *Television and social behavior: Vol. 4. Television in day-to-day life: Patterns of use* (pp. 129–256). Washington, DC: U.S. Government Printing Office.

Newell, A. (1973). You can't play 20 questions with Nature and win: Projective comments on the papers of this symposium. In W. G. Chase (Ed.), *Visual information processing* (pp. 283–308). New York: Academic Press.

Paivio, A., & Csapo, K. (1969). Concrete image and verbal memory codes. *Journal of Experimental Psychology, 80*, 279–285.

Pezdek, K. (1977). Cross-modality semantic integration of sentence and picture memory. *Journal of Experimental Psychology: Human Learning and Memory, 3*, 515–524.

Pezdek, K. (1980). Life-span differences in semantic integration of pictures and sentences in memory. *Child Development, 51*, 720–729.

Pezdek, K., & Hartman, E. F. (1983). Children's television viewing: Attention and comprehension of auditory versus visual information. *Child Development, 54*, 1015–1023.

Pezdek, K., Lehrer, A., & Simon, S. (1984). The relationship between reading and cognitive processing of television and radio. *Child Development, 55*, 2072–2082.

Pezdek, K., & Miceli, L. (1982). Life-span differences in memory integration as a function of processing time. *Developmental Psychology, 18*, 485–490.

Pezdek, K., Simon, S., MacKenzie, L., & MacBride, L. (1985, April). *Individual differences in television and text comprehension.* Paper presented at the meeting of the Society for Research in Child Development, Toronto.

Pezdek, K., & Stevens, E. (1984). Children's memory for auditory and visual information on television. *Developmental Psychology, 20*, 212–218.

Platt, J. R. (1964). Strong inferences. *Science, 146*, 347–353.

Posner, M. I., Nissen, M. J., & Klein, R. M. (1976). Visual dominance: An information-processing account of its origins and significance. *Psychological Review, 83*, 157–171.

Tulving, E. (1979). Memory research: What kind of progress? In L-G. Nilsson (Ed.), *Perspectives on memory research* (pp. 19–34). New York: Halsted, Wiley.

White, M. J. (1983). Prominent publications in cognitive psychology. *Memory & Cognition, 11*, 423–427.

Woodcock, R. W., & Johnson, M. B. (1977). *Woodcock-Johnson Psycho-Educational Battery.* Boston: Teaching Resources Corp.

2 Electronic Technologies, Education, and Cognitive Development*

Patricia M. Greenfield
University of California, Los Angeles

ABSTRACT

Taking a comparative approach to media, this chapter develops an argument about the cognitive effects of media and their role in education. In so doing, it focuses on the interplay of media forms and media content. The first theme is that because of its technical nature, each medium transmits certain kinds of information easily and well, other kinds with difficulty and relatively poorly. Second, because of its particular profile of strengths and weaknesses, a given medium is particularly suited to presenting certain kinds of subject matter in the educational process. Finally, a medium's profile also has implications for cognitive development: each medium calls upon and develops a particular set of abilities to process and produce information. As a consequence, the media—from print to audio, video, and computers—have a complementary role to play both in education and in cognitive development. This point leads to the conclusion that educational policy must not consider media in an either-or framework. Instead, we must move toward a system of multimedia education. By giving each medium—the old ones as well as the new—its place in a child's life and education, each medium will be able to make its own special contribution to a child's learning and development.

In this chapter, I make an argument, based on Greenfield (1984), about the cognitive effects of various media and their role in education. In so doing, I focus

*This article is adapted from an address entitled, Mind and media: Implications of television, video games, and computers for education and cognitive development, presented by the Eleventh Western Symposiom on Learning, Western Washington University, Bellingham, WA, April, 1985. A longer version of this article will also appear in the Proceedings of the Symposium.

on the interplay between media form, media content, and media processing. My approach is comparative: the various media—print, radio (audio), tv, and computer technologies—will be considered not in isolation, but in relation to each other.

EVERY MEDIUM HAS ITS OWN
INFORMATIONAL "BIASES"

A major theme is that each medium has its own biases. Contrary to the common assumption, a medium is not a neutral transmitter of information. Through the filter of its technical and formal characteristics, a medium transforms information while communicating it, emphasizing particular aspects of events and ideas, deemphasizing others. As a consequence, each medium presents certain types of information easily and well, other types with difficulty or relatively poorly.

Print

Let me explain this idea through some examples, starting with the printed word. Print is extremely good at presenting a person's inner reflections. Novels often take advantage of this characteristic in presenting the inner musings of a character. The personal essay is a literary genre that is built around this very strength. Television (or film), on the other hand, presents thought processes less naturally, with greater difficulty. As dynamic, visual media, they seek dynamic visual images to present; but the process of thinking or reflecting involves no visible movement at all: nothing "happens" that can be shown on a screen.

Audio

Radio or other audio media have their own set of strengths. For instance, they make dialogue and figurative language salient. In our research comparing the cognitive effects of radio and television, we gave children the same story presented in one of two media, radio (audio) or television. Each version had exactly the same soundtrack. We found that the children's recall of dialogue was better after the radio version than after the television version (Greenfield & Beagles-Roos, 1983, 1985). Apparently, the visual images distracted attention from dialogue, resulting in poorer recall. It is important to realize in interpreting these results that the information presented in dialogue is generally not reinforced by a visual image; rather it competes with the visual image, generally the image of the speakers themselves. For this reason, dialoque becomes more salient when presented in a purely audio form like radio. For similar reasons, it is not surprising that figurative language, the language of poetry, is also recalled better from a radio story than from a television story with the same soundtrack, at least among certain groups (Beagles-Roos, 1985; Beagles-Roos & Gat, 1983).

Television and Film

Television and film, for their part, have particular strengths in presenting action, three-dimensional space, and several things happening at once. Research findings indicate, for example, that action information is recalled better by both children and adults when a given story is presented on television rather than radio (Greenfield and Beagles-Roos, 1983, 1985; Beagles-Roos, 1985). The addition of moving images to words in depicting action may well explain the great popularity of sports on television and the expansion of the range of sports with which the television public has become involved.

In terms of the presentation of three-dimensional space, a Swiss study was designed to test the effectiveness of television in teaching children spatial information (Sturm & Jorg, 1981). Kindergarten and first-grade children saw or heard a television or radio version of a story. In the story, the main characters, three children, were faced with some spatial problems. For example, they were going to see an owl, and they wanted the owl to think there was only one of them. To solve this problem, they walked in a line, with the tallest child first, so that the shorter children were blocked from the owl's view. After seeing or hearing this story, each child was asked to act out the solutions to the problems, using puppets. More children could solve the problems after seeing the story on television than after hearing it on the radio. (The soundtracks were identical in both versions.) Television apparently made the spatial information necessary to solve the problem clearer, more salient, or both.

Exclusively verbal media such as print or radio (audio) are limited to presenting one thing at a time. To a great extent, information is presented in a linear order, one element at a time. In television or film, in contrast, different things can occur on different parts of the screen simultaneously. For instance, it is commonplace to have several actors or real-life people visible on the screen in a single shot. Carrying this potential for simultaneous information to an extreme, a film such as *Nashville* or a television series such as "Hill Street Blues" uses crowd scenes to present events from several subplots all at once. In sum, television and film, unlike the exclusively verbal medium of print, can easily present several pieces of information simultaneously.

Computers

Computer technology in general has a great strength in allowing users to interact with complex systems having multiple, interacting, dynamic variables. One way it does this is by means of the computer simulation, an interactive model of some real-world system. In addition to the simulation, the video game also represents a complex system, which a player must figure out in order to acquire skill in a particular game. Although most systems in the real world—e.g., an ocean, a forest, a city, a corporation, a country—are complex in this way, the computer is the first medium able to transmit and model this complexity to an audience.

These "biases" toward the presentation of particular sorts of information have implications both for education and for cognitive development.

A MEDIUM'S INFORMATIONAL "BIAS" HAS IMPLICATIONS FOR EDUCATION

In terms of education, the informational strengths of a medium mean that each medium is particularly good at presenting particular subject matter. For example, audio, because it makes figurative language and dialogue salient, should be particularly effective in presenting poetry and drama.

Television or film, because it presents action and transformation so naturally and so well, is particularly suited for presenting scientific topics, for just about all science has to do with some form of action, whether it be transformation or movement. In biology, it might be the growth of a plant; recall here the traditional science films that take slow processes of growth and speed them up on film. In physics, any experiment in mechanics will involve movement of some sort.

Computers are natural for any subject that involves teaching about a complex system. A computer simulation can allow the learner to interact with the kinds of systems that would be relevant to social studies or history—a government or a battle, for example—or the kinds of systems that would be relevant to science—such as an ecological system.

A MEDIUM'S INFORMATIONAL "BIAS" HAS IMPLICATIONS FOR COGNITIVE DEVELOPMENT

The strengths and weaknesses of each medium also have implications for cognitive development. Because of its informational "biases," each medium also calls upon and develops a particular set of abilities to process and produce information. Again, I present examples from the various media.

Print and Radio

Compared with television, print and radio seem to be relatively stimulating to the cognitive process of *imagination*. As an example, my research group did a study comparing radio and television in this respect. Again we used two versions of the same story, a radio version and a television version, each one having the identical soundtrack. This time we stopped the story a little bit before the end, and we asked the children to continue the stories. Our measure of imagination was how many novel elements were introduced into the continuation. An element was considered novel if it had not appeared in the stimulus story just heard or seen by the child. We found that the story continuations were more imaginative following the radio presentation than following the television presentation (Greenfield, Farrar, & Beagles-Roos, in press).

This pattern of results makes sense in terms of the design features of each medium. An audio medium, lacking visual images, leaves more to the imagination. The listener must do imaginative work to create an image of the scene from words alone. Television or film, in contrast, creates the images for you. Other research has shown that a story presented in print stimulates the imagination in the same way that audio does and, again, more so than television (Meline, 1976).

Television

But television has its own set of strengths in stimulating cognitive development. For example, television develops skill in the mental representation of space, the ability to visualize space in your mind. Salomon (1979), working in Israel, has found a whole set of skills of this type that are related to viewing and understanding television and film. Figure 2.1 presents an item from one of Salomon's tests,

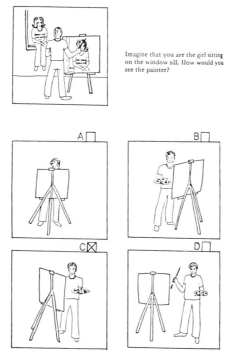

Imagine that you are the girl sitting on the window sill. How would you see the painter?

FIG. 2.1.   Item from Changing Points of View Test (Salomon, 1979).

the Changing Points of View Test. At a time in Israel when "Sesame Street" was the only children's program available, Salomon found that heavy viewers of the show did better on this test than light viewers. But why should skill on such a test correlate with amount of television viewing? Salomon hypothesizes that this has to do not with the content of television, but with its technical nature as a medium and the forms that the techniques produce. A technique that is all-pervasive in television and film is to show the same scene from different camera angles, i.e., different points of view. Apparently, the effect of such repeated exposure to changes in physical points of view is to develop skill in shifting points of view in your mind, the requirement of the test illustrated in Fig. 2.1.

Such a result lends experimental evidence to McLuhan's (1964) assertion that "the medium is the message." The message, here a perceptual one, lies in a technique that is not specific to any particular type of program, but occurs in presenting almost any type of content in the medium of film or TV.

Video Games: Building Upon the Visual-Spatial Skills Developed through Television

Video games and computers can, among other things, be considered an interactive television. It turns out that many forms of computer technology build upon and utilize the *visual-spatial skills* being developed through television. Let me focus on some examples from video games, the first form of computer technology to have a mass impact on the socialization process.

The first example illustrates how the ability to mentally shift points of view is also required by some video games. Figure 2.2 shows two screens from a computer game called Tranquillity Base. In this game, the task is to land your spaceship safely on some flat terrain. At the beginning of the game the player sees a picture on the screen of the spaceship at a distance. The small size of the spaceship conveys this distance information. As the spaceship gets closer to the terrain where it must land, the point of view shifts to a close-up perspective on a part of the landscape. This perspective shift is conveyed by the relatively larger size of the spaceship. In order to be successful, the player must be able to understand the shift in point of view from the long-shot to the close-up.

My hypothesis is that children who have been socialized with a lot of television and film will be very familiar with two-dimensional representations of shifting points of view and that this familiarity then gives them a head start in understanding the screen displays of a game like Tranquillity Base. Although Tranquillity Base is a game for home computers, the requirement to shift visual point of view is found in a number of arcade games as well, so the visual experience in question is generally available.

The visual skills developed by television and film are not limited to two-dimensional representations of shifting points of view, but are, in fact, quite diverse. Figure 2.3 presents another such example. This is an item from another

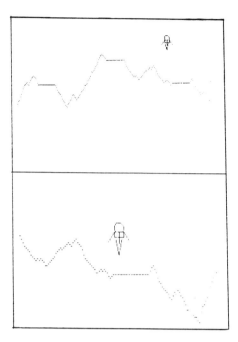

FIG. 2.2.   Two screens from Tranquillity Base (Stoneware).

test of Salomon (1979), the Space Construction Test. In this item, the task is to put the four picture fragments together so that they form a room. Salomon found that children who did well on this test were better able to understand edited films than children who did less well.

Why? Again, Salomon hypothesized that the answer lies in a visual technique that is intrinsic to the film and television media. When a three-dimensional space, such as a room, is filmed, the camera does not and cannot reveal the whole space in a single shot. Instead the camera pans or cuts from one part of the room to another, showing but one fragment at a time. To have a sense of the whole space, the viewer must mentally integrate the fragments, constructing the room for himself or herself. Apparently, learning to interpret and integrate the fragmentary shots in a film creates a cognitive skill which then transfers to this paper-and-pencil test.

A number of video games require this cognitive process of spatial integration. Figure 2.4 shows three screens from a game called Castle Wolfenstein, which utilizes this skill. The goal of Castle Wolfenstein is to escape from the Castle, which represents a Nazi prison. The Castle consists of a series of mazes, only one of which is visible at a time. Yet the mazes are interconnected vertically by stairways (e.g., top right-hand corner of top maze) and horizontally by doorways (e.g., top middle of middle maze). In order to have an overview of the whole

FIG. 2.3.   Item from Space Construction Test (Salomon, 1979).

castle, the player must mentally put together the individual mazes and construct the space.

My own experience in playing the game indicates that this is not a skill to be taken for granted. After my first session with the game, I assumed each maze was independent of the others and that the order of mazes was essentially random. I had not only failed to integrate the fragments, but failed to realize that the fragments *could* be integrated. My son's amazement at my ignorance ("Most people realize *that,* even if they are not paying attention!") gave me a clue that spatial integration may be a well-understood convention, as well as a habit, for expert game players like him more than for other people.

The important point for present purposes is that the need to integrate fragments of space into a single structure in the video game Castle Wolfenstein closely parallels the task of the Space Construction Test, performance on which was found to be related to an understanding of film. Thus, socialization by the visual media of television and film may again provide informal training that is relevant to understanding the screen displays of video games. There is evidence that the games further develop the spatial skills which they require.

Gagnon (in press) found that giving Harvard College students 5 hours of arcade-game play improved performance on standardized paper-and-pencil tests of visual-spatial skills. The positive effect of video game play was, however, found exclusively among inexperienced players (for the Guilford-Zimmerman Spatial Orientation Test) and among women (for the Guilford-Zimmerman Spatial Visualization Test). In fact, there was a great deal of overlap between these two groups, for the majority of women in the sample were classified as novice players, the majority of men as experts.

Furthermore, the two groups, novices and females, for whom the experimental game experience made the biggest difference, also started out with lower scores on the visual-spatial tests, so the games served something like a remedial

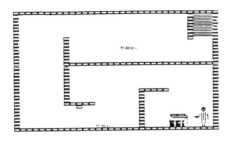

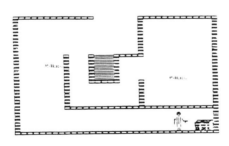

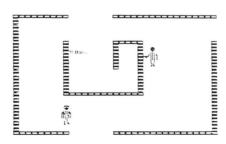

FIG. 2.4.   Three interlinked mazes from Castle Wolfenstein.

function for people with relatively undeveloped spatial skills. Indeed, Gagnon found that scores on the visual-spatial tests were generally correlated with amount of past game experience: the more experienced the player, the better the performance on the test.

Visual-Spatial Skills, Computers, and Technological Education

The particular tests that were affected by video game experience in Gagnon's experiment are considered to measure factors that are important for mechanical occupations, engineering, and architecture. Recent research has gone one step further, suggesting that all sorts of computer skills are quite dependent on visual abilities.

For example, a surprising finding about word processing was that the best predictor of how easily novice adults would learn to do it was their spatial memory (for arrangements of objects) (Gomez, Bowers, & Egan, 1982; Gomez, Egan, Wheeler, Sharma, & Gruchacz, 1983). Young children picked up programming LOGO better if they were able to shift visual perspectives at the outset (Roberts, 1984). Here, a visual-spatial skill that is part of television and film literacy is relevant not merely to playing video games, but also to computer programming.

In a 1977 article in *Science,* Ferguson pointed out that the language of technology is basically a nonverbal one and that people involved in technology need to be able to think in terms of visual images. He criticized engineering schools for their bias toward educating students to analyze systems using numbers rather than visual images, pointing out that this bias has produced a lack of people who have skills to deal with real machines and materials.

Ferguson's point has applicability way beyond engineering now that so many different kinds of learning and work are being done on a computer screen. Our educational system ignores the visual requirements of the new technologies in both teaching and testing. It is concerned about print literacy, but not about visual-spatial literacy. Until this situation changes, television and video games can provide informal education in this important domain.

Learning to Deal with Complex Systems

In addition to presenting visual stimuli that demand interesting spatial skills, a video game is also a *complex system* that must be mastered. Let us take as an example Tranquillity Base, the computer game previously discussed. This relatively simple game involves six variables. In order to land the spaceship safely, the player must take account of altitude, horizontal speed, vertical speed, direction, amount of fuel, and horizontal location. These are the *multiple variables.* In addition, all the variables *interact* with each other: The effect of one variable differs depending on the values of others. For instance, running out of fuel has a very different effect depending on whether you are on the ground or 5,000 feet up in the air. This is an example of a simple interaction between the two variables, amount of fuel and altitude. In order to land the spaceship safely, the player must take account of the variables not only one at a time, but also as they influence one another. Note too that the variables are *dynamic* because their values are changing over time. For example, fuel is constantly being used up and either horizontal or vertical position must always be changing.

Learning to deal with complex systems having multiple, interacting, dynamic variables is a significant accomplishment because the world is not a simple system, but rather many complex and dynamic systems. As we shall see in the next section, video games, although not always presenting realistic models of real-world systems, do foster skill in figuring out how a complex system works, skill that can transfer to figuring out the workings of a more realistic simulation.

Video Games and the Process of Inductive Discovery

Perhaps the most interesting point about the video game as a complex system is that no one tells you its rules in advance. The rules must be figured out by observation, trial and error, and a process of hypothesis testing.

Let me begin with an example from Pac-Man. When I first played Pac-Man, I was terrible at the game. I assumed that my reaction time was simply too slow, but thought I basically understood the game. Then I read a book called *The Video Master's Guide to Pac-Man* (Sykora & Birkner, 1982) and discovered that I had missed about 90% to 95% of the game! The game had a myriad of rules and patterns programmed into it that I had not realized existed, let alone tried to figure out. At this point, I had my first realization that even the simplest of video games (like Pac-Man), far from being simple-minded, were extremely complex and offered many cognitive challenges.

I shall present one example of a rule-bound pattern built into Pac-Man that is not explained to a player in advance, but, when discovered, will help in playing the game. Basically, Pac-Man must clear a maze of small dots, avoiding monsters. During play, the monsters, who are each a different color, come out of their corral at the center of the maze and move around. What is not obvious, however, is that each of the monsters has its own behavior pattern. One, for example, is very slow and unaggressive. Another is fast and aggressive to Pac-Man. Knowledge of these patterns can aid a player in avoiding the monsters, a key element of successful play, but they must be empirically induced through observation and trial and error.

Note the parallel to the precomputer game of chess; there, too, each piece (the rook, the bishop, etc.) has its own rules of allowable behavior. There is a major difference, however: In chess, the player is told the rules in advance; in Pac-Man the player must figure them out for himself or herself. This process of making observations, formulating hypotheses, and figuring out rules through a trial-and-error process is basically the cognitive process of *inductive discovery*. It is the process by which we learn much about the world, and at a more formal level, it is the thought process behind scientific thinking and discovery. If video games function to train this process, it would have great educational and social importance.

Video Games as Informal Training in Scientific Thinking

To test this idea, we did an experiment to document this inductive discovery process in the course of video game mastery and to see whether video games could function as a method of informal training for scientific-technical thinking. Details of the study can be found in Greenfield and Lauber, 1985. Our experiment involved using the game of Evolution, an arcade-style game for Apple computers, as an experimental treatment. Each of the treatment conditions included 2½ hours of playing Evolution.

Because video games are widely considered to have little if any redeeming social value in themselves, we were particularly interested to see if the processes of inductive discovery that they engage might transfer to problem solving in a scientific or technical context, an area of undisputed social importance. We therefore developed two parallel transfer tasks, one given as a pretest, one given as a posttest; these involved demonstrations of the operation of electronic circuits presented schematically on a video screen.

Subjects were told nothing about the demonstrations, not even that what they were seeing were circuits; they were simply told to watch carefully so that they could answer questions later about what was going on. After every few demonstrations on the screen, subjects were given written questions to answer. The questions were such that the subjects had not only to understand what they had been shown on the screen, but also to generalize their conclusions to new instances of circuits.

Our results showed that there was indeed a carry-over from video game practice in the experiment to the posttest that involved *scientific-technical thinking*. Novice game players improved significantly from pretest to posttest after 2½ hours of playing Evolution. A control group of novice players who were not given an opportunity to play Evolution did not, in contrast, show any change in test performance from pretest to posttest. A group of expert game players was also tested. They tested as high on the pretest of scientific-technical problem solving as the novice players did after their experimental treatment. This result shows that video game play in the real world may have an effect similar to that of our experimental treatment.

One puzzling question is why our expert game players, after hundreds of hours of play, did not do better on our test of scientific-technical thinking than novices after 2½ hours of play in our experiment. Although our results show value in video games as informal training for scientific discovery processes, this limitation of the effect suggests a law of diminishing returns; a relatively small quantity of practice or mastery of a single game produces as much effect on scientific thinking as hundreds of hours of play on many different games.

Other Aspects of Computer Technology: The Example of Word Processing

There are a number of beneficial effects of word processing. At this point, however, we do not know exactly why word processing is effective. Most probably it relates to ease of revising and the motivational value of always having a clean, printed copy of your work.

Perhaps, also, word processing is an instance of learners benefiting from the availability of multiple representations of a subject area. A consortium including IBM has recently developed a successful multimedia approach to reading instruction called "Writing to Read" (Evans, 1985). In this program, word processors are just one of the media tools available to young children for coding and decoding the written word. Indeed, the most reliable finding in the area of media and education is the superiority of multimedia over single-medium instruction.

Educational Favoritism Toward Print: It is Not the Only Kind of Literacy

In education, we have, by and large, acted as though print were good at teaching everything, as though it were a "transparent" medium that simply revealed a subject without imposing any of its own distortions on the subject being present- ed. I hope that by now it is clear that this assumption is not correct. Print has its own set of strengths and weaknesses, just like any other medium, and these cause it to "distort" some subjects, while presenting others more accurately and easi- ly. Like other media, it transforms information while it transmits it.

Nevertheless, our bias toward the use of the printed word in education is so strong that we have actually equated reading and writing with education. This is understandable historically, because formal education originated as a way of transmitting print literacy.

Television and Film Literacy

But literacy is not just something required by reading and writing. Just as we learn to decode the written word, we also must learn to decode other media, television and film for example. These media have their own code too. Most interesting here is the code of visual editing or montage techniques. Each tech- nique has its own meaning, which must be learned (Andrew, 1976; Rice, Huston, & Wright, 1982; Salomon, 1979). For example, a cut between shots indicates a new perspective on the scene; a dissolve or a fade is a cue that time or place has changed; a split screen denotes an act of comparison. Understanding these conventions of the code is parallel to understanding the sounds communicated by the alphabetic code in reading. As in reading, such understanding constitutes basic literacy in film and TV. A conscious awareness of the nature of the code and how it creates different effects constitutes a still higher level of literacy skills in these media.

The idea of computer literacy is also becoming accepted, although no one is sure exactly what it involves. However, this tentative acceptance shows an opening in society toward the idea that the printed word is not unique in requiring and fostering literacy skills.

Each form of literacy has its own function and its own value. Print literacy (reading and writing) is not the only worthwhile literacy in education. Indeed, I would present the shocking hypothesis that print has become "educational" not because of the intrinsic qualities of the medium, but simply because the printed word is used in education. That is, printed material is made the subject of discussion and analysis; and students are made responsible for mastering its content (Greenfield, 1985).

My argument is that the same processes of discussion and analysis can be applied to television (and to other electric and electronic media). Indeed, there is a body of evidence, summarized in Greenfield (1984), showing that discussion of televised material with a teacher in a classroom setting enhances learning above that resulting from simply viewing the program alone. We need to remove our prejudices against television and bring it into the educational process in a number of ways, if its full educational potential is to be realized.

One such way is through analyzing the forms of television and film (such as the editing techniques discussed above) in the classroom. This treatment would be analogous to the treatment of literature that is now commonplace in English classes. This kind of study would make learners more conscious of the language or code of television and film, and would take them to that higher level of literacy.

CONCLUSIONS: THE CASE FOR MULTIMEDIA EDUCATION

The biases of each medium are such that each differentially utilizes particular cognitive skills. Not one but many media are therefore necessary to socialize and educate a well-rounded and balanced individual, a person who can relate to the world of visual images as well as to the world of words, who can figure out a complex system or imagine the setting of a novel, who can process linear inputs or comprehend several things happening at once. This is one important argument for multimedia education.

Multimedia education would also give a more equal chance to students who learn best through different modalities. Similarly, it would give a more equal chance to students who arrive at school with unequal background experience with certain media, such as the world of print. This is another line of argument for multimedia education.

From the point of view of information transmission, each medium presents a different point of view on a topic by selectively emphasizing different kinds of information in its particular representation. If multiple representations and multiple points of view are best, then multimedia methods are required. This is another argument for multimedia education.

Indeed, educational thinking about the computer (and new media in the past) has focused too much on either-or questions of media selection: Should computers replace books, or even teachers? My argument is that each medium (the teacher most of all) has its own distinctive contribution to make to education and to cognitive development and that the media should be used in complementary fashion in a process of multimedia education.

For all these reasons, we should move toward a system of multimedia education in which audio, video, and computer technologies will surely play a key role. By giving each medium—the old ones as well as the new—its place in a child's life and education, each medium will be able to make its own special contribution to children's learning and development.

REFERENCES

Andrew, J. D. (1976). *The major film theories*. Oxford: Oxford University Press.

Beagles-Roos, J. (1985, September). *Specific impact of radio and television on adult story comprehension*. Paper presented at the meeting of the American Psychological Association, Los Angeles.

Beagles-Roos, J., & Gat, I. (1983). Specific impact of radio and television on children's story comprehension. *Journal of Educational Psychology, 75*, 128–135.

Evans, P. L. (1985, May). The appropriate use of microcomputer technology in education. In L. N. Bolen (Chair), *Future educational delivery systems: Technology in education*. Symposium conducted at the meeting of the American Association for the Advancement of Science, Los Angeles.

Ferguson, E. S. (1977). The mind's eye: Nonverbal thought in technology. *Science, 197*, 827–836.

Gagnon, D. (1985). Videogames and spatial skills: An exploratory study. *Educational Communication and Technology Journal*.

Gomez, L. M., Bowers, C., & Egan, D. E. (1982, March). Learner characteristics that predict success in using a text-editor tutorial. *Proceedings of Human Factors in Computer Systems Conference*, Gaithersburg, MD.

Gomez, L. M., Egan, D. E., Wheeler, E. A., Sharma, D. K., & Gruchacz, A. M. (1983, December). How interface design determines who has difficulty learning to use a text editor. *Proceedings of the Human Factors in Computing Systems Conference*, Boston.

Greenfield, P. M. (1984). *Mind and media: The effects of television, video games, and computers*. Cambridge, MA: Harvard University Press.

Greenfield, P. M. (1985). The case for multimedia education: Why print isn't always best. *American Educator*, fall,

Greenfield, P. M. & Beagles-Roos, J. (1983). *Cognitive effects of television and radio on children from different socio-economic and ethnic groups.* Paper presented at the meeting of the Society for Research in Child Development, Detroit.

Greenfield, P. M. & Beagles-Roos, J. (1985). Television vs. radio: The cognitive impact on different socio-economic and ethnic groups. Submitted for journal publication.

Greenfield, P. M., Farrar, D., & Beagles-Roos, J. (in press). Is the medium the message? An experimental comparison of the effects of radio and television on imagination. *Journal of Applied Developmental Psychology.*

Greenfield, P. M. & Lauber, B. A. (1985). *Inductive discovery in the mastery and transfer of video game expertise.* Submitted for journal publication.

McLuhan, M. (1964). *Understanding media: The extensions of man.* New York: McGraw-Hill.

Meline, C. W. (1976). Does the medium matter? *Journal of Communication, 26,* 81–89.

Rice, M. L., Huston, A. C., and Wright, J. C. (1982). The forms of television: Effects on children's attention, comprehension, and social behavior. In D. Pearl, L. Bouthilet, & J. Lazar (Eds.), *Television and behavior: Ten years of scientific progress and implications for the eighties: Vol. 2. Technical reviews* (pp. 24–38). Rockville, MD: National Institute of Mental Health.

Roberts, R. (1984, April). The role of prior knowledge in learning computer programming. In D. Kaye (Chair), *Computers, video games, children: New research perspectives.* Symposium conducted at the meeting of the Western Psychological Association, Los Angeles.

Salomon, G. (1979). *Interaction of media, cognition, and learning.* San Francisco: Jossey-Bass.

Sturm, H., & Jorg, S. (1981). *Information processing by young children: Piaget's theory applied to radio and television.* Munich: K. G. Saur.

Sykora, J., & Birkner, J. (1982). *The video master's guide to Pac-Man.* New York: Bantam.

3 Learning Programming Languages: Research and Applications

Richard E. Mayer
University of California, Santa Barbara

Piraye Bayman
AT&T Bell Laboratories

Jennifer L. Dyck
California State University, Fresno

ABSTRACT

This chapter is concerned with the study of how novices learn computer programming. Four research issues addressed in this chapter are (1) users possess many misconceptions of machines and procedures, (2) learning to program involves building a concrete model of the system, (3) successful learning depends on the availability of prerequisite cognitive skills and knowledge, and (4) learning to program may be a vehicle for teaching students about their own thinking processes. Research findings and applications are described for each of these issues.

INTRODUCTION

During the past 10 years, we have been engaged in a research program aimed at understanding how novices learn computer programming (Bayman, 1983; Bayman & Mayer, 1983, 1984; Dyck, 1986; Dyck & Mayer, 1985; Mayer, 1975, 1976, 1979, 1980, 1981, 1985; Mayer & Bayman, 1981; Mayer & Bromage, 1980; Shneiderman & Mayer, 1979; Shneiderman, Mayer, McKay, & Heller, 1977). The purpose of this chapter is to summarize four of our research findings and to describe possible applications for each.

The four research findings and applications are:

1. Users possess many misconceptions—diagnose and remediate users' ineffective mental models.
2. Programming requires going beyond what is taught—use concrete models to foster transfer.
3. All learners are not created equal—assess and pretrain for prerequisite cognitive skills.
4. Programming can enhance cognitive skills—use computers as a way of teaching students about their thinking processes.

USERS POSSESS MANY MISCONCEPTIONS— DIAGNOSE AND REMEDIATE USERS' INEFFECTIVE MENTAL MODELS

Research on Misconceptions

Recent research by Bayman (1983) and Bayman and Mayer (1983) has identified many misconceptions held by beginning BASIC programmers. In a series of studies, college students learned to program in BASIC via a standard hands-on mastery course. Following successful mastery of the material in the course, students were interviewed concerning their "mental models" of the computer. In particular, students were asked to describe the steps that go on inside the computer for each of 10 elementary BASIC statements, such as INPUT A or READ A or LET A = B + 1.

Typical incorrect interpretations of INPUT A were "Write A in memory" or "Wait for someone to type A on the keyboard." Apparently, users have difficulty in conceiving where the to-be-input data comes from (i.e., the keyboard) and how it is stored in memory (i.e., in the specified memory space). Very few students (only 3%) correctly stated that a prompt is printed on the screen, the computer waits for the user to type in a number followed by pressing RETURN, and this number is stored in a specified memory space. Apparently, many users fail to understand the nature of executive control, i.e., that when the computer gives a ready prompt it is waiting for some action from the user.

A typical incorrect interpretation for READ A was "Print the value of A on the screen." Only 10% of the students correctly stated that READ A means to take the next number from the data stack and store that number in memory space A. Apparently, users do not understand where the to-be-read data comes from (i.e., the data stack or DATA statement) or how it is stored in memory (i.e., memory space).

Typical incorrect interpretations for LET A = B + 1 were "Write an equation in memory" or "Print the value of A on the screen." Only 27% of the subjects gave the correct answer: store the value of B + 1 in memory space A. Apparently, users seem to interpret a LET statement as an equation (i.e., treating the equal sign as an equality) rather than as an assignment. Those who understand the concept of assignment often have trouble conceiving of how and where to store the assigned value.

Similarly, misconceptions were found for PRINT statements and IF-GOTO statements. In spite of many hours of hands-on training with apparent mastery of the material, subjects only provided correct interpretations of about 25% of the statements they learned about.

Applications of Research on Misconceptions

The "misconceptions" research suggests that users employ mental models for the computer system they learn about and that these mental models are often incorrect or incomplete. Learning to read and write in BASIC also involves acquiring a mental model of the system. Although all of our subjects showed some proficiency in reading and writing simple BASIC programs similar to those presented in the training materials, most of our subjects failed to acquire useful mental models.

Why should we be concerned with users' mental models? One reason is that certain mental models may be better able to support transfer than other models. For example, Bayman (1983) taught BASIC to college students and then gave them tests measuring their mental models (such as the "misconceptions" interview) and their ability to use BASIC to solve novel programming problems. Students who had acquired good mental models (i.e., who mainly acquired correct conceptions of the actions carried out in the computer for each BASIC statement) scored an average of 75% on the programming problem-solving test whereas students who acquired poor mental models (i.e., who mainly acquired incorrect conceptions of the actions carried out by the computer for each BASIC statement) scored an average of 42% on the problem-solving test. These results are consistent with the assertion that useful mental models are related to transfer to creative problem solving.

The implication of these results is that direct instruction in appropriate mental models—along with traditional instruction in BASIC—would enhance students' ability to use BASIC creatively. For example, Bayman (1983) developed BASIC instruction that either included training in appropriate mental models or did not. The mental models training explicitly stated what happened "inside the comouter" for each BASIC statement. For less skilled learners, the training resulted in better learning of BASIC than standard training; for more skilled learners the reverse pattern was obtained. Apparently, less skilled learners benefit from direct

TABLE 3.1
Protocols for READ A that Suggest Useful and
Unuseful Mental Models

Useful Mental Model
The computer will put the number from DATA into space A.
Unuseful Mental Model
The computer will print out a number from its memory on the screen.

instruction of mental models; in contrast, more skilled learners may be able to generate their own mental models so the teacher's model might interfere.

In summary, a recommendation that follows from this line of research is that teachers should be sensitive to the mental models of students. Mental models may be assessed by asking the student to describe (or role play) what is going on inside the computer for each elementary BASIC statement. For example, Table 3.1 compares the protocol of a student who has a useful mental model versus a student who has an unuseful mental model. When a student displays a mental model that is incorrect or inefficient, direct instruction for a more efficient mental model is needed. Students need practice describing the "hidden" information processes that go on inside the computer—with special focus on where data come from, where data are stored, the concepts of executive control and assignment.

PROGRAMMING REQUIRES GOING BEYOND WHAT IS TAUGHT—USE CONCRETE MODELS TO FOSTER TRANSFER

Research on Concrete Models

Suppose that students learn some elementary BASIC statements such as READ, DATA, LET, PRINT, IF, and END by reading a manual and having hands-on access to a computer. To evaluate their learning we could ask "near transfer" questions that are very similar to the material covered in the manual; for example, we could present fill-in questions such as, "READ and   statements have to exist together in a program." In contrast, we could ask "far transfer" questions that require going beyond information in the manual. For example, we could ask a student to determine whether the following program will run and to repair this program if needed:

```
10 READ A,B
20 LET C = A − B
```

```
30 PRINT C
40 IF C > 0 THEN GOTO 10
50 END
```

As you can see, this program needs a DATA statement such as 15 DATA 6,3,8,8. Although most students are able to perform well on near transfer, students differ greatly in their ability to succeed on far transfer items. What do good problem solvers have that poor problem solvers do not have? The previous section suggested that "going beyond the information in the manual" requires that the user build a useful conceptual model of the system.

Table 3.2 presents a concrete model of the computer similar to that used in many of our research studies on learning of BASIC (Mayer, 1975, 1976, 1981; Mayer & Bromage, 1980). As you can see, the model provides a concrete representation for the main components in a computer system: memory scoreboard represents memory storage of data, input window represents data input from a data list, output pad represents the printing out of data, program list represents executive control of the order of statement processing, scratch pad represents the arithmetic and logic unit, and the run-wait light represents the processing status of the system. These functions are described in detail in Mayer (1986).

In our studies, some computer-naive students were exposed to this kind of model prior to reading a computer programming manual whereas other students were either not exposed to the model or exposed to the model after reading the same manual. All students performed well on tests covering material that was like that in the manual; however, the "before" group performed much better than other students on transferring what they learned to solve novel problems. This finding was particularly strong for low-ability learners, suggesting that more skilled learners could invent their own models.

Applications of Research on Concrete Models

Consistent results, over a series of experiments, suggest that concrete models can enhance problem-solving performance on tasks that require going beyond what was taught. The instructional implications are clear: inexperienced or less skilled students need help in formulating a conceptual model of the system. Before learning, students should be exposed to a concrete model of the system presented at an appropriate level of detail for the students. During learning, students should be encouraged to make connections between information in the manual and their conceptual model of the system. These learning activities can involve orally answering questions during learning or physically role playing the actions of the computer.

TABLE 3.2
Concrete Model of the Computer

Before you start studying the first lesson of the minicourse we want you to study six components of the computer that we think will be helpful to you in the process of learning the course material.

1. The display screen and the keyboard:

The display screen may look like the above, where], the cursor, indicated the computer is ready to accept any command or instruction from you. Numbers and letters you type in and the messages the computer sends may be printed on this display screen.

The keyboard is like a typewriter. It consists of keys for letters; digits, special characters such as *, +, =, and so on; and special keys such as RETURN and CONTROL.

2. The memory spaces

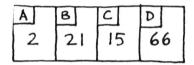

Suppose that inside the computer there are memory spaces labeled A, B, C, D, and so on. The computer can store only one value at a time in each space. In the above diagram, the values stored in A, B, C, and D are 2, 21, 15, and 66 respectively.

3. The control monitor light:

WAIT   ○

GO   ●

When the computer is executing a statement or running a program it turns on the GO light indicating that it is busy. When the computer is ready to accept a command or a statement from the keyboard it turns on the WAIT light indicating that it is waiting for an instruction from you. In the above diagram the computer is running.

4. The data line:

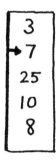

Numbers that are entered with a DATA statement are put in line as shown in the above diagram. 3 is the first number in line to be processed. 7, 25, 10, and 8 are next in line. There is a pointer that indicated the number to be processed. For example, if 3 has already been processed the pointer would point to the next number in line, i.e., 7, as shown in the above diagram.

5. The work space:

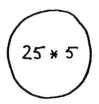

Suppose that inside the computer there is an area where all the arithmetic and logical operations and the computations take place; we call this area the work space. In the above diagram, the computer multiplies 25 by 5 in this space. What the computer does with the result of this calculation depends on the specific instruction typed into the computer.

6. The program memory:

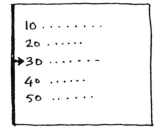

Suppose that you typed in a five-line computer program at a computer terminal and want to computer to execute it. The computer used its program memory to store these lines so that it can keep track of the specific statements you typed in for each line as it runs your program. A pointer shows which line the computer is on during program execution. In the above diagram, the computer is executing the statement on line 30.

In a moment, you will be given the first lesson of the minicourse. Please note that the described parts of the computer will appear in the following arrangement all through the text.

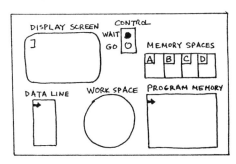

From Bayman (1983).

ALL LEARNERS ARE NOT CREATED EQUAL—ASSESS AND PRETRAIN FOR PREREQUISITE COGNITIVE SKILLS

Research on Prerequisite Skills

Previous research has demonstrated that learning computer programming is not a passive process of pouring information into the learner's head. Instead, learning involves an active integration of new information with existing knowledge and skills. Thus, in order to understand the learning process, it is necessary to determine which prerequisite skills are most relevant to learning a programming language.

General intellectual ability—such as measured by the nonverbal logical reasoning tests of the IBM Programmer Aptitude Test (PAT) or the Aptitude Assessment Battery:Programming (AABP)—often correlates moderately with success in learning programming as measured by exam grade (Webb, 1984). However, such results do not clearly show which specific skills are related to learning a new programming language such as BASIC. In addition to the general skill of nonverbal logical reasoning, there are two specific prequisite skills that have been identified in research studies: procedure comprehension and problem translation.

Snow (1980) found that a "diagramming test"—a test aimed specifically at comprehension of BASIC-like procedures—correlated strongly with success in learning BASIC. This result is consistent with the observation that learning BASIC programming involves building upon one's concept of a procedure—i.e., procedure comprehension skill. Soloway, Lochhead, & Clement (1982) found that students who used BASIC to represent algebra word problems made fewer translation errors than students who did not. This result is consistent with the observation that writing a BASIC program requires translation from English into another formal language—i.e., problem translation skill.

Jennifer Dyck, Bill Vilberg, and I have carried out a series of four studies to examine how these three skills—logical reasoning, procedure comprehension, and problem translation—relate to success in learning BASIC. Logical reasoning represents a measure of general intellectual ability whereas procedure comprehension and problem translation are subcomponent skills in BASIC programming. These latter two skills are specifically related to learning BASIC because they can be identified in a cognitive task analysis of BASIC (see Mayer, 1985).

In our study, computer-naive college students took a battery of pretests including measures of each of these three target skills. Example test items are given in Table 3.3. Then, the students learned BASIC. Finally, the students took posttests to evaluate their success in learning BASIC. As expected, measures of logical reasoning (similar to tests of general intelligence) correlated strongly with performance in learning BASIC. More interestingly, measures of two skills that are specific subcomponents in BASIC programming—procedure comprehension and problem translation—each correlated strongly with performance on the

TABLE 3.3
Example Test Items for Three Predictive Thinking Skills

Problem Translation Skill
(Test item from Word Problem Translation Test)

A car rental service charges $20.00 a day and 15¢ a mile to rent
a car. Find the expression for total cost (C), in dollars, of
renting a car for (D) days to travel (M) miles.

    (a)   C = 20D + .15M
    (b)   C = 15D + .20M
    (c)   C = 20D + .15M
    (d)   D = .15D + 20M
    (e)   none of the above

Procedure Comprehension Skill
(Test item from Following Procedures Test)

1. Put 5 in Box A.
2. Put 4 in Box B.
3. Add the number in Box A and the number in Box B, put result
   in Box C.
4. Add the number in Box A and the number in Box C, put result
   in Box A.
5. Write down the numbers from Box A, B, C.

What is the output of this program?

    (a)   5, 4, 9
    (b)   14, 4, 9
    (c)   14, 9, 9
    (d)   9, 4, 9
    (e)   none of the above

Logical Reasoning Skill
(Test item from Logical Reasoning Test)

Draw an X through the set of letters that is different.

BCDE   FGHI   JKLM   PRST   VWXY

BASIC posttest. In fact, the measures of specifically relevant skills correlated more strongly with success in learning BASIC ($r = .4$ to $r = .6$) than measures of general intellectual ability such as logical reasoning ($r = .3$). These results are particularly interesting because they suggest that some of the most predictive prerequisite skills for initial learning of BASIC are relatively specific and teachable. In contrast, tests of skills such as arithmetic computation or verbal ability did not correlate strongly with success in learning BASIC. These skills are not specific subcomponents of BASIC programming. Apparently, successful learning of BASIC depends partly on students' existing knowledge and skills, including knowledge and skills that are specifically relevant to the processes required to program in BASIC.

Applications of Research on Prerequisites

One implication of the foregoing results is that students' prerequisite skills should be assessed prior to instruction. Pretraining should be provided for students who lack the appropriate prerequisite skills. For example, in one recent study carried out in our labs, Jennifer Dyck provided pretraining in comprehension of English-language procedures to some learners but not to others. Pretraining involved a series of items in which the student had to predict the output of an English-language procedure. For example, one item was the following:

1. Put the first number shown below in Box-A.
2. Put the second number shown below in Box-B.
3. Add the numbers Box-A and Box-B together; and put this new result in Box-C.
4. Write down the number that is Box-C. The first number is 3. The second number is 2.

If the subject was unable to produce the correct answer, the correct answer was provided. The pretrained group subsequently learned BASIC at a much faster rate than the untrained group. Apparently, pretraining can be successfully provided for specific skills such as procedure comprehension and problem translation; however, it is doubtful whether pretraining can greatly influence general skills such as logical reasoning.

PROGRAMMING CAN ENHANCE COGNITIVE SKILLS— USE COMPUTERS AS A WAY OF TEACHING STUDENTS ABOUT THEIR THINKING PROCESSES

Research on Teaching Cognitive Skills

Teaching thinking skills has a long and disappointing history in American education. As Rippa (1980) points out, the Latin School movement, which began several centuries ago, was based on the idea that learning Latin would foster proper "habits of mind," including disciplined and logical thinking. However, the practical demands of an emerging industrialized society, and the results of educational research, helped to bring on the demise of Latin Schools. For example, Thorndike's (1923) famous transfer of training studies reported that a year's study of Latin had very little effect on learning in other disciplines.

More recently, educators have expressed renewed interest in "teaching students how to think" rather than "what to think" (Lochhead, 1979, p. 1). In particular, many strong claims have been made concerning the effects of learning a programming language on students' cognitive development (Papert, 1980). However, there has been relatively little research support for these claims (Clements & Gullo, 1984; Linn, 1985). One promising result is Clements & Gullo's (1984) finding that elementary school children who learned LOGO showed gains in several measures of creative problem solving as compared to children who did not learn LOGO.

In order to provide some new information on this issue, Jennifer Dyck, Bill Vilberg, and I conducted a study involving 57 computer-naive college students who were taking a course in BASIC. The students took pretests—including tests of logical reasoning, procedure comprehension, and problem translation. Then, the students learned BASIC during a semester-long course, and finally, they took versions of the same tests. A comparison group took the same pretests and posttest but did not take an intervening course in BASIC.

The results indicated that the students who learned BASIC showed large gains in specific cognitive skills such as procedure comprehension and problem translation; in contrast, the comparison group did not. Apparently, learning of BASIC also increased certain cognitive skills that were related to programming in BASIC. However, both the BASIC group and the comparison group showed large gains in logical reasoning, so it is not possible to attribute the logical reasoning gains to BASIC instruction. There was also no evidence that learning BASIC enhanced performance on tests of spatial ability or verbal ability. These results suggest that learning of BASIC may serve to enhance cognitive skills that are directly related to BASIC—such as procedure comprehension and problem translation—but may not serve to enhance general cognitive skills—such as logical reasoning, spatial ability, or verbal ability.

Applications of Research on Teaching Cognitive Skills

These results encourage the idea that teaching computer programming may serve as a vehicle for teaching certain thinking skills. Thus, teaching programming should be done in a way that enhances thinking skills—with specific cognitive skills targeted for evaluation. However, the current results serve to place some limitations on our expectations concerning the breadth of thinking skills that can be enhanced. In particular, it is most fruitful to view learning to program as an experience that may enhance cognitive skills that are specific and are direct prerequisites. It may not be fruitful to expect learning of a simple language such as BASIC to have a major influence on general intellectual abilities such as logical reasoning, spatial reasoning, or verbal reasoning.

CONCLUSION

The goal of this chapter, and indeed of this book, is to examine the applications of cognitive research. In cognitive psychology, the interplay between theory and application can be a fruitful one. The demands of real-world domains—such as learning computer programming—offer important challenges to cognitive theory; similarly, the theories of cognitive psychology have potential for improving the educational process in the real world.

The research-to-applications theme, however, is not without serious obstacles and limitations. A major obstacle in writing this chapter has been the relative lack of research on how novices learn computer programming. In short, the research base needs continued growth and a more comprehensive theory. A major limitation is that the applications suggested in this chapter are largely untested. Although the applications seem to follow from the research, additional work is needed to evaluate the applications. The four research-to-application components of this chapter are based largely on our own work over the past decade. We have not attempted to review the growing body of research on how novices learn programming languages; instead, we have given an example of how the results of our research program may eventually be applied to the design of computer literacy curricula.

ACKNOWLEDGMENTS

Our research on learning programming languages has been supported by the following grants: Grant EC-44020 from the National Science Foundation, "Instructional Variables in Computer Programming," 1974–75; Grant SED77-19875 from the National Science Foundation, "Increasing the Meaningfulness of Technical Information for Novices," 1977–80; Grant NIE-G80-0118 from the National Institute of Education, "Diagnosis and Remediation of Computer Programming Skill for Creative Problem Solving," 1980–82; Grant MDR84-70248 from the National Science Foundation, "Cognitive Prerequisites and Consequences of Learning Computer Programming," 1984–87.

REFERENCES

Bayman, P. (1983). *Effects of instructional procedures on learning a first programming language.* Doctoral dissertation, University of California, Santa Barbara.

Bayman, P., & Mayer, R. E. (1983). A diagnosis of beginning programmers' misconceptions of BASIC programming statements. *Communications of the ACM, 26,* 677–679.

Bayman, P., & Mayer, R. E. (1984). Instructional manipulation of users' mental models for electronic calculators. *International Journal of Man-Machine Studies, 20,* 189–199.

Clements, D. H., & Gullo, D. F. (1984). Effects of computer programming on young children's cognition. *Journal of Educational Psychology, 76,* 1051–1058.

Dyck, J. L. (1986). *Acquisition of the cognitive skill of computer programming.* Doctoral dissertation, University of California, Santa Barbara.

Dyck, J. L., & Mayer, R. E. (1985). BASIC vs. natural language: Is there one underlying comprehension process? In L. Borman, & B. Curtis (Eds.), *Human factors in computing systems* (pp. 221–3). Amsterdam: Elsevier.

Linn, M. C. (1985). The cognitive consequences of programming instruction in classrooms. *Educational Researcher, 14,* 14–16, 25–29.

Lochhead, J. (1979). An introduction to cognitive process instruction. In J. Lochhead & J. Clement (Eds.), *Cognitive process instruction* (pp. 1–4). Philadelphia: Franklin Institute Press.

Mayer, R. E. (1975). Different problem solving competencies established in learning computer programming with and without meaningful models. *Journal of Educational Psychology, 67,* 725–734.

Mayer, R. E. (1976). Some conditions of meaningful learning for computer programming: Advance organizers and subject control of frame order. *Journal of Educational Psychology, 68,* 143–150.

Mayer, R. E. (1979). A psychology of learning BASIC. *Communications of the ACM, 22,* 589–593.

Mayer, R. E. (1980). Elaboration techniques for technical text: An experimental test of the learning strategy hypothesis. *Journal of Educational Psychology, 72,* 770–784.

Mayer, R. E. (1981). The psychology of how novices learn computer programming. *Computing Surveys, 13,* 121–141.

Mayer, R. E. (1985). Learning in complex domains: A cognitive analysis of computer programming. *The Psychology of Learning and Motivation, 19,* 89–130.

Mayer, R. E. (1986). *BASIC: A short course.* Boston: Houghton-Mifflin.

Mayer, R. E., & Bayman, P. (1981). Psychology of calculator language: A framework for describing differences in users' knowledge. *Communications of the ACM, 24,* 511–520.

Mayer, R. E., & Bromage, B. (1980). Different recall protocols for technical text due to advance organizers. *Journal of Educational Psychology, 72,* 209–225.

Papert, S. (1980). *Mindstorms.* New York: Basic Books.

Rippa, S. A. (1980). *Education in a free society: An American history.* New York: Longman.

Shneiderman, B., & Mayer, R. E. (1979). Syntactic/semantic interactions in programmer behavior: A model and experimental results. *International Journal of Computer and Information Sciences, 8,* 219–238.

Shneiderman, B., Mayer, R. E., McKay, D., & Heller, P. (1977). Experimental investigations of the utility of detailed flowcharts in programming. *Communications of the ACM, 20,* 373–381.

Snow, R. E. (1980). Aptitude processes. In R. E. Snow, P. Federico, & W. E. Montague (Eds.), *Aptitude, learning, and instruction* Vol. 1 (pp. 27–63). Hillsdale, NJ: Lawrence Erlbaum Associates.

Soloway, E., Lochhead, J., & Clement, J. (1982). Does computer programming enhance problem-solving ability? Some positive evidence on algebra word problems. In R. J. Seidel, R. E. Anderson, & B. Hunter (Eds.), *Computer literacy* (pp. 171–185). New York: Academic Press.

Thorndike, E. L. (1923). The influence of first-year Latin upon the ability to read English. *School and Society, 17,* 165–168.

Webb, N. M. (1984). Microcomputer learning in small groups: Cognitive requirements and group processes. *Journal of Educational Psychology, 76,* 1076–1088.

4 An Investigation of Groups Working at the Computer

David Trowbridge
Carnegie-Mellon University

ABSTRACT

Computer-based learning materials can provide ample opportunities for interactive learning. Materials can be particularly effective when more than one student works at the computer. This paper reports results of an investigation of interactivity among young adolescent students working at the computer. Groups ranged from individuals working alone to four students working together. Interactivity was enhanced when students worked in twos or threes.

INTRODUCTION

As microcomputers gradually become available in schools and other learning environments, many questions arise about how they can best be used. Since (at least in the near term) computers are expensive tools of instruction, and limited in number, it is important to consider the advantages and disadvantages of having students use computers in small groups.

This chapter presents a program of research that examines learning by individuals and groups in a computer environment. Individual interactivity as a function of group size was investigated by focusing on the various modes of interaction available to students using a computer. Achievement was measured by administering brief paper-and-pencil tests and individual interviews. In addition, a description of social interaction among students using computers was developed by making global assessments of the learning sessions.

Which context is better for learning: group or individual? Clearly, individuals working alone at the computer have exclusive access to the program,but normally do not articulate their ideas verbally. Students working as members of groups, on the other hand, may have less access to the keyboard, but have many opportunities for verbal and social interaction with other members of the group. How do these opportunities for interaction affect learning?

A number of research efforts have focused on the effects of instructional group size on learning in non-computer environments. The results vary. Klausmeier, Wiersma, and Harris (1963) examined the efficiency with which concepts were learned by students who participated in instructional groups of various sizes. They concluded that students working in pairs and quads grasped concepts faster than individuals (triads were not examined). However, on transfer tests, subjects who had learned as individuals generally exhibited greater concept retention than those who had learned in a group.

In another study, Sharan, Ackerman, and Hertz-Lazarowitz (1980) found no differences in the learning of low-level information between those students who worked individually and those who worked in small groups. In the learning of higher-level concepts, however, they found that groups did better. Sharan (1980), Johnson and Johnson (1974), Slavin (1980), and Webb (1977) report similar findings.

The current study used instructional materials that emphasize high-level learning: reasoning skills and conceptual understanding. The materials utilized simulations of science experiments that students performed on the screen. A Socratic dialogue format encouraged active participation by the learner.

RESEARCH METHODS

The science materials were produced by the Educational Technology Center at the University of California, Irvine, under two previous development projects. They were designed specifically to develop formal reasoning skills and scientific literacy, and have been described elsewhere (Arons, Bork, & Kurtz, 1981; Arons, Bork, & Trowbridge, 1983; Trowbridge & Bork, 1981a, 1981b). Middle-ability student subjects were drawn from seventh- and eighth-grade classes in the Irvine Unified School District. They participated in unsupervised activities at the computer individually or in groups of 2, 3, or 4. Sessions lasted about 40 minutes each.

Each session was videotaped; an interface device connecting the videotape recorder to the computer enabled researchers to review the course of the computer program during their observations of student behavior. Three components of the group activity were recorded on videotape: (a) video of the students working together, (b) audio of their conversation, and (c) all key pushes of the computer keyboard.

The videotape data collection system consisted of a microcomputer that ran the interactive learning materials, a video cassette recorder with two separate audio channels (one channel for voice, the other for keystrokes), an interface device for connecting the computer to the recorder, and associated utility software for handling input and output during recording and playback sessions.

An observational instrument, akin to the systems of interactional analysis pioneered by Bales (1950) and Flanders (1970), was developed to categorize behaviors representing various kinds of interactivity. The videotaping system and observational instrument were tested and refined during a pilot study which has been described elsewhere (Potter, 1982; Trowbridge & Bork, 1982; Trowbridge & Durnin, 1983). The coupling of computer and videotape recorder provides an authentic reconstruction of the original learning session which yields to systematic and reliable observation. Several experiments were then conducted in a systematic formal study. Details of the two studies are reported in a doctoral dissertation by Robin Durnin (1985), then at The Claremont Graduate School.

REVIEW OF FINDINGS FROM THE PILOT STUDY

The purpose of the pilot study was to determine relevant variables and establish a means of analysis. Early observations of groups in this highly interactive environment had indicated a high incidence of cognitive and social behaviors which were indicative of important thinking and learning activity.

Several questions arose: Is access to the keyboard dominated by one member of the group to the exclusion of others? In the group setting, is behavior mainly beneficial to learning (e.g., restatement of questions or problems in one's own words, articulation of one's own thinking, formulation of hypotheses, predictions, evaluations and explanations, tutorial assistance to other members of the group, etc.), or detrimental to learning (e.g., distracting or irrelevant conversation, non-cooperation, or withdrawal)? To what extent is the social interaction among members of groups supportive, and to what extent is it disruptive?

Thirty-five students in grades 6–8 took part in the pilot study. They worked at the computer individually, in pairs or in triads. A wide cross-section of students was represented, ranging from high to low ability. The composition of groups varied in terms of previous group history, ability, and sex. In addition, the computer-based learning materials varied in several respects, including their emphases on textual and graphical input. Students worked in a room by themselves, unsupervised. Findings of the pilot study are summarized as follows:

1. Generally, engagement was high throughout the learning session (mean percentage of time on task: 95%).
2. Students working in pairs generally displayed greater interactivity than those working alone or in groups of three.

3. Cognitive behavior, indicated by verbalization, accounted for a slightly larger fraction of interactivity among pairs than among triads.
4. Students working in pairs made fewer incorrect responses to program questions (about 30% fewer) than individuals or triads.
5. In groups consisting of members who had a prior group history, the tenor of the session was sometimes dictated by previously established social roles.

On the basis of these findings, we began a more controlled and more extensive investigation of this particular instructional setting.

DESIGN OF THE FORMAL STUDY

In the formal study, the sample was limited to middle-ability students with roughly equal numbers of groups who had worked together on academic tasks before and those who had not. The study involved a single sequence of computer-based learning activities.

Fifty-eight 7th- and 8th-grade students participated in this part of the study. On the basis of their teacher's knowledge of their ability levels and prior group-learning experiences, we selected a sample of students that excluded individuals with exceptionally high or low academic abilities. In addition, we chose roughly equal numbers of groups with and without prior academic group experience. Thus, our population reflected the social groupings in a typical school. Our sample is summarized in Table 4.1.

Data were collected for each subject on age, sex, grade point average, and family income. A one-way analysis of variance on individuals indicated that none of these factors varied significantly with group size.

Students worked in a quiet area separate from their classroom, in the presence of one researcher who unobtrusively monitored the videotaping but did not intervene during the session. The camera was in full view of the students. As we had discovered early in the pilot study, students quickly became involved in the computer program during these sessions, and seemed to ignore the fact that they were being taped.

A sequence of four activities from the computer dialogue "Batteries and Bulbs" was used for all sessions. Students manipulated images of batteries, bulbs, and wires on the computer screen to perform experiments with simple DC circuits. The purpose of the materials was for students to discover the idea of current flow through a complete circuit. Titles of the first four activities were, "Light the Bulb," "Arrangements of Batteries and Bulbs," "Other Things in the Circuit," and "A Scientific Model." Immediately before and immediately after the session, students took a brief quiz on their understanding of electrical circuits. Three months after the computer sessions, the paper-and-pencil quiz

TABLE 4.1
Subject Sample for the Formal Study

	Group Size			
	1	2	3	4
Numbers of Groups	8	8	6	4
(with, without) group experience	(5,3)	(5,3)	(4,2)	(2,2)

was repeated, and a brief interview was conducted involving a simple task of lighting a flashlight bulb using actual equipment.

Three major goals of the study were established: (a) to measure frequencies of interactivity and to look for variations as a function of group size, (b) to measure students' grasp of the concepts being taught by having students apply their knowledge to appropriate non-computer tasks, (c) to judge certain global aspects of the group session in order to provide generalizations of typical social and psychological behavior in the computer-based learning environment.

RESULTS

Interactivity

The observational instrument consisted of 19 observable behaviors. Behavior codes fell into three categories of interaction: keyboard, cognitive, and social. The first category represents interaction between a student and the program via the computer screen and keyboard. The cognitive category encompasses those verbal behaviors that were suggestive of thinking activity. We did not attempt to infer cognitive behavior beyond that which was directly observable in speech. The third category, social, includes the verbal and nonverbal behaviors that though not specific to the intellectual content of the lesson, nevertheless appeared to facilitate the learning process. A summary of these three categories of behaviors is presented in Table 4.2.

The original list of behavior codes included a category for reading from the screen, and a few categories of off-task behavior. Reading from the screen was so frequent and continuous, however, and off-task behaviors were so infrequent that these categories were not deemed useful for the subsequent analysis of interactivity based on frequency counts.

For purposes of reducing the magnitude of the task of reviewing videotapes, observations were limited to Activities 2-4 of the Batteries and Bulbs dialogue. During playback of the videotapes, raters focused attention on one student at a time and recorded behavior codes in 10-second intervals.

TABLE 4.2
Summary of Behaviors Included in the Keyboard,
Cognition, and Social Categories

1. Keyboard Category

    types at keyboard

2. Cognitive Category

    tells, directs others
    queries, asks for suggestions
    accepts, responds to suggestions
    interprets in one's own words
    explains, formulates reasons
    formulates question or answer
    formulates prediction
    evaluates using criteria
    disagrees with program

3. Social Category

    neutral conversation, opinions
    approval, agrees with another
    disapproval, disagrees
    shares keyboard with others
    takes turns
    gives help, assists another
    polls others, solicits, votes
    delegates task to another
    encourages another

Time to complete these activities ranged from 15 to 35 minutes, with an average time of 25 minutes. Differences in average completion times for groups of different sizes were not significant. Nevertheless, observations of interactive behaviors were normalized by dividing the number of observations by the elapsed time of the session. Thus, we compare "Interactivity Rates" rather than behavior counts. Table 4.3 displays the mean Individual Interactivity Rates by group size for each category of interactivity. Percentages of the totals are shown in parentheses.

Because members of groups of any size have opportunities for verbalization that individuals working alone do not have, we have separated the consideration of groups of 2–4 from the overall consideration of groups of 1–4. The analysis of variance has been carried out first by considering all four sizes as conditions, then second, by considering pairs, triads, and quads as a set of three conditions on which the interactivity rates depend.

A significant difference in total individual interactivity rates is evident whether or not the condition of working alone is included. The figures suggest not only that members of pairs and triads had higher rates of interactivity than individuals working alone, but that among groups of 2–4, members of pairs and triads experienced greater rates of interactivity than members of quads.

The breakdown of various modes of interactivity is displayed in the first three rows. For example, in the row labeled keyboard, we see that as the size of the group increased, the keyboard activity of each member decreased correspon-

TABLE 4.3
Individual Interactivity Rates Interactions per 100 Seconds With Percentage
of Total Shown in Parentheses

| | Group Size | | | | Values (see note) | | |
	1	2	3	4	A	B	C
Keyboard	3.36 (91)	1.82 (34)	1.36 (24)	0.87 (23)	13.94***	4.01**	1.34
Cognitive	0.23 (6)	1.61 (30)	2.10 (38)	1.45 (39)	15.02***	4.15**	1.71
Social	0.12 (3)	1.90 (36)	2.10 (38)	1.43 (38)	14.11***	3.06	3.26**
Total	3.71 (100)	5.33 (100)	5.56 (100)	3.75 (100)	4.51**	4.66**	3.26**
Sample size	8	16	18	16			

Note.   A: Anova on means, $F(3,54)$: conditions 1-4; $(N = 58)$
B: Anova on means, $F(2,47)$: conditions 2-4; $(N = 50)$
C: F test for equality of variances, $F(15,15)$: conditions 4 vs. 2

*$p < 0.05$, **$P < 0.025$, ***$p < 0.01$.

dingly. Rates of cognitive and social interactivity for individuals working alone were negligible; non-zero values were due to the fact that individuals occasionally talked to themselves.

Pairs and triads had higher levels of cognitive and social in!eractivity than either individuals or quads. Consideration of groups of 2–4 alone led to the same conclusion: Members of quads do not experience as high a level of interactivity in any category as either members of pairs or triads.

An *F* test for equality of variance was also performed for groups of 2–4. As the size of the group increased, so did the dispersion in interactivity rates. The ratio of variances for quads to pairs was significant for total interactivity rates, suggesting that members of quads are more likely to vary in interactivity from high to low.

TABLE 4.4
Percentage of Total Group Interactivity Exhibited
by Each Group Member as a Function of Group Size

| | Group Size | | |
Rank	2	3	4
Highest	59	44	43
2nd Highest	41	31	33
3rd Highest		26	18
Lowest			6

Another result of the analysis of Interactivity Rates was obtained by ranking members of each group according to their interactivity rates and comparing mean values. These data are presented in Table 4.4. In groups of 2 and 3, there is a spread of 18 percentage points between the most and least interactive members; in groups of 4, the spread is 37 points. Thus in quads, we often observed one person "left out" of the group activity.

Achievement

Immediately before and after each computer session, students were tested individually using a paper-and-pencil task in which they were shown a picture of a battery and a light bulb and were asked to draw an arrangement of wires in which the bulb would light. After 3 months, students were again tested with the picture, and immediately afterward with an interview task.

In the interview, students were presented with an actual battery, bulb, and wires, and were asked to light the bulb. They received a passing score only if they lighted the bulb successfully on their first attempt, without trial and error. On both the paper-and-pencil version of the quiz, and in the interview with actual equipment, students were scored only as having passed or failed.

Before using these instructional materials, very few of these students (12%) knew how to light a bulb. Immediately after the session with the computer, nearly all (95%) could light the bulb. On an interview task involving actual batteries, bulbs, and wires, essentially all students who had used the computer materials (86%) could light the bulb immediately, without trial and error. Thus, for this particular task, transfer of learning to the actual physical case was straightforward and successful.

Another paper-and-pencil test was administered immediately after the computer session and again 3 months later. This test involved eight items, each illustrating an arrangement of battery, bulb, and wires, in which the student had to judge whether the given arrangement would light the bulb. Results are summarized in Table 4.5.

TABLE 4.5
Mean Scores (and Standard Deviations) on 8-Item Posttest
"Which Arrangements Will Light the Bulb?"

	Group Size			
	1	2	3	4
Posttest	5.8 (0.9)	6.4 (1.3)	5.9 (1.0)	5.7 (1.4)
Delayed Posttest	6.2 (1.3)	6.2 (1.0)	6.2 (0.9)	6.1 (1.1)
Control	4.5 (1.4)			

Although students working in pairs had the highest mean score by a slight margin on the posttest that was administered immediately after the instructional session, differences were not significant. On the delayed posttest, administered 3 months later, differences were even less. As expected, students who had used the computer materials did better than control students who had not participated ($t = 6.45$, $df = 152$; $p < 0.001$).

Global Aspects

In addition to the above measures which assessed individuals, another set of measures was developed to describe the group as a whole and the tenor of each session. Immediately after viewing the videotape of the session, a researcher (R.D.) scored the session with respect to each of the nine characteristics listed in Table 4.6. Each characteristic was scored on a 3-point ordinal scale (1 = low, 3 = high). These scores represent a subjective assessment by an individual with several hundred hours of experience in videotape observation. Results were obtained as shown in Table 4.6.

The following conclusions were drawn from global assessments:

1. Students working in pairs or quads were more likely to cooperate with each other than students working in triads.
2. Students working in triads were more likely to compete with one another than students working in pairs or quads.
3. Students working in pairs were more likely to give or receive tutorial assistance than students in triads or quads.
4. Students working in pairs made fewer incorrect entries and formulated

TABLE 4.6
Median Scores Describing Session as a Whole

	Group Size			
	1	2	3	4
Tenor of Session:				
(a) Cooperative	n.a.	3	2	3
(b) Competitive	n.a.	1	3	1
(c) Tutorial	n.a.	3	1	2
Success with Material:				
(a) Error Frequence	2	1	2	2
(b) Response Quality	2	3	2	2
Engagement:				
(a) Attentiveness	3	3	3	3
(b) Off-Task	1	1	1	1

Note.   Scale: 1 - low, rarely; 2 - medium, sometimes;
3 - high, usually

higher quality responses to program questions than individuals, triads, or quads.

5. Whether working individually or in groups, students were uniformly attentive during the instruction sessions and displayed little off-task behavior.

In addition, researchers observed that students working alone seemed to have a more difficult time answering program questions correctly on their first attempt than those in groups of any size. However, individuals were also more likely to review earlier parts of the instructional materials than those students who worked in groups. Among eight individuals, six spontaneously returned to earlier material to review; among eight pairs, one pair returned to review; none of the six triads nor four quads did so.

SUMMARY

This study has shown that small-group usage of highly interactive computer-based learning materials has certain advantages over individual usage. On the whole, verbalization among pairs, triads, and quads was relevant to the learning material and socially supportive. We found no evidence for any detrimental effects among students working in pairs or triads. Quads, however, seemed to be too large, in general, for all four members to maintain high levels of interactivity either with the program or with other members of the group. On post-session achievement measures of individual competence, no differences were found among individuals and members of groups.

Students working in groups seemed more likely to interpret program questions as the authors of the materials had intended. Often, discussion about multiple interpretations would converge to the correct interpretation. On the other hand, individuals working alone were more likely to misinterpret program questions and to pursue incorrect paths through the material than students working in groups. Individuals showed a greater willingness to go back and review material that gave them trouble, however, which may explain why we found no inferiority of individuals' performance on achievement measures.

A comparison of achievement between those students who had used the materials and a control group who had not indicated clearly that students had learned some elementary ideas of electric current flow by using the computer simulation. In addition, these students had no difficulty applying their knowledge to a task involving actual physical equipment.

CONCLUSION

Teachers and school administrators who are considering the use of computer-based learning materials in the classroom need to examine the desirability of more than one student working at the computer. With the limited availability of computers in schools, teachers may wish to consider the advantages of having students work in groups.

Although it is difficult to measure gains directly attributable to social interaction, a student working with one or two others at the computer typically verbalizes his or her own thoughts so frequently that an inference of cognitive gain is not unreasonable. Furthermore, performance is generally unimpaired.

Our findings suggest that the use of computer-based learning materials should not be restricted to individuals working alone. On the contrary, many benefits are to be gained by having pairs and, under some circumstances, groups of three working together.

ACKNOWLEDGMENT

This work was supported by NSF grant no. SED-8112633. The project was conducted at the Educational Technology Center, University of California, Irvine.

REFERENCES

Arons, A., Bork, A., & Kurtz, B. (1981). *Science literacy in the public library—Batteries and bulbs.* Paper presented at the National Educational Computing Conference, Iowa City, IA.

Arons, A., Bork, A., & Trowbridge, D. (1983). *Observation and inference—A computer based learning module.* Paper presented at the National Educational Computing Conference, Silver Spring, MD.

Bales, R. (1950). *Interaction process analysis: A method for the study of small groups.* Chicago, IL: University of Chicago Press.

Durnin, R. (1985). *Computer based Education: A study of student interactions and achievement in small group and individual settings.* Unpublished doctoral dissertation, The Claremont Graduate School, Claremont, CA.

Flanders, N. (1970). *Analyzing teaching behaviors.* Menlo Park, CA: Addison-Wesley.

Johnson, D., & Johnson, R. (1974). Instructional goal structure: Cooperative, competitive or individualistic? *Review of Educational Research, 44,* 213–240.

Klausmeier, H., Wiersma, W., & Harris, C. (1963). Efficiency of initial learning and transfer by individuals, pairs, and quads. *Journal of Educational Psychology, 54,* 160–164.

Potter, M. (1982). *Audio tape interface unit: Technical documentation.* Educational Technology Center, University of California, Irvine, CA.

Sharan, S. (1980). Cooperative learning in small groups: Recent methods and effects on achievement, attitudes and ethnic relations. *Review of Educational Research, 50,* 241–271.

Sharan, S., Ackerman, Z., & Hertz-Lazarowitz, R. (1980). Academic achievement of elementary school children in small-group versus whole-class instruction. *Journal of Experimental Education, 48,* 125–129.

Slavin, R. (1980). Cooperative learning. *Review of Educational Research, 50,* 315–342.

Trowbridge, D., & Bork, A. (1981a). Computer based learning modules for early adolescence. In R. Lewis & D. Tagg (Eds.), *Computers in Education,* New York: North-Holland.

Trowbridge, D., & Bork, A. (1981b). *A computer-based dialogue for developing mathematical reasoning of young adolescents.* Paper presented at the National Educational Computing Conference, Iowa City, IA.

Trowbridge, D., & Bork, A. (1982). *Groups and computer based learning materials.* Paper presented at the National Educational Computing Conference, Columbia, MO.

Trowbridge, D., & Durnin, R. (1983). *A study of student-computer interactivity.* Paper presented at the National Educational Computing Conference, Silver Spring, MD.

Webb, N. (1977). *Learning in individual and small group settings.* Technical Report 7, School of Education, Stanford University.

5 Applying Cognitive-Developmental Theory to the Acquisition of Literacy

George Marsh
*California State University,
Dominguez Hills*

ABSTRACT

This chapter describes our efforts to apply cognitive developmental theory to the applied problem of the acquisition of literacy. The genesis of the theory in the context of developing a reading program at an educational research and development laboratory is related. Behavioristic principles of instructional technology that failed to take cognitive-developmental factors into account caused serious problems in this reading program.

The search for a general cognitive developmental model appropriate for this applied problem is related. A model of developmental reading stages is described in detail. The relationship between logical development and reading development is discussed in this context.

A FAILURE OF LEARNING THEORY

This chapter represents a somewhat personal case history in the problem of applying cognitive psychology to an applied educational problem—the acquisition of literacy. When I was in graduate school 20 years ago at Berkeley, psychology was in the throes of a major paradigm shift from behaviorism to cognitive psychology. Behaviorism has now been eclipsed as a major theory of human behavior in academic psychology. However, behaviorists have gone on to apply principles of behavior modification to a wide range of applied problems in mental health, industrial psychology, and education, to name but a few examples. Cognitive psychology has only more recently begun to attempt to apply its theories and principles to the real-world problems of applied domains. The chapters in this book represent some examples of applications of cognitive psychology research and theory to situations outside of the psychological laboratories of the university.

I first came to grips with the task of applying cognitive psychology to an educational problem when I went to work for one of the numerous regional laboratories of educational research and development that mushroomed as a part of the Great Society programs of the 1960s. My assigned task was no less than to ascertain the underlying cognitive skills necessary for learning to read and write. At that time I considered the cognitive developmental theory of Jean Piaget as the basis for developing a theory of cognitive skills involved in learning to read (Marsh, 1969). This was prompted partly by the tremendous impression made upon me when I heard Piaget speak in graduate school and also by Einstein's maxim that "one can see farther if one stands upon the shoulders of giants." However, for reasons that are discussed in detail later, Piaget's theory did not offer me fertile ground for the construction of a theory of educational change.

The laboratory I worked for was engaged in developing a kindergarten reading program involving two major components. The goal of the program was to get the children to learn by *rote* a list of 100 words by the end of the year. The motto of the program director, a dedicated behaviorist, was "We could teach a chimpanzee a hundred words in a year!"

The basic theoretical principles of instruction involved were behavioristic—repetition, and reinforcement. The vast educational literature on reading instruction primarily consisted of atheoretical comparisons of method A versus method B. Usually method A was some variant of the *whole word* approach and method B was some variant of the *phonics* approach. The general consensus of experts at that time was that the phonics approach was superior to the whole-word approach (cf. Chall, 1967).

The major purported advantage of the phonics approach was the promise of transfer to reading unknown words. The child could take advantage of a major cultural innovation, the invention of the alphabet, to figure out the pronunciation and consequently the meaning of new words made up of previously learned letter-sound combinations. The educational laboratory therefore included a secondary phonics component in its instructional program for the kindergarten children. The same words that were used in the whole-word lists were used as examples in the phonics instruction, which involved learning letter-sound combinations as well as practice in combining these letter-sound pairs to form words (i.e., blending).

The initial tryouts of the reading program in the schools were impressive. The children were indeed able to learn the 100 words during the kindergarten year. They also did well on learning the component skills in the phonics program such as letter-sound pairs and blending the sounds together. It was not until the program was well under way that some laboratory researchers looked for the transfer that should be forthcoming if the children in fact were learning the alphabetic principle in the phonics part of the program. This transfer test consisted of new words that had not been learned in the program but were made up of previously learned letter-sound combinations.

The kindergarten children by and large could *not* read the new words on the transfer tests. They appeared to be relying on their whole-word strategies to read the known words in the phonics component of the instructional program. So it appeared that there might be some limits after all on the kindergarten child's ability to absorb the phonics instruction despite the best efforts of program developers and teachers. The failure of this instructional program impressed me with the need to take developmental factors as well as instructional factors into account in describing the child's reading performance.

WHICH COGNITIVE THEORY TO APPLY TO THE ACQUISITION OF LITERACY?

The problem of what theory to apply to learning presented itself several years after I had left the educational laboratory for academia. While at a summer seminar on learning to read sponsored by Society for Research in Child Development, I heard talks by many of the leading researchers in the area of reading and interacted with many bright young researchers in this area. Several theories were popular.

Human Information Processing Models

The Zeitgeist at the conference was clearly the *human information processing* (HIP) approach to cognitive psychology. Using the computer metaphor, researchers in cognitive psychology were busily constructing models of cognitive processing involving flow charts of information processing systems. Several such models of the reading process were presented at this conference. After reviewing the literature on areas that seemed germane to reading such as word recognition, I came to several conclusions. The HIP models were based upon artificially controlled situations, using restricted response measures and adult subjects.

A typical experiment might involve tachistoscopic recognition of a small subset of words using reaction time as a dependent measure and college students as subjects. Having fairly recently come from an applied setting, it was hard for me to see how such experiments could be helpful in understanding the process young children engage in while learning to read and write in the real world of school classrooms. The HIP research lacked two essential components: ecological validity and a conception of developmental processes.

My first critical view of the HIP models of the mid-1970s was elaborated in a monograph that emanated from the conference (Marsh, 1978). Most of the criticisms in my opinion are still valid in the mid-1980s, although an interactive compensatory model of the reading process has included a developmental component, and data from laboratory research are converging with data from more ecologically representative settings (Stanovich, 1980).

Psycholinguistic Approaches

Several speakers at the reading conference were psycholinguists and educators promoting a *psycholinguistic approach* to reading. The general theories of this group emphasized the analogy between reading and Chomsky's notion of the development of spoken language (cf. N. Chomsky, 1968). Because children were endowed with an innate language acquisition device, they should be endowed with an innate reading acquisition device. Because all normal children exposed to speech develop spoken language, then all children exposed to print should learn to read spontaneously without much explicit instruction. This view certainly has a developmental component, but the component is primarily the unfolding of an innate maturational process with minimal need for environmental input.

According to this view, the teacher should basically not get in children's way as they develop their reading ability. The psycholinguistic view thus is at the opposite pole to the learning theory view on the role of nature versus nurture. I had seen many children who were having great difficulty learning to read even though exposed to print daily for years in the classroom. Although it was possible that this was due to the negative effects of confusing instruction, it seemed hardly credible to ascribe all children's reading problems to this source.

Cognitive-Developmental Theories

Piaget's Theory. I have found that Piaget's theory provides little basis for application to the problem of how children learn to read and write (cf. Piaget, 1977). First, Piaget minimized the applicability of his theory to education. In his talk at Berkeley, for example, Piaget dismissed questions concerning the effects of instruction on cognitive development as the "American question." The general point of his theory has been that cognitive development in the normal child in a normal environment is universal and spontaneously occurs without explicit instruction.

Second, Piaget's theory has dealt with logical development. Logical development concerns that which must be true under all conditions, not that which is culturally agreed upon. For example, it must be true that the quantity of water poured from one container to another is identical or that two plus two equals four. On the other hand, reading and writing represent an arbitrary culturally determined symbolic system. Although Piaget's theory might be educationally applied to logic-based systems such as mathematics instruction, it seems to have little applicability to reading and writing.

This impression was reinforced by another monograph from our summer conference concerning the relationship of Piaget's theory to reading (Waller, 1978). The literature as reviewed consisted mainly of studies correlating children's performance on Piagetian measures of logical development with performance on standardized reading tests. The core assumption was that certain levels of logical development were either necessary or sufficient for certain levels of reading development. This hypothesis was embodied in the title of Waller's monograph, "Think First, Read Later." This represented a formulation based on Piaget's ideas concerning language and thought that are discussed later. Suffice to say the correlations between these measures were not very impressive.

Bruner's Theory.   An alternative to Piaget's cognitive developmental theory was the theory proposed by Bruner (1960). Piaget's theory uses a central metaphor of the "child as logician" whereas Bruner's theory uses the central metaphor of the "child as inheritor of cultural tools." Primary among these cultural tools are language and, in our society, the language-based systems of reading and writing. Piaget's theory is largely based upon observations of children interacting with the physical environment. Bruner, following earlier work of the Russian cognitive theorist Vygotsky (1962), emphasized the child's interaction with the social-cultural universe of peers, parents, and school. The two theories thus deal with different domains of cognitive development.

Another difference between these two views is that, according to Piaget, cognitive development occurs primarily from an autoregulated process occurring from the "inside out," whereas Bruner sees cognitive development occurring as a result of interaction with the social environment or from the "outside in."

Case's Theory.   A recent theory of cognitive development has been proposed by Case (1985). Case's work incorporates both Piaget's position and information processing concepts. Instead of logical development as the driving force behind intellectual development, Case has adopted the concept of M-space from Pascal-Leone (1970). M-space is essentially the capacity of working memory or the capacity to process several chunks of information simultaneously. According to Pascal-Leone, this capacity increases from one chunk to seven chunks as the child develops.

Case proposes the metaphor of the "child as problem solver" to reconcile the divergent views of previous theories and to accommodate recent evidence on cognitive development. The essential elements of Case's theory are a problem situation, an objective or goal, and strategy for obtaining this goal. The notion of strategy is the central one in this approach. According to Case, young children have strategies that are reasonable but simplified versions of those used later in development. Case's theory maintains the central core of Piaget's mechanism of cognitive-developmental growth. Cognitive growth is the result of a conflict between existing strategies and the requirements of a new problem situation. The child's existing strategies are determined by limitations of M-space and by previous problems (assimilation in Piagetian terms). New strategies are discovered to be inadequate by the child (accommodation in Piaget's terms). Case's theory is especially compatible with the cognitive developmental approach my colleagues and I have devised to describe the stages of reading development.

A MODEL OF READING DEVELOPMENT

It was not until I was on sabbatical at UCLA in mid-1970s that I was able to again comprehensively survey the literature on reading to attempt to formulate a descriptive theory of reading development. In the intervening years since my stint in the applied laboratory, there had been considerable progress in experimental reading research. One fertile area of research was naturalistic observation of children's reading behavior in school classrooms (Barr, 1974–75; Biemiller, 1970; Cohen, 1974–75). In line with Piaget's insight that more could be discerned from children's errors than from their correct responses, these studies focused on the mistakes children made while reading orally in the school classroom.

This research had the great advantages of all naturalistic research—ecological validity. But it also had the disadvantages of naturalistic research such as the inability to test specific hypotheses. This problem caused Piaget to move from purely naturalistic observation to more controlled observation involving specific tasks.

A second fruitful new line of research was the work of Venezky, a linguist who had developed the first comprehensive description of English spelling to sound correspondence rules (cf. Venezky, 1967). Venezky and his colleagues used a technique devised earlier by Berko (1958) to test for children's knowledge of orthographic rules. This technique involved the use of invented or nonsense words to test children's knowledge of rules.

I was particularly interested in children's ability to read new or unknown words because this was the task that kindergarten children failed in our previous laboratory reading program. My colleagues and I hypothesized that children went through four qualitatively different developmental stages when faced with the problem of reading a novel unknown word. This view has been elaborated elsewhere (cf. Marsh & Desberg, 1983; Marsh, Friedman, Desberg, & Saterdahl, 1981; Marsh, Friedman, Welch, & Desberg, 1981). An overview of these stages follows.

Stage 1: Rote Strategies and Linguistic Guessing

In Stage 1, children have learned by rote memorization a relatively small subset of written words. This rote strategy is the initial strategy used by all individuals when encountering an unfamiliar symbolic system. It is found as the initial strategy, for example, in children's learning of morphophonemic rules (Mac-Whinney, 1978) and in adults' learning of an artificial grammar. This strategy was exemplified by the kindergarten children's acquisition in the research laboratories of 100 sight words during the first year of instruction. The diagnostic criterion of a rote strategy is the individual's inability to generate related forms that could be generated by the symbolic system. Thus, the kindergarten children were not able to read the new words presented in isolation if they were made of previously learned letter-sound pairs. This is because they had not acquired the combinatorial rules of the orthographic system.

Children at this stage are able to generate responses to unknown words when these words are presented in the context of a sentence, a picture, or both. The response, however, will be generated on the basis of the context. Thus, a child reading the sentence "The cime went to the story," would read "The boy went to the store." This linguistic substitution strategy is very often successful in children's early reading. Suppose the child does not have the word "boy" in the sentence, "The boy went to the store," when the sentence is accompanied by a picture of a boy walking to the store. If the child reads the sentence correctly, the linguistic substitution problem-solving strategy will be strengthened.

According to our theory the longer and more frequently the strategy is successful, the longer it will persist. This strategy is compatible with several approaches to teaching beginning reading. A basal approach presents relatively few words, which are visually distinctive in a sentence and picture context (e.g., See Jane, see Jane-run, accompanied by a picture). Linguistic context is also heavily emphasized in the language experience approach and in the approach used by the research laboratory in its story books.

The reason for the failure of the laboratory's phonics program now became clearer. The children were able to use the rote strategy successfully to read the relatively few words and the simple stories in their readings. They also successfully transferred this strategy to the phonics portion of the program. They successfully learned the letter-sound combinations by rote. When they were asked to "blend" these letter-sound to read the words already in their reading vocabulary, they had little difficulty because they already could rotely read the target words. Only when they were presented with unknown words made up of previously learned letter-sound combinations did their poor performance make clear their reliance on stage one strategies.

The initial reliance of young children on rote-reading strategy is also reported in an observational study by Barr (1974–75). Barr studied the reading errors of children in two first-grade classrooms using different instructional approaches. One classroom used a basal reading whole-word approach and the other classroom used a phonics approach. Regardless of instructional approach, all of the children started out using a *linguistic guessing* strategy on unknown words. This is an important point because it makes clear the interaction between the child's natural sequence of strategies and the sequence of instruction. Clearly a basal reading or language experience approach is more compatible with the child's initial natural strategies than a phonics approach. Some theories, such as the psycholinguistics approach, take the position that the child never abandons this "meaning-driven" or "top-down" linguistic guessing approach. Barr's study makes clear that this is not the case, for the children seemed to develop other strategies. However, the rate of development was a function of the type of instruction.

Most children in the basal reading classroom continued to use the linguistic guessing strategy when encountering the problem of unknown words. This is not surprising because this strategy will be a successful heuristic in most cases in a basal reading program. However, the best reader in this classroom went on to develop a more advanced strategy by the end of the first year, on his own, without explicit instruction. In contrast, most children in the phonics classroom did use more advanced strategies by the middle of the first year.

Stage 2: Discrimination Net Guessing

The second stage of development according to our theory is *discrimination net guessing*. The term *discrimination net* comes from a computer simulation program called EPAM (Elementary Perceiver And Memorizer) produced by Feigenbaum and Simon (1963).

In our model of reading, the process of rote learning from Stage 1 is generalized from the child's reading of known words to reading of unknown words at this stage. Given the sentence, "The cime went to the store," the child might produce, "The cats went to the store." This response has several new characteristics. First, "cats" shares the same initial letter and word length as the nonword "cime," in contrast to "boy," which shared neither. Second, "cats" is not as syntactically and semantically appropriate as the word "boy"; the response represents a compromise between the "top-down" meaning-driven strategy and a "bottom-up" print-driven strategy.

At this stage, the young reader also has a strategy for dealing with unknown words presented out of sentence or picture context. The strategy is simply to assign the unknown word a value based on the location of the nearest known word in the memory network. This will be determined by the number of shared elements between the known and unknown words such as first letter, and so forth. The classroom reading situation forms a general context for this memory retrieval process since the substitutions almost always have two characteristics: (a) they are real words, and (b) they are real words found only in the child's reading vocabulary. The latter characteristic is found in adults' rote learning in the laboratory where almost all of the substitutions or intrusions come from the list being learned in the laboratory setting.

According to our theory, the child progresses from Stage 1 to Stage 2 as a result of two factors. The first factor is cognitive maturity, which is discussed later. The second factor is environmental or task demands. The environmental demands are of two sorts, those imposed by the structure of the task itself and social demands in the instructional situation. As an example of the first type of demand, a child who substitutes a known for an unknown word might produce a semantically or syntactically anomalous sentence. Better readers catch these errors sooner than poorer readers. The child in the first stage has no adequate strategy for dealing with words out of context except a random guess.

The correction of the child's oral reading errors by the teacher is an example of a social factor that may cause a child to abandon the linguistic guessing strategy. Paying attention to print as well as linguistic context will increase the accuracy of responding to unknown words. However, it is a heuristic rather than an algorithm for pronouncing unknown words.

Stage 3: The Sequential Decoding Stage

The third stage of reading development involves the attempted application of an algorithmic procedure rather than a heuristic procedure for solving the problem of reading unknown words. This is referred to as a decoding strategy. This is the strategy that the laboratory reading program attempted to teach in its phonics programs for kindergarten children. In this strategy the reader uses knowledge of the alphabetic principle to decode the unknown word. The alphabetic principle in its simplest form involves the concept that each letter from left to right represents a sound in the word. These *grapheme-phoneme* correspondences can therefore be used to pronounce an unknown word. This strategy used in reference to the previous example would produce "the Cimme went to the store." The initial *C* would be pronounced as the sound /K/ because (a) it is the most frequent pronunciation of the letter *C* and (b) the reader is processing sequentially from left to right so the initial consonant is not constrained by the following vowel. The vowel would be given the short form because that is the initial form of the vowel taught and the long vowel silent *E* rule is not used.

There are two general diagnostic criteria for determining that the child has entered Stage 3. First, children will substitute known words for unknown words that are not in their reading vocabulary. This is a sign that they are aware that all words written in alphabetic system are potentially readable. The second more important diagnostic criterion is the production of nonwords in an attempt to read an unknown word. This results from an attempt to decode words that do not conform to simplify alphabetic principle (e.g., cite as kitee). This stage is marked by three cognitive advances. The first cognitive advance is the notion of one-to-one correspondence. The second is the principle of sequential order. The third principle is that of concatenation of elements to form new combinations. All of these principles have been used before in terms of larger units of words in sentences. Now they are employed in the metalinguistic domain of letters and their associated sounds.

Stage 4: Hierarchical Decoding

The transition to Stage 4 involves the use of higher order relationships between elements in the word. In order to read the nonword *cime* as *sim* the child must first process the entire word to determine the relationship between the parts. The pronunciation of the initial consonant is dependent on the following vowel. If the vowel is *i, e,* or *y,* the letter *c* is pronounced as /s/ (e.g., city). If the following vowel is *a, o,* or *u,* the letter *c* is pronounced as /k/ (e.g., can). The pronunciation of the medial vowel itself is dependent on the presence or absence of a final silent *e* marker (e.g., cut vs. cute).

The cognitive demands are greater at this stage because the entire word must be scanned in order to determine the relationship between the whole and its parts. For example, in *cime* the child must look at the last letter in order to pronounce the second letter correctly. This represents an abandonment of the sequential left-to-right strategy. In addition the child must deal with conditional if-then relationships that are cognitively more complex than the single letter-sound relationships used in the previous stage. Again the factors producing transition from Stage 3 to Stage 4 are the child's cognitive maturity and the demands of the task environment.

Many reading programs use a strategy of restricting the reading vocabulary to simple consonant-vowel-consonant words (e.g., cat) in order to make a sequential decoding strategy successful. In this approach the reader always encounters words where the *c* is pronounced as /k/ and the medial vowel is short rather than long. In i.t.a. (the initial teaching alphabet) more complex words are spelled using a one-to-one correspondence strategy (e.g., cime would be spelled siem). It is only when the child is exposed to more complex words that a hierarchical strategy is developed and the rate of development depends on the number of examples. The child is exposed to long vowel silent *e* words and learns this rule relatively early in development. In contrast the child only rarely encounters words where *c* is pronounced as /s/, and this rule is slow to develop.

As a child's reading vocabulary increases in size and diversity, another Stage 4 strategy develops. This is the strategy of reading unknown words by analogy to known words. We have diagnosed the development of this strategy by giving the child nonwords to read that can be read either by analogy to irregular real words or by a decoding strategy. An example would be this nonword *faugh* which can be pronounced as *faff* in analogy to laugh or as *faw* by a decoding strategy. Children by Stage 4 have developed the analogy strategy as a viable alternative strategy. There is evidence from reaction time tasks that adults rely on analogy type strategy even in pronouncing regular words (Glushko, 1981). This strategy is particularly useful with complex multisyllabic words that are often analogous in spelling to other words related in meaning (C. Chomsky, 1970).

RELATIONSHIP BETWEEN COGNITIVE DEVELOPMENT
AND READING DEVELOPMENT

Piaget and his followers have proposed that cognitive development (i.e., logical development) is at the core of other developmental domains. A strong form of this hypothesis is that specific stages of logical development are necessary and/or sufficient for the development in other domains.

In our initial work on reading development we adopted the weaker form of this hypothesis with regard to reading development; that is that logical development is a necessary but not sufficient condition for reading development. This was suggested to us because children made the transition from Stage 2 to Stage 3 in reading development at about the same age that Piaget reported for the transition from the preoperational to the concrete operational stage, approximately age 7.

To test our view we gave children tests of logical development and tests of reading development (Marsh, Desberg, & Bridge, in press). We have found the same rather small positive correlations between performance on the conservation tests of logical development and tests of reading development reported by Waller (1978). However, when we looked at results of individual children we found a number of cases where children were in Stage 3 yet not in concrete operations on the conservation test. Logically, only one negative case is needed to disprove the hypothesis that concrete operations is necessary for Stage 3 in reading development. Thus, we must conclude that the hypothesis is disproven. Additional evidence against the hypothesis has been found in spelling development where stages of spelling development do not seem to depend on stages of logical development (Marsh, Desberg, & Buhl, in press).

We suggest that logical development and reading development are separate parallel streams of development. However, there may still be developmental factors underlying both performance on tests of logical development and tests of reading development. The most promising possibility is the capacity of working memory or M-space. This has been shown to be a basic factor in children's performance on Piagetian logical tasks (Case, 1985). We are currently conducting research to determine if working memory capacity is related to reading development. It appears that cognitive immaturity restricts the range of strategies that children employ in both logical tasks and reading tasks. The strategies utilized in both domains are age-related.

A cognitive developmental stage model has been very fruitful in understanding many aspects of reading development. Our model has been applied to learning to read in languages other than English (e.g., Carraher, 1985) and to the thorny problem of developmental dyslexia (e.g., Frith, in press). It is hoped that it will some day provide a better pedagogical model for teaching children to read and write.

REFERENCES

Barr, R. (1974–75). The effect of instruction on pupil reading strategies. *Reading Research Quarterly, 10,* 555–582.

Berko, J. (1958). The child's learning of English morphology. *Word, 14,* 150–177.

Biemiller, A. J. (1970). The development of the use of graphic and contextual information as children learn to read. *Reading Research Quarterly, 6,* 75–96.

Bruner, J. (1960). *The process of education.* Cambridge, MA: Harvard University Press.

Carraher, T. N. (1985, May). *Illiteracy in a literate society: Understanding reading failure.* Paper presented at The Conference on Future of Literacy in a Changing World: Syntheses from the Industrialized and Developing Nations. University of Pennsylvania, Philadelphia.

Case, R. (1985). *Intellectual development: Birth to adulthood.* New York: Academic Press.

Chall, J. (1967). *Learning to read: The great debate.* New York: McGraw-Hill.

Chomsky, C. (1970). Reading, writing and phonology. *Harvard Educational Review, 40,* 287–309.

Chomsky, N. (1968). *Language and mind.* New York: Harcourt, Brace & World.

Cohen, A. S. (1974–75). Oral reading errors of first grade readers taught by a code emphasis approach. *Reading Research Quarterly, 10,* 616–650.

Feigenbaum, E. A., & Simon, H. A. (1963). Performance of a reading task by an elementary perceiving and memorizing program. *Behavioral Science, 8,* 72–76.

Frith, U. (in press). Beneath the surface of developmental dyslexia. In K. E. Patterson, J. C. M. Marshall, & M. Coltheart (Eds.), *Surface dyslexia: Neuropsychological and cognitive studies of phonological reading.* Hillsdale, NJ: Lawrence Erlbaum Associates.

Glushko, R. J. (1981). Principles for pronouncing print: The psychology of phonography. In A. M. Lesgold & C. A. Perfetti (Eds.), *Interactive processes in reading* (pp. 61–84). Hillsdale, NJ: Lawrence Erlbaum Associates.

MacWhinney, B. (1978). Processing a first language: The acquisition of morphophonology. *Monographs of the Society for Research in Child Development, 39* (3, pt. 2).

Marsh, G. (1969, July). *Conceptual skills in beginning reading* (Technical report #18). Los Alamitos, CA: Southwest Regional Laboratory.

Marsh, G. (1978). The HIP approach to reading. In F. Murray (Ed.), *Models of efficient reading* (pp. 62–70). Newark, DE: International Reading Association.

Marsh, G., & Desberg, P. (1983). The development of strategies in the acquisition of symbolic skills. In D. Rogers & J. A. Sloboda (Eds.), *The acquisition of symbolic skills* (pp. 149–154). New York: Plenum.

Marsh, G., Desberg, P., & Bridge, E. (in press). Relationship between cognitive development and reading strategies. In M. K. Poulsen & G. I. Lubin (Eds.), *Piagetian theory and its implication for education.* Los Angeles: University of Southern California Press.

Marsh, G., Desberg, P., & Buhl, J. (in press). The relationship between cognitive development and spelling strategies. In M. K. Poulsen & G. I. Lubin (Eds.), *Piagetian theory and its implication for education.* Los Angeles: University of Southern California Press.

Marsh, G., Friedman, M. P., Desberg, P., & Saterdahl, K. (1981). Comparison of reading and spelling strategies in normal and reading disabled children. In M. P. Friedman, J. P. Das, & N. O'Conner (Eds.), *Intelligence and learning* (pp. 363–368). New York: Plenum.

Marsh, G., Friedman, M. P., Welch, V., & Desberg, P. (1981). A cognitive developmental approach to reading acquisition. In T. G. Waller & G. E. MacKinnon (Eds.), *Reading research: Advances in theory and practice* (Vol. 3, pp. 199–221). New York: Academic Press.

Pascal-Leone, J. (1970). A mathematical model for the transition rule in Piaget's developmental stages. *Acta Psychologica, 32,* 301–345.

Piaget, J. (1977). *The development of thought: Equilibration of cognitive structures.* New York: Viking Press.

Stanovich, K. E. (1980). Towards an interactive-compensatory model of individual differences in the development of reading fluency. *Reading Research Quarterly, 16,* 32–71.

Venezky, R. L. (1967). English orthography: Its graphical structure and its relation to sound. *Reading Research Quarterly, 2,* 75–105.

Vygotsky, L. S. (1962). *Thought and language.* Cambridge, MA: MIT Press.

Waller, T. G. (1978). Think first, read later: Piagetian prerequisites for reading. In F. Murray (Ed.), *Development of the reading process* (pp. 1–34). Newark, DE: International Reading Association.

II THE TEACHING OF THINKING AND PROBLEM SOLVING

College and high school teachers have long been concerned that many students do not have the basic tools of logical thinking that are so important for education, especially in mathematics and the sciences. Only recently has improvement of critical thinking skills among college and high school students become a goal recognized at the national level. Although extensive work will be needed to establish the best ways to incorporate appropriate instruction into the curriculum, much can be learned from the experience of those who have attempted to teach courses in thinking skills. The authors of the next three chapters have each taught college-level courses designed to improve general thinking skills. They provide three perspectives on the value of such courses, their limitations, and aspects that are most successful.

In her chapter ''Analogies as a Critical Thinking Skill,'' Diane Halpern examines the limitations of methods that have commonly been used to evaluate the effectiveness of instruction in critical thinking skills. Increasing awareness of these limitations is an important first step toward improving the quality of evaluation research in this area. Halpern reports her own work where she focuses on the use of analogies as a particularly important skill for enhancing comprehension and memory of new concepts. Her research demonstrates one way in which the use of analogies can be taught, and her evaluation methods verify the effectiveness of the instruction.

Susan Nummedal's chapter ''Developing Reasoning Skills in College Students'' describes some of the issues that were faced as she and others developed a course in critical thinking skills for science majors in the California State University system. A goal was to expand the range of processes to be taught, especially in the domain of metacognitive processes such as planning and representing. In this chapter she presents her own work on the ability of college students to represent relationships between events and assess the degree of covariation. Nummedal's work provides us with a better understanding of the strategies and processes used by both skilled and unskilled persons, an understanding that is necessary if we hope to teach successful strategies.

Kenneth Pfeiffer, Gregory Feinberg, and Steven Gelber have been associated with a course on ''patterns of problem solving'' that was developed at UCLA by Moshe Rubinstein. In their chapter, ''Teaching Productive Problem Solving Attitudes,'' they discuss the importance of HOW problem solving is taught as compared to WHAT is taught. Using the model of the teacher as a coach, they emphasize the role of practice, motivation to practice, and attitudes toward problem solving.

Over the years, algebra word problems have frustrated legions of students and their teachers. Few people have contributed as much to our understanding of the cognitive processes involved in solving algebra story problems as Richard Mayer. In his chapter, ''Learnable Aspects of Problem Solving: Some Examples,'' Mayer examines four major issues in the cognitive literature that are relevant to instruction for mathematical problem solving: translation training, schema training, strategy training, and algorithm automaticity. For each issue, he summarizes recent cognitive psychology research and the implications for the teaching of mathematical problem solving.

Dale Berger and Jeffrey Wilde present ''A Task Analysis of Algebra Word Problems.'' Their analysis identifies specific ways in which information must be integrated in the process of solving algebra word problems. A comparison of ''expert'' and ''novice'' problem solvers demonstrates how experts make use of their knowledge of the overall structure of the problems to guide them to solution. Instruction focused on clarifying the structure of problems substantially improved the performance of novices.

Instruction in problem solving skills represents an area of especially rich opportunity for applied cognitive psychology to test and extend psychological theories. The issues to be addressed have genuine significance for the education of the next generation of American scientists. The five chapters in this section illustrate directions that future resarch might take.

6 Analogies as a Critical Thinking Skill

Diane F. Halpern
*California State University,
San Bernardino*

ABSTRACT

Evidence in support of the position that thinking skills can be enhanced with critical thinking courses is reviewed, and research on the effectiveness of analogies as a critical thinking skill is presented. Although analogies are a common component in many critical and creative thinking courses, there is little empirical evidence on the extent to which they can serve as an aid in comprehension, recall, and problem solving. Results suggest that well-chosen analogies can improve understanding and memory for events explicitly stated in scientific prose passages.

Analogy is inevitable in human thought.

—Oppenheimer (1956, p. 129)

There has been a recent growing interest among colleges and universities across the United States and Canada, and in other countries around the world in the development of courses that are designed to help students improve their ability to think critically. These courses have been instituted in the belief that, far too often, instruction in traditional college classrooms has not encouraged the development of critical thought. Although there has been considerable debate over exactly what sorts of skills comprise critical thinking, the term is usually used to refer to systematic, goal-directed thinking that includes evaluation of the assumptions, processes, and outcome in making a decision, solving a problem, or formulating inferences from information given.

Traditionally, our schools have required students to learn, remember, make decisions, analyze arguments, and solve problems without ever teaching them how. There has been a tacit assumption that adult students already know "how to think." Recent research has shown, however, that this assumption is not warranted. Psychologists have found that only 25% of first-year college students scored at the Formal Level of thought on Piagetian tests designed to assess the thinking skills needed for logical thought (McKinnon & Renner, 1971). Bertrand Russell summed up this situation well when he said, "Most people would rather die than think. In fact, they do."

Although virtually everyone agrees that critical thinking instruction is an idea whose time is long overdue, the mandate to teach college students how to think has raised numerous questions. The most important question is, "Can we teach college students how to think?" Or, more appropriately, "Can thinking skills be enhanced with proper instruction?"

Critical thinking and problem-solving courses are predicated on two basic assumptions: (1) that there are clearly identifiable and definable thinking skills that students can be taught to recognize and apply appropriately, and (2) that if these skills are recognized and applied, the students will be more effective thinkers. A list of such skills typically would include understanding how cause is determined, recognizing and criticizing assumptions, analyzing means-goals relationships, reducing complex problems to simpler ones, making appropriate inferences, and, one that I have chosen to focus on, using analogies as an aid to comprehension, memory, and problem solving.

As the number of critical thinking and problem-solving courses has proliferated, so has the number of skeptics claiming that it is not possible to produce long-lasting enhancement of students' ability to think effectively outside of domain-specific courses, that is, outside of courses that deal with a specific subject matter (Glaser, 1984; Resnick, 1983). I disagree. There is evidence to suggest that general thinking skills courses have positive effects that are transferable to a variety of content-specific domains (Block, 1985; Halpern, 1984).

Critical thinking instruction poses a unique assessment problem. Unlike other courses in which students are taught a specific content and then tested for their knowledge of that content, thinking and problem-solving courses aim to teach students how to improve their "ability to think"—a much more global and amorphous goal. In this chapter, I consider briefly some of the instruments that have been used as criterion measures to support claims that a course or other type of instruction has resulted in an improvement in the ability to think. I then present some research that I have conducted on the effectiveness of analogies as a critical thinking skill. Since the use of analogies is an important part of any critical thinking course, it is important to ascertain whether they are an effective aid to comprehension and problem solving.

EMPIRICAL STUDIES OF CRITICAL THINKING COURSES

At least six different forms of outcome evaluations for thinking and problem-solving programs have been conducted. I argue that since positive results have been obtained with each measure, it is reasonable to conclude that students have improved their ability to think critically. However, the data are still incomplete, and this remains an area in need of additional and improved research.

The most usual assessment instrument is the standard midterm and final exam written by the professor. Such exams have the benefit of being tailor-fit to the course content and objectives, but contain the obvious disadvantage of unknown reliability and validity. Most people view with skepticism any professor's claims that she or he has improved a student's ability for critical thought if such claims are supported solely on the basis of good grades earned on the professor's final exam.

A second approach to the assessment problem has been the evaluation of pre-course and post-course student self-reports regarding their thinking ability (Wheeler, 1979). There are obvious problems with using student self-reports to support the proposition that they have learned to think better. Self-reports may not reflect reality. Students may report that they can make decisions more intelligently when they cannot, or conversely, that they have not improved when they have. I would like my students to think more clearly and to know that they can, but I would not rely upon students' beliefs about their abilities as an index of those abilities.

A third way of measuring thinking improvement is with gains in IQ points on standardized intelligence tests. For example, Rubinstein (1980) reported on a midwestern study in which 82.4% of the students who participated in the problem-solving course he developed showed gains in IQ points. The reasoning behind this claim is that when people improve the way they think, they become more intelligent. It is difficult to know how to interpret claims like this one. (This particular study was flawed because the researcher failed to use a control group.) Hayes (1980) has said that he questions the data in support of this claim because he does not believe that the types of skills taught in these courses are the same ones that are tapped in intelligence tests. Experts have argued for years about the many bitterly disputed issues that surround the IQ controversies. There is always the lingering question of whether or not any gain in IQ points is merely the result of training in test taking or drill on the topics addressed in intelligence tests rather than a general enhancement of "intelligence." The students may not show similar gains when out of the classroom or away from testing situations. Whatever your point of view on the IQ issue, few would argue that IQ is a good way to measure the thinking skills that we hope to sharpen in our students.

One promising approach to the quantification of course-related improvement in the ability to think is the measurement of growth in cognitive development using Piagetian tasks. Such assessment will typically involve comparisons between students who have taken a thinking course and a control group of students who have not taken a thinking course on a variety of Piagetian tasks that measure an individual's level of cognitive development. Consider for example, Piaget's "mixing chemicals" task. In this task, students are given four colorless liquids and an activating agent. They are told to mix the chemicals and agent until they discover which combinations produce a yellow color. The correct answer requires a systematic approach, first mixing the chemicals with the activating agent one at a time, then two at a time, then three at a time, then all four together. A random or unsystematic approach is not a good strategy. There are many other tasks originally devised by Piaget that are used to determine the level of thought at which an individual is functioning. In one study that employed this method of assessment, the results generally supported the superiority of the students who had taken the thinking course (Fox, Marsh, & Crandall, 1983). Although this is a promising line of research, it requires that the Piagetian tasks used for assessment be novel to the students and that the professor eschew the temptation to teach tasks like the ones that appear on the test.

A fifth approach is the use of scores on standardized tests of critical thinking, such as the Watson-Glaser Critical Thinking Appraisal, the Ennis Weir Argumentation Test, and the Cornell Critical Thinking Test. Although such tests have a considerable literature attesting to their reliability and validity, they are designed to assess a narrow range of thinking skills, specifically understanding short prose passages, and thus do not match well with many course objectives. Most of these tests are concerned only with argument analysis including inductive and deductive reasoning.

One of the most recent and theoretically advanced means of exploring course-related changes in thinking ability is to examine the underlying structure of cognitive skills and knowledge. Much of the research in this area is based on comparisons between skilled and unskilled problem solvers. From these studies, we have learned that experts approach problems in ways that novices do not. Experts possess complex problem representations or schemata that allow them to make appropriate inferences from problem statements. Schemata are theoretical constructs that denote organized bodies of knowledge. According to cognitive theory, all of the information we possess about a topic is organized into a structural framework that represents the properties and relations that pertain to the topic. For example, a cognitive psychologist would have a complex schema or knowledge structure for "mental chronometry." It would contain information about the relationship between componential analysis and reaction time, and the underlying assumption that reaction times can be subtracted to isolate simpler thought processes. Information about mental chronometry can be encoded, utilized, and retrieved more efficiently by a cognitive psychologist (the "expert" in this example) than by someone who is less familiar with this topic. A novice's problem representation or schema is presumably less differentiated, contains fewer connections to other related schemata, and often may be faulty (c.f. Glaser, 1984; Kintsch & Greeno, 1985).

One excellent approach for measuring course-related cognitive growth is to demonstrate that novices who are given instruction in thinking and problem solving have underlying knowledge structures or schemata that are more similar to those of experts than a control group of novices who had some other educational experience. Following this line or reasoning, Schoenfeld and Herman (1982) had subjects categorize mathematical problems. The task for the subjects was to sort problems into different piles on the basis of their similarity. They found that novices tended to classify problems on the basis of *surface similarity* or topic. For example, problems about people working together might be perceived as being similar to problems about people traveling together because both types of problems involved group activities. However, both mathematics professors and students who had taken an 18-day course on problem-solving strategies classified problems according to problem-solving principles or what is sometimes called *deep structure*.

USE OF ANALOGIES

Although positive results supporting the hypothesis that it is possible to improve students' critical thinking ability with general thinking courses have been reported with each of the six assessment approaches discussed above, there are weaknesses and pitfalls inherent in each of these approaches. A better way to examine the efficacy of critical thinking instruction is to look at the components of a typical critical thinking course to ascertain whether they are effective aids to comprehension and problem solving. To this end, I have begun research on the use of analogies. I chose to focus on analogies for several reasons. First, a national survey that I conducted with the help of a publisher (Lawrence Erlbaum Associates) revealed that virtually every college-level critical and creative thinking course, regardless of discipline, included instruction on the use of analogies.

A second reason for studying analogies is that they readily lend themselves to assessment by examining underlying knowledge structures, an assessment approach that I believe to be the most promising demonstration that general thinking skills courses can lead to improvements in domain-specific knowledge. I became intrigued with the possibility that an expert's representation of a problem space could be transferred to a naive subject or novice in a simple straightforward manner. One method to speed this transfer is to provide subjects with an analogy selected from a subject matter domain familiar to the novice. This method would be effective, however, only to the extent that the use of analogies is an effective cognitive tool.

Unlike some of the more artificial topics taught in many critical thinking courses, like drawing Venn diagrams or calculating Bayesian post hoc probabilities, analogies are used spontaneously by most adults. Sternberg (1977) has noted the ubiquitous nature of analogies in our everyday thinking: "Reasoning by analogy is pervasive in everyday experience. We reason analogically whenever we make a decision about something new in our experience by drawing a parallel to something old" (p. 353). Analogies are also frequently used in explaining scientific concepts. Analogies in cognitive psychology, for example, have always reflected the most advanced technology at the time, and include likening the human mind to a hydraulic system, indoor plumbing, a telephone switchboard, and, more recently, a computer and a hologram. Each of these anlogies provides a framework for understanding the transfer or flow of information and its storage in the human memory system.

Consider, for example, that in learning about the structure of an atom, you are told that it is like a miniature solar system. Suppose further that you already have a great deal of knowledge about the solar system. If you don't, then there is no advantage in learning about the solar system. There is an important point because a working theory of analogies assumes that new information is efficiently acquired because of its parallel relationship to preexisting (i.e., already known) information. If the structural properties of the atom are highly similar to that of the solar system, then a new, but highly complex cognitive structure is quickly created. In the jargon of cognitive psychology, this is known as *structure mapping* because the structure of a base (or known) complex knowledge system is mapped onto a target (or unknown) domain (Gentner & Gentner, 1983). According to this view, analogies are much more than weak comparisons; they play a geneiative role in the formation of new schemata in which the relations between objects in 'he base domain are preserved in the target domain (D. Gentner, 1983).

A good analogy can facilitate comprehension and recall in several ways. It can function as an advanced organizer by providing a structural framework for interpreting new information (Mayer, 1979; Mayer & Bromage, 1980). The fact that recall is dependent on the organization of information that is to be learned is a well-known learning principle (Mandler, 1967). One of the functions of analogies is to provide a logical interrelationship among ideas, which could serve as a means of organizing separate "facts" or initially disparate segments of information (Meyer & Mc Conkie, 1973). Kintsch and Greeno (1985) have argued that the ability to comprehend and solve problems depends on the nature of the internal representation. If analogies speed the formation of differentiated schemata, then comprehension and solution of the problem should be facilitated.

Analogies often make abstract concepts more concrete, usually by providing a memorial mental image. Concrete nouns are more easily remembered than abstract nouns, probably because they evoke clear mental images (Paivio, 1969). Thus, analogies to concrete objects should also function as a visual-imagery mnemonic aid in the retention of the new information presented. In addition to creating complex schemata and concrete images, analogies also evoke novel comparisons. All analogies suggest similarity between two disparate concepts. When the two concepts are very different, or in the jargon of cognitive psychology, the between-domain distance is great, the analogy becomes more striking, as in an analogy between love and a rose or between the mentally ill and weeds in a flower garden (Tourangeau & Sternberg, 1981). Early research in memory showed that people tend to remember the unusual or unexpected, a finding that is commonly called the von Restorff effect. The unexpected or surprise aspect of good analogies could also be a comprehension and retention aid.

The ability of analogies to function as a cognitive tool is important for both theoretical and practical reasons. Notwithstanding the widespread use of analogies in critical thinking courses, and the fact that there are several theoretical mechanisms by which they should serve as a thinking skill, very few studies have investigated the extent to which they improve comprehension, recall, and problem solving. The following research, which I conducted with the help of three students at California State University, San Bernardino (Cheryl Eberhardt, Joan Gonzales, & Carol Hansen) was designed to investigate this possibility.

Research Report

One hundred fifteen college students were presented with two different short prose passages about technical scientific topics. One passage described the purpose and the operation of the lymphatic system. The other passage described retrograde motion of the planets. Each of these passages was presented either with or without an analogy. The lymphatic analogy described it as being like "a wet sponge with spaces filled with water. If you squeeze it, you can force the water from one end of the sponge to another." The analogy for retrograde motion of the planets was that of "a car traveling westward in the fast lane of a freeway that overtakes another car. If you are a passenger in the faster moving car, it appears as though the car you passed is going in the opposite direction, that is, eastward."

One problem in conducting research of this sort is that highly motivated subjects are needed. Considerable effort is required if subjects are to learn about complex scientific topics. We tried various motivating tricks. First, we only used students in intact classrooms in which the instructors were willing to give extra credit for participation. In addition, the students in each classroom who answered the greatest number of questions correctly were awarded prizes.

Subjects were assigned at random to one of two testing groups. Group 1 subjects were tested for comprehension and recall immediately after reading each passage and again 2 days later. Subjects in Group 2 were tested for comprehension and recall only after a 2-day intervening period. Subjects were blind to the nature of these conditions and the purpose of the experiment. Filler activities were used immediately after reading the passages for subjects in Group 2 (de-layed-recall-only group) to control for time variables and to disguise the nature of this manipulation.

All subjects read both the lymphatic and retrograde motion passages, with only one of the passages containing the analogy. Order of presentation was counterbalanced to control for order effects. Immediately after reading each passage, subjects were asked to rate how much they had learned from the pas-sage. Subjects in Group 1 (the immediate and delayed-recall group) were then asked to list as many facts as they could remember about the passage they had just read. Following the free-recall task, they then responded to 10 multiple-choice questions, two of which required a thoughtful inference about information that was not explicitly stated. We believed that if analogies facilitate the estab-lishment of differentiated knowledge structures, then subjects who read passages with analogies would be better able to make valid inferences about information that was not explicitly stated than subjects who read the same passages without an analogy. The ability to make correct inferences would result directly from the complex problem representation.

Two days later, all subjects were asked to list as many facts as they could recall from each passage. The same multiple-choice test that had been given to Group 1 immediately following each passage was given again, this time to all subjects in both groups. The test questions and possible alternative answers, however, were presented in a different order from that used earlier.

Overwhelmingly, the 115 students who participated in this experiment re-ported that they had learned a great deal about each topic (all p's $< .001$), with no significant differences with respect to the analogy/ no analogy manipulation. We had expected to find a difference on this measure such that when subjects read passages with analogies they believed that they learned more than when they read passages without analogies; however, this didn't happen.

Figure 6.1 shows the results for subjects who were tested immediately after reading each passage. Results for free recall and multiple-choice questions for each passage were tested for statistical significance with separate analyses. Peru-sal of Fig. 6.1 reveals that when the retrograde motion passage contained an analogy, subjects in a free-recall paradigm recalled an average of 1.2 more facts about it than when it did not. All analogy/ no analogy comparisons with the retrograde motion passage either obtained statistical significance ($p < .05$) or approached statistical significance ($p < .06$ or $.07$). Results with the lymphatic system passage were less dramatic, with the analogy offering only a small advantage. For the most part, although the analogy/ no analogy mean differences for the lymphatic system passage were in the predicted direction, they failed to obtain statistical significance.

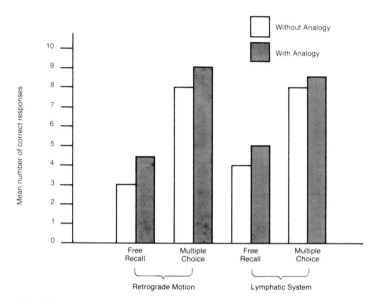

FIG. 6.1. *Immediate recall condition* Mean number of free recall and multiple choice responses for students who read scientific passages (retrograde motion or lymphatic system) either with or without an analogy.

Results from the multiple-choice test that immediately followed the free-recall test mirrored the free-recall results. Out of a possible 10 questions, the analogy improved comprehension of the retrograde motion passage an average of almost one question, with a smaller mean difference for the lymphatic system passage.

The analysis of the results from the delayed test that was administered 2 days later was more complex, as shown in Fig. 6.2. Free-recall and multiple-choice data from the delayed recall test were analyzed separately for each passage. In general, subjects who were tested immediately following each passage tended to perform better than subjects who were tested only after a 2-day delay. This result was expected, although not directly relevant to the experimental question. Again the superiority of the analogy can be seen with seven out of eight comparisons favoring the analogy passage and more reliable results for the retrograde motion passage. However, the two questions written to require subjects to draw inferences about material not explicitly stated failed to differentiate between the analogy/ no analogy conditions. I believe that this negative result was probably due to the relatively insensitive measure that was used. It is extremely difficult to get subjects to read highly technical material and then take a lengthy test on that material. For that reason, the number of test questions was kept small. I am currently conducting research to investigate the use of analogies for deducing information that has not been stated, using a more sensitive measure.

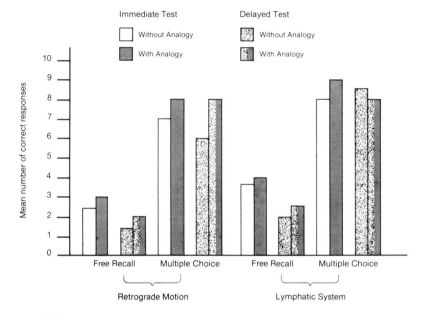

FIG. 6.2. *Recall after a 2-day delay interval* Mean number of free recall and multiple-choice correct responses for passages about a scientific topic (retrograde motion or lymphatic system) that either did not contain (left-most bar of each pair) or contained an analogy.

CONCLUSIONS

Experimental results support the position that analogies can be a useful tool in the comprehension and recall of scientific information. A logical follow-up question is whether college students can learn to generate their own analogies as a strategy to improve the comprehension and recall of technical material. The small amount of research that has addressed this question is mixed (e.g., Gick & Holyoak, 1980). It seems that this is not a spontaneous process, but one that can be learned. Many scientists and mathematicians report that their ideas or solutions to problems come to them by recognizing analogies drawn from different academic domains (Hadamard, 1945), and it seems likely that college students, our future scientists, mathematicians, and other professionals, would benefit from instruction on generating and utilizing analogies. There are, however, potential problems in teaching students to generate their own novel analogies when faced with new information that has to be acquired and assimilated into existing knowledge structures. Analogies are always imperfect because they suggest a similarity between objects and events that are not identical, and thus can be misleading. The strength of the analogy and the nature of the comparison also must be considered. Yet, despite any possible limitations on the use of analogies, they are one way of "making the unfamiliar known" (Halpern, 1984).

The present research provides a strong case for at least one of the types of skills taught in thinking and problem-solving courses. Much work must yet be done to determine the effects of the other types of skills taught in such courses. When this work is completed, we will be in a better position to ascertain the relative value of each of these skills. This will not only help us determine course content, but will help us determine the relative value of different approaches to critical and creative thinking courses.

Traditionally, instruction in how to think has been a neglected component in American education. Students were taught what to think more often than how to think. Education within most academic disciplines has primarily been concerned with presenting students with the "facts" on a variety of topics—the "knowing that"—while offering little on how to utilize this information or how to discover facts on their own—the "knowing how." Domerique (cited in Parnes, Noller, & Biondi, 1977) summarized this situation well when he said, "Some people study all their life, and at their death they have learned everything except to think" (p. 52). It is hoped that the introduction of critical thinking courses into college curricula will alter the perception that modern education is a mindless exercise and demonstrate that improvement in basic thinking skills can be an outcome of higher education.

ACKNOWLEDGMENTS

I thank Cheryl Eberhardt, Joan Gonzales, and Carol Hansen for their help with the research project described in this chapter.

REFERENCES

Block, R. A. (1985). Education and thinking skills reconsidered. *American Psychologist, 40*, 574–575.

Fox, L. S., Marsh, G., & Crandall, Jr., J. C. (1983, April) *The effect of college classroom experiences on formal operational thinking.* Paper presented at the 1983 Annual Convention of the Western Psychological Association, San Francisco, CA.

Gentner, D. (1983). Structure-mapping: A theoretical framework for analogy. *Cognitive Science, 7*, 155–170.

Gentner, D., & Gentner, D. R. (1983). Flowing water or teeming crowds: Mental models of electricity. In D. Gentner & A. L. Stevens (Eds.), *Mental models* (pp. 99–129). Hillsdale, NJ: Lawrence Erlbaum Associates.

Gick, M. L., & Holyoak, K. J. (1980). Analogical problem solving. *Cognitive Psychology, 12*, 306–355.

Glaser, R. (1984). Education and thinking: The role of knowledge. *American Psychologist, 39*, 93–104.

Hadamard, J. (1945). *The psychology of invention in the mathematical field.* Princeton, NJ: Princeton University Press.

Halpern, D. F. (1984). *Thought and knowledge: An introduction to critical thinking.* Hillsdale, NJ: Lawrence Erlbaum Associates.

Hayes, J. R. (1980). Teaching problem solving mechanisms. In D. T. Tuma & F. Reif (Eds.), *Problem solving and education: Issues in teaching and research* (pp. 141–147). Hillsdale, NJ: Lawrence Erlbaum Associates.

Kintsch, W., & Greeno, J. G. (1985). Understanding and solving word arithmetic problems. *Psychological Review, 92,* 109–129.

Mandler, G. (1967). Organization and memory. In K. W. Spence & J. T. Spence (Eds.), *The psychology of learning and motivation: Vol. 1. Advances in research and theory* (pp. 328–379). New York: Academic Press.

Mayer, R. E. (1979). Can advanced organizers influence meaningful learning? *Review of Educational Research, 49,* 371–383.

Mayer, R. E., & Bromage, B. K. (1980). Different recall protocols for technical texts due to advanced organizers. *Journal of Educational Psychology, 72,* 209–225.

McKinnon, J. W., & Renner, J. W. (1971). The college student and formal operations. In J. W. Renner, D. G. Stafford, A. E. Lawson, J. W. McKinnon, F. E. Friot, & D. H. Kellogg (Eds.), *Research, training, and learning with the Piaget model* (pp. 110–129). Norman: University of Oklahoma Press.

Meyer, B. J. F., & Mc Conkie, G. W. (1973). What is recalled after hearing a passage? *Journal of Educational Psychology, 65,* 109–117.

Oppenheimer, J. R. (1956). Analogy in science. *American Psychologist, 11,* 127–135.

Paivio, A. (1969). Mental imagery in associative learning and memory. *Psychological Review, 76,* 241–263.

Parnes, S. J., Noller, R. B., & Biondi, A. M. (1977). *Guide to creative action: Revised edition of creative behavior guidebook.* New York: Charles Scribner's Sons.

Resnick, L. B. (1983). Mathematics and science learning: A new conception. *Science, 220,* 477–478.

Rubinstein, M. F. (1980). A decade of experience in teaching an interdisciplinary problem-solving course. In D. T. Tuma & F. Reif (Eds.), *Problem solving and education: Issues in teaching and research* (pp. 25–38). Hillsdale, NJ: Lawrence Erlbaum Associates.

Schoenfeld, A. H., & Herman, D. J. (1982). Problem perception and knowledge structure in expert and novice mathematical problem solvers. *Journal of Experimental Psychology: Learning, Memory, and Cognition, 8,* 484–494.

Sternberg, R. J. (1977). Component processes in analogical reasoning. *Psychological Review, 84,* 353–373.

Tourangeau, R., & Sternberg, R. J. (1981). Aptness in metaphor. *Cognition, 13,* 27–55.

Wheeler, D. D. (1979). A practicum in thinking. In D. D. Wheeler & W. N. Dember (Eds.), *A practicum in thinking* (pp. 6–18). Cincinanti, OH: Department of publications and printing services of the University of Cincinnati.

7 Developing Reasoning Skills in College Students

Susan G. Nummedal
California State University, Long Beach

ABSTRACT

The majority of college students are unable to use the strategies and processes of formal reasoning consistently and reliably. The goal of improving students' reasoning generally has been accepted by educators. However, there is disagreement about which reasoning skills to teach and how best to teach them. Several approaches to improving reasoning skills in college students are discussed. Understanding how to teach any reasoning skill requires knowledge of how both the skilled and unskilled try to solve problems. An example of research on one reasoning skill—correlational reasoning—that provides such knowledge is presented. Implications for instruction are discussed.

According to classic cognitive developmental theory (Inhelder & Piaget, 1958) the thinking of 16- to 18-year-olds is at last free from its earlier dependence on concrete referents. Along with this freedom comes the ability to differentiate reality from possibility, form from content. The result is reflective thinking (i.e., thinking about one's own thoughts) and the generalized application of the operations of formal reasoning across varied domains. It is in this sense that the reasoning of the older adolescent has been described as formal, abstract, and general. But research has failed to support this hypothesis about adolescent reasoning.

Reasoning Abilities of College Students

Over the past 15 years, the results of numerous studies of the reasoning abilities of college students have shown a consistent pattern, namely, that less than 50% of the students in our universities are able to use formal reasoning processes confidently and reliably. For example, McKinnon and Renner (1971) found that fully one half of the college freshmen tested were operating at a concrete, or nonformal, level of reasoning, and thus were unable to demonstrate formal reasoning abilities, such as elimination of contradiction, isolation and control of variables, and reciprocal implication. Tomlinson-Keasey (1972) reported that less than 50% of her sample of female college students were able to reason at the formal level on problems requiring the ability to isolate and control variables and proportional reasoning. Lawson, Nordland, and DeVito (1975) found that only 20% of the college freshmen and sophomores sampled were able to separate and identify variables in a complex problem, and even fewer (14%) could exclude irrelevant variables from consideration when solving problems. In these and other studies (e.g., Keating & Clark, 1980; Kuhn & Brannock, 1977; and Moshman, 1979), even when students did demonstrate the use of a particular reasoning skill, they were unable to apply it across a variety of problem-solving situations; i.e., they were only able to use the skill under limited circumstances.

If one closely examines the level of instruction of college courses and contrasts this with the above findings on the reasoning abilities of the students in these courses, a dilemma emerges. In college courses, the understanding of most concepts and principles in the various subject matter domains is developed through the very formal reasoning processes so many students lack. Indeed, most of the materials, lecture presentations, and assignments encountered in college-level study implicitly assume either that these thinking processes are already developed in the students, or that they will automatically evolve with the study of the subject matter.

The research shows clearly that it is incorrect to assume students have already developed these thinking skills. Furthermore, the ability to think critically about a variety of problems does not flow inevitably, or even particularly commonly, out of the curriculum students generally obtain. Research also suggests that without the explicit teaching of formal reasoning processes, only a small proportion of college students—perhaps only the upper 25% of the ''brightest,'' as Arons (1979) has estimated—will develop them.

Teaching Reasoning Skills

As a result, in the 1970's, faculty at a number of universities began designing curricula that have as an explicit goal the teaching of reasoning processes in students. Such curricula were developed at the University of Nebraska-Lincoln (Project ADAPT), University of Massachusetts (Cognitive Skills Project), California State University, Fullerton (Project DORIS), Xavier University in Louisiana (Project SOAR), and University of California, Los Angeles (Patterns of Problem Solving). More recently, in the fall of 1983, concern with the critical thinking abilities of college students led the largest university system in the country, The California State University, to require all graduating students to complete course work in critical thinking. This requirement has resulted in the construction of different kinds of university-level critical thinking courses.

I would like to describe one such course in greater detail. Beginning in 1977, I participated in the design of a course at California State University, Fullerton, entitled *Development of Reasoning in Science* (DORIS). The purpose of this National Science Foundation funded project was to develop a course for college science majors that would have as an explicit instructional goal the teaching of the models of reasoning that form the basis for understanding the subject matter of chemistry, earth science, mathematics, and physics. Concepts from first-year course offerings in these disciplines provided the grist for teaching five models of reasoning: (1) hypothetico-deduction, (2) combinatorial reasoning, (3) isolation and control of variables, (4) proportional reasoning, and (5) correlational reasoning. These general models are assumed to mediate the acquisition of more specialized methods of reasoning characteristic of these particular subject matter domains. Although the acquisition of subject matter knowledge was considered important, the primary instructional goal was the teaching of these models in the context of the subject matter domains in which they would be applied. (See Collea & Nummedal, 1980, for a more complete description of the DORIS course.)

Mathematicians and philosophers would remind us that it is not new to assume that general reasoning models can be taught in separate courses, and that transfer across specific subject matter domains will occur. For a very long time, it has been common practice for mathematics departments to teach the quantitative models of reasoning (e.g., algebra, calculus, etc.) assumed necessary for acquiring and applying concepts in other disciplines. We do not assume that the disciplines utilizing these models (i.e., chemistry, physics, psychology, etc.) should themselves be responsible for teaching algebra, for example. Indeed, we find it efficient to require mathematics courses as prerequisites to the study of a variety of complex subject matter domains. That students can generalize reasoning models is assumed also for the logic courses offered by philosophy departments. The development of the DORIS course was founded on the same basic reasoning. What is new about the course is that it expands the range of general reasoning models and processes to be taught in separate *thinking* courses.

Few would find the educational goal of improving the reasoning abilities of students particularly controversial. Over half a century ago, John Dewey (1933) stated that the major purpose of education is learning to think. He argued that "education . . . is vitally concerned with cultivating the attitude of reflective thinking, preserving it where it already exists, and changing looser methods of thought into stricter ones whenever possible" (p. 78). Educators generally have assumed that not only should students be taught to think, but that in fact they *can* be taught to think. What is controversial is how this goal might best be achieved.

Some have rejected outright the very idea of a separate "thinking" course. McPeck (1981), for example, has argued that critical thinking occurs only within particular fields and that it "can only be taught as part of a specific subject and never in isolation" (p. 158). He asserts that most of the important thinking skills are domain-specific, and therefore there should be no critical thinking courses per se.

However, most educators do accept the idea of separate critical thinking courses. There is even some agreement about what to teach in such courses. Virtually all "thinking" courses place at least some emphasis on the training of metacognitive processes (e.g., planning, representation, monitoring, etc.) since it is generally accepted that these meta-processes have a critical role in directing the application of other reasoning processes and in the transfer of training across different content domains (Sternberg, 1982). But there is considerable disagreement about exactly what other reasoning processes should be taught. The disagreement is basically over the role of domain-specific knowledge in the acquisition of reasoning processes and the associated issue of transfer of training across subject matter domains (Glaser, 1984).

As Glaser's (1984) recent review of a large number of programs attests, there is a broad range of thinking skills being taught in the name of improving students' reasoning abilities. In addition to metacognitive processes, they include general problem-solving heuristics, decision-making models, formal operational reasoning models, and the skills of logic and inquiry. Glaser expresses concern over the fact that these programs tend to focus on general reasoning processes (as opposed to domain-specific processes), and that they systematically avoid complex domain-specific knowledge. He does not say that we should abandon these thinking programs. Rather, he suggests that we "consider the teaching of thinking not only in terms of general processes, but also in terms of knowledge structure-process interactions" (p. 97). He bases his position on the research in cognitive psychology on expert problem solving (e.g., Chase & Simon, 1973; Wilkins, 1980), which describes the interaction between structures of knowledge and reasoning processes.

Questions of what should be taught arise primarily because no single thinking course can create THE complete thinker. It is not possible to teach everything in one course. Within the context of the general goal of improving the reasoning abilities of students, more specific course objectives must be formulated. Decisions must be made about which reasoning processes to include and which to omit. For example, the DORIS course was designed specifically for college science majors with the principal objective being to teach the reasoning models that mediate the acquisition of more specialized reasoning processes in the domains of chemistry, physics, and so on. The course developed by Rubinstein (1975), entitled Patterns of Problem Solving, serves the general student population and teaches general problem-solving heuristics, such as described by Polya (1957). Unfortunately, no amount of research can answer the question of what should be taught. "Should" questions, even in the guise of a controversy over general versus domain-specific processes, are not empirical research questions.

They are fundamentally questions of values. As Bruner (1985) has said with respect to another controversy in education (i.e., what a learner should be), ''at the heart of the decision process there must be a value judgment about how the mind should be cultivated and to what end'' (p. 5).

This is not to say that research has no bearing on educational practice. It does! Evaluation research, for example, potentially should be able to tell us something about the relative effectiveness of various critical thinking programs in reaching particular objectives, although clear answers are not yet forthcoming from this type of research (Halpern, this volume). Research on the performance of skilled and unskilled problem solvers has enabled us to develop an increasingly clear picture of the processes used by both experts and novices. Results from these kinds of studies have been very useful, indeed, for those teaching reasoning skills. They have helped to define more precisely the nature of (a) the expert performance that is the desired outcome of instruction, and (b) the difficulties those who are less than expert have in applying particular reasoning processes. My own research on the ability of college students to assess the covariation between events is an example of this type of work. A brief discussion of what is involved in the assessment of covariation should help in introducing this research.

The Skill of Correlational Reasoning

The detection of covariation between events is basic to perceiving order, regularity, and predictability in the world (Kuhn & Phelps, 1979). It is surely one of the fundamental processes used both in scientific and in everyday reasoning. At the earliest stages of development, infants exhibit an understanding of covariation when they intentionally kick their feet to make the mobile overhead move. These action-outcome linkages are common occurrences. The inferences made from them form the foundation for the development of the formal reasoning schema identified by Piaget (Inhelder & Piaget, 1958) as correlational reasoning.

Inhelder and Piaget have proposed a three-stage model to characterize developmental changes in the understanding of correlational reasoning. To illustrate this model, consider a task (Ward & Jenkins, 1965) in which subjects are asked to determine if cloud seeding causes rainfall. The task requires the assessment of the relationship between two binary events, P and Q, where P stands for cloud seeding (present or absent) and Q stands for rainfall (present or absent). These two events combine to produce the following four associations:

1. cloud seeding and rainfall $(p.q)$
2. cloud seeding and no rainfall $(p.\bar{q})$
3. no cloud seeding and rainfall $(\bar{p}.q)$
4. no cloud seeding and no rainfall $(\bar{p}.\bar{q})$

According to Inhelder and Piaget, then, the first stage of correlational reasoning involves defining the relationship between two binary events by considering only the frequency of co-occurrence of cloud seeding and rainfall $(p.q)$. At the next stage, judgments are made by comparing the frequency of the cloud seeding and rainfall cases to the frequency of either the cloud seeding and no rainfall cases or the no cloud seeding and rainfall cases (i.e., $p.q$ vs. $p.\bar{q}$ or $p.q$ vs. $\bar{p}.q$). Only at the final stage are correct judgments made by comparing the difference between the confirming cases (cloud seeding and rainfall plus no cloud seeding and no rainfall) and disconfirming cases (cloud seeding and no rainfall plus no cloud seeding and rainfall), that is, $p.q + \bar{p}.\bar{q}$ versus $p.\bar{q} + \bar{p}.q$.

Thus, the Inhelder and Piaget model of correlational reasoning specifies that the accurate assessment of covariation between binary events requires both the correct identification of confirming and disconfirming cases, and the comparison of the differences between these correctly identified cases. The critical feature would seem to be knowledge of the confirming and disconfirming cases. Yet, there has been little research on the development of knowledge of confirming and disconfirming evidence, and how this knowledge is used in the process of judging the covariation between two binary events. Crocker (1981) obtained judgments from subjects as to which of the four types of information in a 2×2 contingency table would be necessary and sufficient for estimating the relationship between two events. Seggie (1975) asked subjects to rate the degree of influence each of the four cases had on their judgments. Data from both studies make it clear that adults do not attach equal importance to the cases corresponding to each of the four cells in the 2×2 contingency table. Still, these results do not reveal exactly how adults actually *used* the four types of cases in arriving at a judgment (i.e., which cases they thought to be confirming and disconfirming of a relationship and which of these cases they compared to arrive at a judgment).

The purpose of the study to be reported here (Nummedal, 1982) was to investigate students' use of confirming and disconfirming evidence when judging the covariation between two binary events. Results from the analysis of the judgment process should enable instructors to understand more precisely the nature of the difficulties students have with correlational reasoning and to design instruction accordingly.

METHOD

Two types of covariation relationships, causal and noncausal (or correlational), were included for study since previous research (i.e., Adi, Karplus, Lawson, & Pulos, 1978) has indicated that judgments may be influenced by the type of relationship to be assessed. The causal relationship problems were based on the cloud seeding task of Ward and Jenkins (1965) in which students were asked to determine if cloud seeding causes rain. Pictured in each problem were the four

TYPE OF CORRELATION

Positive   Negative   Zero

FIG. 7.1. Cell frequencies used for causal and correlational problems. From "Intellectual Development Beyond Elementary School VI: Correlational Reasoning" by Adi et al., 1978, *School Science and Mathematics,* II 78, p. 677.

possible associations between the two binary events, P (cloud seeding) and Q (rainfall); that is, presence (q) or absence ($\bar{q}$) of rainfall as a possible function of the presence (p) or absence ($\bar{p}$) of cloud seeding. For the noncausal, or correlational, relationship problems, the Smedslund (1963) symptom-diagnosis problem was used. To determine whether there was a relationship between symptom A and diagnosis of illness F, each of the problems pictures the presence (p) or absence ($\bar{p}$) of symptom A in association with the presence (q) or absence ($\bar{q}$) of illness F.

For each type of covariation relationship, there were three problems in which the set of frequencies used was varied to correspond to a positive, negative, and zero correlation. Actual cell frequencies were those used by Adi et al. (1978) and are presented in Fig. 7.1.

Participants in the study were 60 college students (30 females and 30 males) enrolled in introductory psychology at a large state university. Each student made judgments about either causal or correlational relationships. For each of the three problems, the student was presented with a set of cards. Each card pictured one of the four possible associations between the two binary events (e.g., cloud seeding and rainfall [$p.q$]). The student was asked to examine the cards and sort them into groups. The way in which the student sorted and organized them was noted. Then, the student was asked a series of structured questions to determine (a) what data were considered confirming and disconfirming, and (b) what judgment was made about the hypothesized relationship and why (Inhelder & Piaget, 1958).

RESULTS

Examination of the students' judgments of confirming and disconfirming cases revealed that for all three problems, 51 of the 60 students consistently judged the same evidence to be confirming and disconfirming. The remaining 9 students (3 for the causal problems and 6 for the correlational problems) made consistent judgments in two of the three problems. Therefore, it was possible to classify subjects according to their dominant judgment strategy based on the evidence they judged to be confirming and disconfirming.

Table 7.1 presents the numbers of students using each of the five judgment strategies. These data revealed quite clearly that students had great difficulty identifying both the confirming and the disconfirming cases. All students saw the cases corresponding to $p.q$ as confirming, but only 10% correctly included the $\bar{p}.\bar{q}$ cases in this category. In identifying the disconfirming cases, different errors occurred depending upon the type of relationship evaluated. For the causal relationship, 67% of the students saw as disconfirming the cases corresponding to only one of the two correct associations ($p.\bar{q}$ or $\bar{p}.q$). For the correlational relationship, 57% of the students designated the cases corresponding to the confirming association $\bar{p}.\bar{q}$ as either (a) the only disconfirming cases in the set, or (b) disconfirming along with the other correct disconfirming cases. Clearly students did not know the meaning of the cases corresponding to the $\bar{p}.\bar{q}$ association. In all, 58% ignored it completely, and 32% identified it erroneously as disconfirming.

Judgments of covariation were scored according to whether or not a student correctly evaluated the data in the three problems as corresponding to a positive, negative, and zero correlation, respectively. These responses were scored as correct or incorrect independent of the judgment strategy used. Overall, most judgments of covariation were correct, with 88% correct for the causal problems and 77% correct for the correlational problems.

The covariation judgments then were compared with the judgment strategies used. For both the causal and correlational problems, the cases initially identified as confirming and disconfirming formed the basis for the subsequent judgments of covariation. For the particular data sets judged by the students, this resulted in 80% to 91% of all correct judgments (depending on the problem) being based on the incorrect identification of confirming and disconfirming cases. For example, for the 67% of the students in the causal relationship condition who judged the $p.q$ cases to be confirming and the $p.\bar{q}$ (or $\bar{p}.q$) cases to be disconfirming, the

TABLE 7.1
Number of Students Using Each Judgment Strategy
for the Causal and Correlational Relationship Problems

Judgment Strategy		Type of Relationship Problem		
Confirming	Disconfirming	Causal	Correlational	Total
$p.q$	$\bar{p}.\bar{q}$	1 (3)	8 (27)	9 (15)
$p.q$	$p.\bar{q},\ \bar{p}.q,\ \bar{p}.\bar{q}$	1 (3)	9 (30)	10 (17)
$p.q$	$p.\bar{q}$ or $\bar{p}.q$	20 (67)	4 (13)	24 (40)
$p.q$	$p.\bar{q}$ and $\bar{p}.q$	5 (17)	6 (20)	11 (18)
$p.q$ and $\bar{p}.\bar{q}$	$p.\bar{q}$ and $\bar{p}.q$	3 (10)	3 (10)	6 (10)

Note. Numbers in parentheses are percentages.

ratio of confirming to disconfirming cases in the positive correlation problem was 7:2 (or 7:3). Students using this strategy could conclude (correctly) that cloud seeding causes rainfall. And in the correlational relationship condition, for the 30% of the students who judged the $p.q$ cases to be confirming and the $p.\bar{q}$, $\bar{p}.q$, and $\bar{p}.\bar{q}$ cases to be disconfirming, the ratio of confirming to disconfirming cases in the negative correlation problem was 2:18. Students using this strategy could conclude correctly that having symptom A was associated with not having illness F.

Examination of the ways in which the students sorted and organized the cards revealed a basic difficulty in problem representation as well. Those who were unable to identify correctly the confirming and disconfirming cases also failed to sort these cards into the four associations they represented. For example, after initially inspecting the cards, it was common for those in the correlational problem condition to organize the cards into two groups, one corresponding to the cases judged to be confirming (i.e., $p.q$) and one corresponding to all those cases judged to be disconfirming (i.e., $p.\bar{q}$, $\bar{p}.q$, and $\bar{p}.\bar{q}$). In the causal problem condition, often the cases corresponding to $\bar{p}.q$ and $\bar{p}.\bar{q}$ were grouped together and set aside as irrelevant to the problem. Problem representations, such as these, suggest a basic lack of understanding of the process of inferring covariation—a process which, at the minimum, requires consideration of all four associations obtained from the cross-classification of two values on each of two variables.

DISCUSSION

The results clearly demonstrate that students were unable to generate an appropriate problem representation, and that this difficulty, in turn, was associated with an inability to identify correctly both the confirming and disconfirming cases. Students in this study had particular difficulty with the cases corresponding to the confirming $\bar{p}.\bar{q}$ and the disconfirming $\bar{p}.q$. Both of these cases represent the non-occurrence of an event ($\bar{p}$) that is explicitly the causal event for the causal relationship, and implicitly so for the correlational relationship. As Einhorn and Hogarth (1978) have argued, these are precisely the cases that also are usually nonobservable in the natural environment. It seems reasonable to assume that in our natural environment, we have learned to pay more attention to outcomes that are associated with occurring (observable) rather than nonoccurring (nonobservable) causal actions. To the extent that conditions in the natural environment influence the development of the ability to make covariation judgments, it is not surprising that adults experience difficulty in evaluating the data corresponding to the nonoccurrence of events in laboratory-type tasks.

Interestingly, however, these difficulties did not necessarily prevent the students from making correct judgments of covariation. Of course, these "correct" judgments were possible because of the particular cell frequencies used in this study. Presumably, for many data sets in everyday life, more simplistic judgment strategies can yield correct judgments. For example, if there is a strong positive relationship, then commonly looking only at the $p.q$ cases will lead to a correct judgment at least most of the time. And, as noted above, sometimes in everyday life, data on all four cases are not even available. Hence, students may well have experienced a good deal of success making judgments based on more simplistic strategies (i.e., ones that utilize only a portion of the relevant information or ones that group together different types of information) that are approximations to the more complex ones we might like them to use. Like other heuristics, these simplistic strategies are efficient, and often lead to correct judgments, although sometimes they are in error. The results of this study help us to understand more precisely the judgment strategies students do use and how these strategies relate to actual judgments of covariation.

Conclusions

Research has shown that the majority of college students are unable to use the strategies and processes of formal reasoning consistently. Although the goal of improving these reasoning skills generally has been accepted by educators, there is disagreement about which reasoning skills to teach (e.g., general problem-solving heuristics, formal operational schema, etc.) and how best to teach them (e.g., in separate "thinking" courses, in specific subject matter domains, etc.). However, in order to develop *any* reasoning skill in college students, it seems clear that one must know both (a) the strategies and processes of skilled performance—the desired outcome of instruction, and (b) the strategies and processes less skilled students already possess and necessarily must abandon in order to acquire new ones. Research on specific reasoning skills that provides a clearer picture of both is critical for teaching reasoning skills. The tactics of successful instruction must focus on the formidable task of changing these well-practiced, yet more simplistic, skills into the more complex ones that will consistently and reliably yield correct judgments.

ACKNOWLEDGMENT

I gratefully acknowledge Earl R. Carlson and Gerard L. Hanley for their helpful comments on an earlier draft of this chapter.

REFERENCES

Adi, H., Karplus, R., Lawson, A., & Pulos, S. (1978). Intellectual development beyond elementary school VI: Correlational reasoning. *School Science and Mathematics, 78,* 675–683.
Arons, A. B. (1979). Some thoughts on reasoning capacities implicitly expected of college stu-

dents. In J. Lochhead & J. Clements (Eds.), *Cognitive process instruction: Research on teaching thinking skills* (pp. 209–215). Philadelphia, PA: Franklin Institute Press.

Bruner, J. S. (1985). Models of the learner. *Educational Researcher, 14* (6), 5–8.

Chase, W. G., & Simon, H. A. (1973). Perception in chess. *Cognitive Psychology, 4,* 55–81.

Collea, F. P., & Nummedal, S. G. (1980). Development of Reasoning in Science (DORIS): A course in abstract reasoning. *Journal of College Science Teaching, 10,* 100–102.

Crocker, J. (1981). Judgment of covariation by social perceivers. *Psychological Bulletin, 90,* 272–292.

Dewey, J. (1933). *How we think: A restatement of the relation of reflective thinking to the educative process.* Boston: D. C. Heath.

Einhorn, H. J., & Hogarth, R. N. (1978). Confidence 1n judgment: Persistence of the illusion of validity. *Psychological Review, 85,* 395–416.

Glaser, R. (1984). Education and thinking. *American Psychologist, 39,* 93–104.

Inhelder, B., & Piaget, J. (1958). *The growth of logical thinking from childhood to adolescence.* New York: Basic Books.

Keating, D. P., & Clark, L. V. (1980). Development of physical and social reasoning in adolescence. *Developmental Psychology, 16,* 23–30.

Kuhn, D., & Brannock, J. (1977). Development of the isolation of variables scheme in experimental and "natural experiment" contexts. *Developmental Psychology, 13,* 9–14.

Kuhn, D., & Phelps, E. (1979). A methodology for observing development of a formal reasoning strategy. In D. Kuhn (Ed.), *Intellectual development beyond childhood, No. 5* (pp. 45–57). San Francisco: Jossey-Bass.

Lawson, A. E., Nordland, F. H., & DeVito, A. (1975). Relationship of formal reasoning to achievement, aptitudes, and attitudes in preservice teachers. *Journal of Research in Science Teaching, 12,* 423–431.

McKinnon, J. W., & Renner, J. W. (1971). Are colleges concerned with intellectual development? *American Journal of Physics, 39,* 1047–1052.

McPeck, J. E. (1981). *Critical thinking and education.* New York: St. Martin's Press.

Moshman, D. (1979). Development of formal hypothesis-testing ability. *Developmental Psychology, 15,* 104–112.

Nummedal, S. G. (1982, June). *The role of confirming and disconfirming evidence in judgments of covariation between events.* Paper presented at the 12th Symposium of the Jean Piaget Society, Philadelphia, PA.

Polya, G. (1957). *How to solve it: A new aspect of mathematical method* (2nd ed.). Princeton, NJ: Princeton University Press.

Rubinstein, M. F. (1975). *Patterns of problem solving.* Englewood Cliffs, NJ: Prentice-Hall.

Seggie, J. L. (1975). The empirical observation of the Piagetian concept of correlation. *Canadian Journal of Psychology, 29,* 32–42.

Smedslund, J. (1963). The concept of correlation in adults. *Scandinavian Journal of Psychology, 4,* 165–173.

Sternberg, R. J. (1982). Training of intelligent performance. In D. K. Detterman & R. J. Sternberg (Eds.), *How and how much can intelligence be increased* (pp. 141–146). Norwood, NJ: Ablex.

Tomlinson-Keasey, C. (1972). Formal operations in females aged 11 to 54 years of age. *Developmental Psychology, 6,* 364.

Ward, W. C., & Jenkins, H. M. (1965). The display of information and the judgment of contingency. *Canadian Journal of Psychology, 19,* 231–241.

Wilkins, D. (1980). Using patterns and plans in chess. *Artificial Intelligence, 14,* 165–203.

8 Teaching Productive Problem-Solving Attitudes

Kenneth Pfeiffer
Gregory Feinberg
Steven Gelber
University of California, Los Angeles

ABSTRACT

This chapter presents teachers with some suggestions for improving problem-solving attitudes. We question the commonly held notion that the role of the teacher should be to "give" specific factual information to passive students. We liken learning problem-solving skills to learning a physical skill, such as riding a bicycle. Because this learning requires much active practice, we present the notion that the role of the teacher should be not only to present information but more important to provide appropriate practice, motivation, and feedback. We conclude with some specific characteristics and attitudes of productive problem solvers that teachers might attempt to instill in students by using our suggestions.

Some educators emphasize that one goal of education should be to produce students who are both good thinkers and good problem solvers. These educators believe students should be taught how to solve problems they have never encountered before. Students therefore must be able to identify and classify problems and to restructure and transfer knowledge and skills to new situations. Unfortunately, there has been little research that validates any method of instruction designed to accomplish this. There is little evidence that general problem-solving skills have been taught effectively. As Rubinstein (1979) put it, "Often our solutions apply to problems that do not arise, and we are confronted with problems for which we have no solutions."

WHY DON'T EDUCATORS TEACH PROBLEM SOLVING DIRECTLY?

Gagne has offered some possible reasons why educators spend so little time teaching students to think. Gagne (1980) hypothesized that educators today do not consider learning to think as an important goal. Another possible explanation for the lack of attention to thinking and problem solving is that educators simply have not yet found a method that can successfully teach problem solving. Many cognitive psychologists also share this view.

Gagne recognizes the difficulty of teaching people to think and solve problems. According to Gagne, problem solving, for the most part, is determined by situational factors and by the intellectual capacity of the individual. In other words, the educational environment of the individual has very little room to exert any effect.

Schoenfeld's (1980) work supports Gagne's position regarding the difficulty of teaching general problem solving. His program was successful in teaching students to use algorithms, but not *heuristics*. An algorithm is a sure-fire method for solving a particular problem, such as applying the quadratic formula to solve a quadratic equation. A heuristic is a "rule of thumb" that increases the probability of solution, but does not guarantee it. An example of a heuristic is the rule in chess, "guard your king," or the rule in inferential statistics, "classify the problem as to type of statistical test required." The difficulty with heuristics, as with all rules of thumb, is knowing when, where, and how to apply the rule.

Schoenfeld found he could teach algorithms effectively, but he found it difficult to teach students the heuristic of *when* to apply the algorithms. That is, it was difficult to teach the heuristic of how to classify problems correctly. Teachers of statistics frequently encounter this obstacle. It is relatively easy to teach students to do specific statistical tests, such as a *t* test or a chi square. It is more difficult to teach students when each test is appropriate, or when to use the formulas they have already learned.

Although a number of theories attempt to explain problem solving, they all fall short of generating recommendations for how to teach general problem solving. The major difficulty, we feel, is that researchers have focused too much attention on *what* to teach students to make them better problem solvers, instead of *how* to teach students. We feel the answer to the question of how to teach problem solving lies in the definition of teaching itself.

We believe an examination of the concept of teaching will reveal some clues that will help teachers and researchers find better ways of teaching problem-solving skills to their students. Many people think teaching is a one-dimensional act. They believe the teacher directly imparts knowledge to passive students, much like the teacher might hand the student a gem or a pizza. Even today, the dominant concept of teaching is that the teacher's task is directly to *cause* specific changes in the student, as though there were a direct, one-to-one relationship between what is taught and what is learned. For years this popular "cause and effect" view has guided educational programs. However, researchers are now finding that teaching is not a simple procedure, but one that involves the orchestration of a large number of factors that must be continually altered to accommodate the rapidly changing needs of the student.

Most models and definitions of teaching share one conception: that the teacher *gives* the student knowledge, skills, or attitudes. With this conception of teaching, we are not surprised there is little research that supports the idea that problem solving can be taught. We believe that learning problem-solving skills requires much practice and active participation by the student. We think general problem solving can be taught, but only if we redefine the role of the teacher in the learning process.

PROBLEM SOLVING AS A SKILL TO BE LEARNED

Consider an analogy. We claim that *learning to solve problems is like learning to ride a bicycle, or like learning to play basketball.* It requires active participation by the student, and a lot of practice.

First, let us state what we think effective teaching of problem solving is NOT. Effective teaching does not follow from the traditional "gift" model of instruction. Teachers cannot give students a "gift" of effective problem-solving skills, any more than you can hand a person a "gift" of bicycle-riding skills. Effective teaching does not come from the "osmosis" strategy of tossing students unaided into the situation you want them to master. Throwing a person into a professional basketball game and telling them to "learn" is not an effective strategy for teaching basketball, just as giving students a book and telling them to "learn it" is not an effective strategy in general. Also, effective teaching does not come from the "TV" strategy. A person cannot learn to play basketball very well by simply watching games on TV, just as a person cannot learn to become an effective problem solver by reading a book. Finally, learning to ride a bike takes much time and practice, perhaps more time than researchers spend trying to "teach" problem-solving heuristics.

Many people teach themselves how to ride a bike, or how to play basketball. Many people also teach themselves computer programming, or "computer programming problem solving." Obviously these skills can be learned. What about the question of whether they can be taught?

Teaching a person how to ride a bicycle is very different from teaching them "the name of the President of the United States." Bicycle riding involves *procedural knowledge;* names of United States Presidents is *declarative knowledge* (cf. Anderson, 1982). Acquiring procedural knowledge involves more active participation than does acquiring declarative knowledge. A person can learn the name of the President by watching TV or by reading a book, but they cannot learn to ride a bike by watching it on TV or by reading a book. There is no substitute for the student's own effort and practice, and for *adequate time,* especially when acquiring procedural knowledge.

USEFUL TECHNIQUES FOR TEACHING SKILLS

We believe general problem solving can be taught if the teacher provides not only facts but also practice, feedback, and motivation. The teacher must become more than just a "giver" of knowledge to passive students. The teacher must become a coach, a manager, a motivator. The role of the teacher is to arrange the learning environment in a way that optimizes the student's learning experience. The teacher can create an environment in which students want to learn, and can learn efficiently.

We first suggest, in general, some techniques the teacher might use to teach skills such as general problem solving. Then we present important problem-solving attitudes. We realize some of our suggestions may be controversial. We are presenting these ideas because we have found them effective in our own practice as teachers, and because they all have some research support in the areas of learning and cognitive psychology. Many of the specific techniques and supporting research are summarized in Snelbecker (1974).

Useful techniques for teaching problem solving fall into two important areas, giving students relevant practice and motivating students to practice. Regarding the first point, research from many different areas of psychology supports the idea that active learning is better than passive learning. One must practice solving problems.

Have students practice many real problems, and if possible organize study groups or some other way in which students can attempt to teach one another. Treisman (1985), who teaches mathematics to disadvantaged minority students at the University of California, Berkeley, found that the stronger students benefit from this the most! It is also beneficial to arrange a cooperative, rather than a competitive, environment for students, so they feel free to teach one another. Treisman (1985), Aronson and Osherow (1980), and others have demonstrated the advantage of cooperation over competition, especially with disadvantaged minority students. Treisman found that the worst students always study alone, and the best students generally study with others after they have studied alone. Students who study alone tend to use limited and inefficient problem-solving strategies. Studying with others helps students decide which problems really are the hard ones, allows incorrect ideas to be challenged, and allows students to analyze and test relevant skills. We suggest group efforts and the use of absolute grading scales, rather than curves.

The second important teaching technique is motivating students to practice. Present students with a challenge. Show them a problem they will have some difficulty solving. Then show them how the tools you are going to teach them will allow them to solve the problem more easily.

Research indicates that motivation is highest when the probability of success is close to 50% (Atkinson, 1957). Problems that are too easy are not rewarding to solve; they are just busywork. Problems that are too difficult do not give the student enough success to be motivating; students tend to give up. Students must believe they can solve the problem with a reasonable amount of effort. Expending that effort should be rewarded.

It is also important to make the challenge relevant. Use examples from students' own lives, or examples students are otherwise interested in. Use analogies, metaphors, and images with concepts and skills students are already familiar with. This makes problem solving intrinsically motivating. Also, students should feel they are working on something meaningful.

Observations in many different arenas make it clear that those who are doing what they like, and who thus appreciate the immediate importance of a problem, deal with it in a more adaptive and effective manner. For example, Treisman (1985) reports that the best of his students are those who want to deal with problems *now*, rather than put them off. They want to understand the material at the time it is presented, rather than put it off and ''worry about it tomorrow.'' They want to absorb everything presented in class, and ask questions to clarify the material presented. The good students show a real interest in what they are doing. We have made similar observations among our own students at UCLA. The best students want to ''get it now.''

Another important motivational technique is the use of positive reinforcement rather than negative reinforcement or punishment. According to Skinner (1968), positive reinforcement strengthens behavior without the negative effect associated with aversives. Praise students for good performance. Tell students what they did *right* rather than always telling them what they did wrong. Never put students down, particularly in front of their peers. Emphasize that making mistakes is part of the learning process, and is nothing to be ashamed of. Reward students' good efforts and gently point out errors. Make sure reinforcement is contingent on good performance, and is not random. Improve practice, performance, and learning by rewarding it with your attention and praise.

Having positive expectations about students also enhances their motivation. Expect them to work hard, expect them to practice, and expect them to improve their performance. If you are an effective teacher, students will work hard, practice, and improve. Rosenthal (1966), among others, has shown that positive expectations create far better performance than negative or neutral expectations.

Shaping is another effective teaching technique. As students' skills increase, make problems gradually more difficult. Everyone started as a novice. As much as possible, break complex problems and skills down into component parts. To avoid unnecessary interference and confusion, give practice with each part until the student has a fairly good grasp before you go on to the next part. For the same reason, try to "accrete" component skills, or add onto what students already know.

Finally, be a good model. Teach what most interests you, and what you have the most first-hand personal experience with. Teach what you think will benefit students most. Remember, the more you put into your teaching, the more you will get out of it. Your enthusiasm, practical experience, and good intentions will serve as an inspiration.

PRODUCTIVE PROBLEM-SOLVING ATTITUDES

Good creative problem solvers share certain characteristics, regardless of their specific discipline (Maier, 1970). We state these characteristics in the form of attitudes, rather than as specific skills.

1. They are comfortable with complex situations, and they have a high toler-ance for conflict and uncertainty.
2. They have respect for the facts, and also an interest in the interpretation, significance, and meaning of the facts.
3. They are self-confident; they seem to be in control. They have a strong taste for new experiences and for conceptual adventures.

How would we go about teaching these attitudes? How could we arrange the environment of students so they would be likely to acquire these important characteristics? We feel that if teachers use the teaching techniques we have discussed, students will be more likely to acquire these desirable characteristics. We are suggesting that the *manner* of teaching itself might help instill the above productive attitudes. If teachers model these attitudes, our experience suggests that students will have a higher probability of developing these attitudes.

Let us break down the above general characteristics of creative problem solvers a little further, and suggest more specific attitudes that might be useful in solving any problem.

1. One of the most important attitudes in problem solving is the *attitude of inquiry*. An effective problem solver has a questioning attitude; this person wants to find out "what," "how," and "why." The problem solver should observe more than just the external facts. Equally important is the problem solver's own reaction to those facts. How do I feel about what seems to be going on? Is there a way to look at the situation other than the way I am seeing it now? Can I formulate the problem differently?

Effective problem solvers are aware of their own reactions to the environ-ment. A problem exists when "what is" differs from "what is desired" (Rubinstein, 1975). The observation of "what is" and of "what is desired" both depend on what the problem solver brings to the situation, including values and emotional reactions. For example, a typical American might look at a partially rotted fish and see only the problem of how to dispose of it without smelling up everything. A Korean might view the same situation and see the very different problem of how to prepare this delicacy for a feast.

Another difficulty is thinking you know more than you actually do, and jumping to conclusions on the basis of flimsy evidence (Nisbett & Ross, 1980). For example, suppose you are driving in your car and the red alternator light on the dashboard goes on. A week ago the same thing happened. At that time you took your car into a repair shop and they replaced the alternator. What do you do now? What is the problem?

Some people might conclude the repair shop fouled up and the alternator is faulty again. However, the "fact" is merely that "the light is on." Since there are ways the light can be on when the alternator is not faulty, such as from a short circuit or broken belt, the conclusion of a faulty alternator is not warranted by the facts.

2. A good problem solver should be *open minded, flexible, and should consider a wide range of alternatives.* Effective problem solvers take the time to generate and examine a wide range of alternative solutions, rather than lock themselves into just a few choices. They look at the pros and cons of each possible alternative, carefully weighing what they know about the possible consequences, rather than passing a quick judgment.

The effective problem solver is willing to tolerate some ambiguity or uncertainty, rather than constantly forcing observations into a preconceived hypothetical explanation. Effective problem solvers are willing to change their hypotheses to fit the facts, rather than always trying to explain why the "facts" do not fit preexisting hypotheses. Good problem solving involves a balance between assimilation (trying to fit facts into existing hypothetical frameworks), and accommodation (modifying the framework to provide a better or more elegant fit to the facts).

Rather than seek information that would help clarify a problematic situation, people often force available information into a preexisting hypothetical framework; they defend the preconceptions they want to be true. Rather than trying to generate and consider other alternate solutions to their problem, they restrict the range of alternative solutions. Because of the unpleasantness of conflict, they inflexibly "assimilate" new information into their preconceptions, effectively ignoring the real problem. This is another example of how the old adage, "I'll believe it when I see it," often in truth turns out to be, "I'll see it when I believe it!"

3. Effective problem solvers *believe in their own ability to solve the problem* at hand. This means not only that they feel they have sufficient knowledge, motivation, and skill, but also that they believe the problem at hand has a satisfactory solution. If either of these conditions is not met, then problem solvers will not attack the problem with the kind of attention that increases the

likelihood of a satisfactory outcome. If it appears the problem cannot be solved, the problem solver may ignore or avoid the situation. If the problem solver feels incompetent to solve the problem, then little effort will probably be spent. Instilling confidence in students' ability is a prime example of the importance of *how* the teacher behaves.

4. View a problem as a challenge, or as an opportunity to learn, rather than a source of frustration. Many people become frustrated in their problem-solving endeavors because they inevitably make many mistakes in the process. Yet people can learn just as much, if not more, from their mistakes as they can from their successes.

In the proper application of the scientific method, researchers attempt to find contradictions to their hypotheses. Much more is learned from apparent contradictions than by correct but commonsense predictions. Likewise, when a theory predicts something that seems highly unusual, the theory receives much more confirmation than when it predicts the commonplace (Popper, 1959; Rubinstein, 1975). We can learn much from one negative instance. If problem solvers realized how much is learned by making mistakes, they would be less frustrated by errors.

In spite of all efforts and good intentions, some problems are not solved. If the problem solver has approached the problem with the proper attitudes and has made the best attempt under the circumstances, then all is not lost. All you can do is your best, isn't it? It is better to place the unsolved problem in perspective and go on to the next problem than to worry over the past.

5. Good problem solvers *take a larger perspective*. They get the whole picture, and do not create unnecessary problems for themselves. They ask themselves, "What are all the alternatives? What will probably happen if I do nothing? What are the consequences of trying to deal with this problem? How much difference can I make? How much time, effort, or money will it cost me to focus my attention on this problem?" The effective problem solver tries to weigh the likely consequences of different courses of action.

SUMMARY

We have presented what we consider to be some of the most important attitudes in problem solving, along with some ideas for how to teach these attitudes, and how to improve teaching in general. In summary, we think the extensive controversy over whether problem solving can be taught is based on an overly narrow conception of teaching. If we consider the teacher as more of a manager or coach, rather than as merely a giver of facts, it seems clear that the teacher can play a major role in helping students acquire problem-solving skills and attitudes. The teacher cannot "do it all" for the student. However, the teacher can provide not only specific facts, but an appropriate model, motivation, exercises for practice, and feedback to help students acquire problem-solving skills and attitudes more quickly than they could alone.

REFERENCES

Anderson, J. R. (1982). Acquisition of cognitive skill. *Psychological Review, 89,* 369–406.

Aronson, E., & Osherow, N. (1980). Cooperation, prosocial behavior, and academic performance: Experiments in the desegregated classroom. In L. Bickman (Ed.), *Applied social psychology annual: Vol. 1* (pp. 163–196). Beverly Hills, CA: Sage Publications.

Atkinson, J. W. (1957). Motivational determinants of risk-taking behavior. *Psychological Review, 6,* 365.

Gagne, R. M. (1980). Learnable aspects of problem solving. *Educational Psychologist, 15,* 84–92.

Maier, N. R. F. (1970). *Problem solving and creativity.* Belmont, CA: Brooks/Cole.

Nisbett, R. E., & Ross, L. (1980). *Human inference: Strategies and shortcomings of social judgement.* Englewood Cliffs, NJ: Prentice-Hall.

Popper, K. R. (1959). *The logic of scientific discovery.* New York: Basic Books.

Rosenthal, R. (1966). *Experimenter effects in behavioral research.* New York: McGraw-Hill.

Rubinstein, M. F. (1975). *Patterns of problem solving.* Englewood Cliffs, NJ: Prentice-Hall.

Rubinstein, M. F. (1979). Attitudes productive in problem solving. *Patterns of problem solving vignette #36.* Los Angeles: UCLA.

Schoenfeld, A. H. (1980). *Measures of students' problem solving performance and of problem solving instruction.* Washington, D.C. National Science Foundation RISE research report.

Skinner, B. F. (1968). *The technology of teaching.* New York: Meredith.

Snelbecker, G. E. (1974). *Learning theory, instructional theory, and psychoeducational design.* New York: McGraw-Hill.

Treisman, U. (1985). A model academic support system. In R. B. Landis (Ed.), *Improving the retention and graduation of minorities in engineering* (pp. 55–66). New York: National Association of Minority Engineering Program Administrators, and National Action Council for Minorities in Engineering.

9 Learnable Aspects of Problem Solving: Some Examples

Richard E. Mayer
University of California, Santa Barbara

ABSTRACT

This chapter is concerned with teaching and learning of mathematical problem-solving skill. In particular, the chapter explores four potentially learnable aspects of mathematical problem solving: (1) translation training, which involves teaching students how to transform each sentence of a problem into an internal representation, (2) schema training, which involves teaching students how to integrate the information into a coherent representation, (3) strategy training, which involves teaching students how to devise and monitor solution plans, and (4) algorithm automaticity, which involves teaching students to effortlessly use arithmetic and algebraic procedures. The theme of this chapter is that learning to solve mathematical problems requires the acquisition of large amounts of domain-specific knowledge.

INTRODUCTION

Issue. ''What kind of education does it take to become a productive thinker, a successful problem solver?'' This question, taken from Gagne's (1979) classic ''Learnable Aspects of Human Thinking,'' has a long history in educational psychology (see Mayer, in press). In spite of nearly a century's work on problem solving, however, the answer to this question is still not clear (Mayer, 1983). Gagne (1979) provides a framework for the answer by noting that learning to become a problem solver requires ''learning of stores of knowledge'' (p. 20). In particular, Gagne suggests that several kinds of knowledge are required, including knowledge for representation of problems, knowledge of solution procedures, and knowledge of strategies. This approach seems to be consistent with recent developments in the information processing approach to cognition (see Mayer, 1981b, 1983) as well as some recent research on mathematical problem solving (Carpenter, Moser, & Romberg, 1982; Ginsburg, 1983; Resnick & Ford, 1981; Silver, 1985). In particular, Gagne's framework captures the emphasis on the role of knowledge and on the analysis of cognition into components.

The purpose of this paper is to explore some examples of how problem solving might be taught within the domain of algebra story problems. Consistent with the information processing approach, this chapter examines the kinds of knowledge needed for each of four component processes in mathematical problem solving. In particular, four techniques are examined:

1. Translation training involves teaching students how to transform each sentence of a problem into an internal representation.
2. Schema training involves teaching students how to integrate the information into a coherent representation.
3. Strategy training involves teaching students how to devise and monitor solution plans.
4. Algorithm automaticity involves teaching students to effortlessly use arithmetic and algebraic procedures.

Example.   In order to understand these four types of problem-solving training, let's begin with the tile problem as shown in Table 9.1. First, the cognitive processes required by this problem can be broken down into two main phases—problem representation (i.e., going from the words to some internal representation of the problem) and problem solution (i.e., applying the appropriate operators in proper order). The problem representation phase can further be broken down into translation (i.e., comprehension of each sentence of the problem) and integration (i.e., putting the sentences together into a coherent or meaningful representation of the problem). The problem solution phase can be broken down into planning/monitoring (i.e., determining which operators to apply and when to apply them) and execution (i.e., successfully carrying out each arithmetic or algebraic operation). Table 9.2 provides examples of the four component processes in solving the tile problem. As you can see, Table 9.2 summarizes processes carried out by good problem solvers. However, except for drill and

TABLE 9.1
Tile Problem

Floor tiles are sold in squares 30 cm on each side and weigh 10 g each.   How much would it cost to tile a rectangular room 7.2 m long and 5.4 m wide if the tiles cost $0.72 each?

TABLE 9.2
Components in Mathematical Problem Solving

Components	Examples from Tile Problem
Problem Representation	
Translation	The room is a rectangle with length of 7.2 m and width of 5.4 m. The floor tiles are squares with length of .3 m and width of .3 m. The floor tiles cost $0.72 each. The unknown is the cost of tiling the floor of the room.
Integration	

7.2

.72	.72	.72	.72	...
.72	.72	.72		
.72	.72			

5.4

Problem Solution	
Planning/Monitoring	First, find the area of the room. Second, find the number of needed tiles. Third, find the cost of the needed tiles.
Execution	7.2 x 5.4 = 38.88 38.88/(.3 x .3) = 432 432 x .72 = 311.04

practice in execution, students rarely receive direct instruction in the other three component processes.

Each component process may be supported by a different kind of knowledge, as summarized in Table 9.3. Translation processes require that the problem solver possess linguistic knowledge about the English language and factual knowledge about objects or events in the problem. Integration processes depend on schematic knowledge, that is, knowledge of problem types. Planning and monitoring processes require strategic knowledge, such as how to break the problem into parts and how to tell what to do next. Execution processes require algorithmic knowledge, such as knowing arithmetic computational procedures. Thus, Table 9.3 summarizes the kinds of knowledge that a good problem solver needs in order to solve the tile problem. This framework is consistent with Gagne's (1979) assertion that the learnable aspects of problem solving are specific, e.g., "rules of syntax and mathematics," "knowledge about particular objects and events," "specific cognitive strategies" (p. 19–20).

TABLE 9.3
Types of Knowledge Required for Four Components in Problem Solving

Components	Knowledge	Example from Tile Problem
Problem Representation		
Translation	Linguistics	"Floor tiles" and "tile" refer to the same variable. "30 cm on each side" means that the length is 30 cm and the width is 30 cm.
	Factual	100 cm equals 1 m. Each side of a square is the same.
Integration	Schematic	Area = Length x Width Total Cost = Unit Cost x Number of Units
Problem Solution		
Planning/Monitoring	Strategic	Break problem into subgoals.
Execution	Algorithmic	Procedure for long division and multiplication.

TRANSLATION TRAINING

Research on Translation.   In order to solve the tile problem, a student needs to be able to translate each sentence or proposition into a memory representation. Unfortunately, instruction rarely deals with how to comprehend the sentences in a problem. However, research is accumulating which shows that sentence translation is a major source of errors for many students.

As an example, let's consider students' ability to understand relational propositions such as "the length of a rectangular room is ⅓ greater than its width." Greeno and his colleagues (Greeno, 1980; Riley, Greeno, & Heller, 1982) asked primary-grade children to listen to a problem and then repeat the problem. A problem such as "Joe has three marbles. Tom has five more marbles than Joe; How many marbles does Tom have?" was sometimes repeated as, "Joe has three marbles. Tom has five marbles. How many marbles does Tom have?" As you can see, the relational sentence was not encoded properly by students in this example.

Similar results have been obtained with adults. Soloway, Lochhead, and Clement (1982) asked college students to write equations to represent relational propositions such as "there are six times as many students as professors at this university." Approximately one third of the students produced the wrong equation, such as $6S = P$. In another series of experiments, Mayer (1982b) asked college students to read a series of eight algebra story problems and then recall them. The problems contained both relational propositions, such as "the rate in still water is 12 mph more than the rate of the current," and assignment propositions, such as "the cost of the candy is $1.70 per pound." The recall results indicated a much higher error rate for relational propositions as compared to assignment propositions. In addition, students tended to change relational propositions such as "the rate in still water is 12 mph more than the rate of the current" into assignment propositions, such as "the speed of the boat in still water is 12 mph." In summary, these results indicate that some subjects—both children and adults—lack appropriate linguistic knowledge for translating relational sentences into internal representations.

Examples of Translation Training. What can be done to help students acquire skill in the translation process? Traditionally, students are given story problems and asked to generate a numerical answer. In contrast, Table 9.4 suggests four kinds of questions that seem to better focus on the translation process: restating the problem givens in other words, restating the problem goals in other words, representing a problem sentence as a picture or diagram, representing a problem sentence as an equation. Other techniques that could be used in individual one-on-one instruction include asking the student to repeat or para-

TABLE 9.4
Examples of Translation Training

Restating the Problem Givens

Which of the following sentences is not true?

(a) the room is a rectangle measuring 7.2 by 5.4 meters.
(b) each tile costs 30 cents.
(c) each tile is a square measuring 30 by 30 centimeters.
(d) the length of the long side of the room is 7.2 meters.

Restating the Problem Goal

What are you being asked to find?

(a) the width and length of the room
(b) the cost of each tile
(c) the cost of tiling the room
(d) the size of each tile

Representing a Sentence as a Picture

Floor tiles are sold in squares 30 cm on each side.

Which of the following pictures corresponds to this statement?

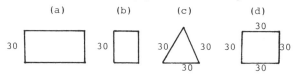

Representing a Sentence as an Equation

The length of a rectangular room is 1/3 greater than its width.

Which of the following equations corresponds to this statement?

(a) width - 1/3 (length)
(b) width + 1/3 (width) = length
(c) width = length + 1/3 (length)
(d) 1/3 (width) = length

phrase a problem sentence or to represent a sentence using concrete objects. Although these techniques are suggested by the research literature, they are offered only as hypotheses that warrant further study. For example, Reed (1985) recently studied the role of computer graphics in helping students represent story problems.

SCHEMA TRAINING

Research on Schemas.   Building a useful representation of a problem may require more than correctly translating each sentence. For example, consider the following problem used in a study by Paige and Simon (1966): "The number of quarters a man has is seven times the number of dimes he has. The value of dimes exceeds the value of quarters by two dollars and fifty cents. How many has he of each coin?" A person who translates each sentence could generate the equations: $Q = 7D$ and $D(.10) = 2.50 + Q(.25)$. However, a person who integrates the information in this problem into a coherent structure would recognize that the problem is self-contradictory. Paige and Simon (1966) found both kinds of problem solvers.

What do skilled problem solvers know about problem representation that helps them to understand problems? Hinsley, Hayes, and Simon (1977) offer some evidence that skilled problem solvers have an extensive knowledge of problem types—i.e., schematic knowledge. For example, in one study, students were given a series of algebra problems like those in standard textbooks. Students were asked to sort the problems into categories. The results indicated that students were able to perform this task with much consistency, yielding a total of 18 problem types such as work, interest, river current, triangle, and so on. The results also indicated that students tended to categorize problems after reading only the first few words. Subsequent studies by Silver (1979) have shown that experienced problem solvers tend to sort problems by solution procedure (as in the Hinsley, Hayes, & Simon study) but novices often use superficial aspects of the problem as the basis for categorization.

More recently, Mayer (1981a) analyzed the problems in secondary school mathematics textbooks and identified over 100 basic problem types. Some problem types were labeled "high frequency" because they occurred at least 25 times per 1000 problems; other problem types were "low frequency" because they occurred less than 4 times per 1000 problems. In a follow-up study, Mayer (1982b) asked college students to read and recall a series of eight problems. Students tended to recall high-frequency versions of problems better than low-frequency versions. In addition, there were many instances of students converting low-frequency versions into high-frequency versions. Apparently, when students lack a schema for a problem—as would be expected for some low-frequency problems—problem representation is more likely to be faulty.

Greeno and his colleagues (Greeno, 1980; Riley, Greeno, & Heller, 1982) have identified three main types of algebra word problems: cause/change problems, such as "Joe has three marbles. Tom gives him five more marbles. How many marbles does Joe have now?" combination problems, such as "Joe had three marbles. Tom has five marbles. How many marbles do they have altogether?" and comparison problems, such as "Joe has three marbles. Tom has five more marbles than Joe. How many marbles does Tom have?" Although

TABLE 9.5
Examples of Schema Training

───

Recognizing Relevant and Irrelevant Information

Which numbers are needed to solve this problem?

(a) 30, 10, 7.2, 5.4, .72
(b) 10, 7.2, 5.4, .72
(c) 30, 30, 7.2, 5.4, .72
(d) 30, 10, 7.2, 5.4

Representing a Problem as a Number Sentence

Which of the following expressions corresponds to this problem?

(a) (7.2 x 5.4) x .72 = __
(b) [(7.2 x 5.4)/.3] = __
(c) [7.2 x 5.4/.3] x .72 = __
(d) [7.2 x 5.4)/(.3 x .3)] x .72 = __

Representing a Problem as an Equation

Which of the following expressions corresponds to this problem?

(a) length x width x cost per tile = total cost
(b) length x width = area
(c) number of tiles x cost per tile = total cost
(d) area x cost per tile = total cost

Representing a Problem as a Diagram

Which of the following diagrams correspond to this problem?

───

each of these problems requires the same computation of adding 3 and 5, children tended to have much more difficulty with comparison problems and the least amount of difficulty with cause/change problems. The pattern of results suggests a developmental trend in which children begin with the idea that all problems are cause/change problems, and later begin to differentiate other problem schemas. According to this view, errors in comparison problems may be due to children's lacking appropriate schemata.

Examples of Schema Training.   How can we help students to develop appropriate problem schemata? One approach is to provide direct instruction on problem types. Unfortunately, this approach can sometimes lead to asking students to senselessly memorize key words, such as "if the problem says 'altogether' then add the numbers" or "if the problem says 'difference' then subtract" (Briars & Larkin, 1984). In contrast to the superficial approach of keyword memorization, Table 9.5 suggests several techniques for teaching problem types: recognizing relevant and irrelevant information, representing the entire problem as a number sentence, representing the entire problem as an equation, representing the entire problem as a diagram. Other techniques include sorting problems into categories and solving a mixture of problem types rather than one type.

STRATEGY TRAINING

Research on Strategies.   Once the problem is represented, the next step is to develop a solution plan. There are many well-known attempts to teach general problem-solving strategies, such as Rubinstein's (1975) *Patterns of Problem Solving,* DeBono's (1983) *CoRT,* or Covington, Crutchfield, Davies, and Olton's (1974) *Productive Thinking Program.* However, courses in general thinking strategies have been plagued by lack of research support (Mansfield, Busse, & Krepelka, 1978; Mayer, 1983, in press).

Better success has been obtained in teaching domain-specific strategies, such as within the domain of mathematical problem solving. Polya (1957, 1968) suggested several strategies for mathematical problem solving, including working backwards, restating the goal, using subgoals, finding related problems, and so on. In a research study, Schoenfeld (1979) was successful in teaching mathematics students to use strategies such as "try to establish subgoals" or "consider a problem with fewer variables." Similarly, Thornton (1978) was able to teach elementary school children to use strategies for deriving number facts in arithmetic computation. One benefit of strategy training is that it might help students to see commonalities among analogous problems, since students do not naturally seem to make connections between analogous story problems (Reed, Dempster, & Ettinger, 1985).

The most studied strategy is means-ends analysis, a strategy of continually setting subgoals and assessing distances to the goal (see Newell & Simon, 1972). Means-ends analysis was once considered to be the primary strategy used in human thinking, but more recent research has shown that means-ends analysis can be an ineffective strategy in mathematical problem solving (Owen & Sweller, 1985). Similarly, Mayer (1982a) and Mayer, Larkin, and Kadane (1984) have found that students use entirely different strategies for solving isomorphic algebra problems stated in words versus equations. Greeno (1978) has observed that a wide variety of goal setting and monitoring skills are required in mathematical problem solving, although these principles are "not mentioned explicitly in any text that I have examined" (p. 60). Greeno (1978) further argues that "the strategic knowledge needed for problem solving can be learned" (p. 62).

Examples of Strategy Training.   In order to teach students strategies for the tile problem, Table 9.6 lists several possible techniques. These include establishing subgoals, identifying necessary operations, and drawing conclusions. Other techniques include having students describe their own thinking process for a

TABLE 9.6
Examples of Strategy Training

Establishing Subgoals

   To answer this question you need to determine:

   (a) how many tiles are needed
   (b) how much longer one side of the room is than the other side
   (c) how much the tiles would weigh
   (d) how much money would be left

Identifying Necessary Operations

   To calculate an answer to this problem you must:

   (a) multiply, multiply, multiply
   (b) multiply, multiply, divide, multiply
   (c) multiply, add, multiply, add
   (d) add, divide, add, divide

Drawing Conclusions

   If the tiles come only in boxes containing 100 tiles each, how many boxes are needed?

   You make the following calculations:

   $7.2 \times 5.4 = 38.88$

   $.3 \times .3 = .09$

   $38.88/.09 = 432$

   $432/100 = 4.32$

   Look back at the question. What is the answer?

   (a) 4
   (b) 4.32
   (c) 5
   (d) 432

---

problem and comparing that to the thinking process of a ''model.'' Simon (1980) suggests that worked-out examples can serve as a ''model'' against which students can compare their own process.

ALGORITHM AUTOMATICITY

Once a problem is represented and a solution strategy is devised, the problem solver must carry out the necessary operations—such as arithmetic computations. In other words, the problem solver needs procedural knowledge, such as computational algorithms. For example, Groen and Parkman (1972) have suggested several computational procedures that children might use for simple addition problems, such as $m + n =$ _____. The counting-all procedure involves setting a counter to zero, incrementing it m times, incrementing it n times, and reciting the result. For $3 + 5$, the child would recite ''1,2,3,4,5,6,7,8.'' The counting-on procedure involves setting a counter to m, incrementing it n times, and reciting the result. For $3 + 5$, the child would recite, ''4,5,6,7,8.'' The choice procedure involves setting the counter to the larger of m or n, incrementing by the smaller of m or n, and reciting the result. For $3 + 5$, the child would recite, ''6,7,8.''

How can we tell which counting procedure a student is using? One approach is simply to observe children, including their use of fingers and their reciting of numbers. Another technique is to measure the time it takes them to answer simple addition problems. According to the counting-on model, response time should be a function of the sum of $m + n$; for example, for $3 + 5 =$ _____ the counter is set once and incremented eight times. According to the counting-all model, response time should be a function of n; for example, for $3 + 5 =$ _____ the counter is set once and incremented five times. According to the choice model, response time should be a function of the smaller of m or n; for example, for $3 + 5 =$ _____ the counter is set once and incremented three times. Fuson (1982) has observed that preschoolers often use counting-all or counting-on procedures. Groen and Parkman (1972) found that the response times of first graders corresponded best to the choice model. As children acquire more experience with simple addition, they acquire ''known facts''—that is, they have memorized answers for the problems (Fuson, 1982). Groen and Parkman (1972) found some evidence that first graders were beginning to acquire a few known facts; for example, first graders were particularly fast on ''doubles'' such as $1 + 1$, $2 + 2$, $3 + 3$, $4 + 4$. Fuson (1982) observed that students may use a strategy called ''derived facts'' in which they use known facts to derive answers for other problems. For example, to answer ''$3 + 5 =$ _____,'' a child may say, ''I borrow 1 from the 5 and give it to 3. $4 + 4$ is 8.'' Fuson (1982) suggests a developmental trend in which students build increasingly more efficient counting procedures, and then move on to derived facts, and eventually to known facts. This progression can be seen as a move from procedural knowledge to declarative knowledge (Anderson, 1983).

Woods, Resnick, and Groen (1975) have observed a similar pattern in children's computational procedures for simple subtraction. Most second graders and all fourth graders seemed to be using a choice model, whereas about 20% of the second graders seemed to use a less sophisticated counting procedure.

Once a child has acquired proficiency in simple addition or subtraction, the child might be ready to build more complex procedures for two- or three-column addition or subtraction. Several researchers have shown that building of complex procedures requires that children have automatized the components (Case, 1978; Siegler, 1978). Thus, learning of the procedure for three-column subtraction requires that the child has reached the level of known facts for simple subtraction. Brown and Burton (1978) analyzed the error patterns of children's answers for three-column subtraction problems. Much of students' performance can be attributed to the systematic use of subtraction procedures that contain one or more *bugs*. Typical bugs include subtracting the smaller number from the larger number in each column (e.g., $322 - 133 = 211$) and borrowing from zero (e.g., $202 - 103 = 109$). These results support the idea that errors in three-column subtraction may not be due to random or careless performance, but rather to students' correct use of an incorrect (or "buggy") procedure.

Example of Algorithm Information Training.   Research on algorithm automaticity suggests that students need experience in computing. Students' procedural knowledge can be analyzed into components, such as counting models or buggy procedures. One strong implication of this work is that students should achieve high levels of automaticity on component skills before moving on to more demanding algorithms. For example, proficiency in counting is required in order to use counting models of addition, and automatic knowledge of number facts is required for efficient use of algorithms for three-column addition. Table 9.7 presents a typical exercise for algorithm automaticity in the tile problem. Because textbooks provide ample opportunity for drill and practice based on

TABLE 9.7
Examples of Algorithm Automaticity Training

Carrying Out Calculations

$$((7.2 \times 5.40 / (.3 \times .3)) \times .72 = \underline{\quad}$$

The correct answer is:

(a) 38.88
(b) 432
(c) 311.04
(d) 28

Thorndike's (1922) classic work, this chapter has emphasized the foregoing three types of training in addition to algorithm automaticity training.

CONCLUSION

How can we help students to improve their mathematical problem-solving performance? This paper has examined four types of training, suggested by the current state of research on mathematical problem solving. Each type of training is aimed at increasing a different kind of knowledge relevant to mathematical problem solving. The approach of the chapter is to propose direct instruction for specific kinds of knowledge needed for representation and solution of the tile problem. The proposals listed in the "example" sections of the chapter and presented in Tables 9.4, 9.5, 9.6, and 9.7 are hypotheses that warrant further research. They do not represent well-established facts, but rather "best guesses" that need to be tested. If this chapter stimulates such testing, I will consider the chapter to be successful.

REFERENCES

Anderson, J. R. (1983). *The architecture of cognition.* Cambridge, MA: Harvard University Press.

Briars, D. J., & Larkin, J. H. (1984). An integrated model of skill in solving elementary work problems. *Cognition and Instruction, 1,* 245–296.

Brown, J. S., & Burton, R. R. (1978) Diagnostic models for procedural bugs in basic mathematical skills. *Cognitive Science, 2,* 155–192.

Carpenter, T. P., Moser, J. M., & Romberg, T. A. (Eds.). (1982). *Addition and subtraction: A cognitive perspective.* Hillsdale, NJ: Lawrence Erlbaum Associates.

Case, R. (1978). Intellectual development from birth to adulthood: A neo-Piagetian interpretation. In R. S. Siegler (Ed.), *Children's thinking: What develops?* Hillsdale, NJ: Lawrence Erlbaum Associates.

Covington, M. V., Crutchfield, R. S., Davies, L. B., & Olton, R. M. (1974). *The productive thinking program.* Columbus, OH: Merrill.

De Bono, E. (1983). The Cognitive Research Trust (CoRT) thinking program. In W. Maxwell (Ed.), *Thinking: The expanding frontier* (pp. 115–127). Philadelphia: Franklin Institute Press.

Fuson, K. C. (1982). An analysis of the counting-on solution procedure in addition. In T. P. Carpenter, J. M. Moser, & T. A. Romberg (Eds.), *Addition and subtraction: A cognitive perspective.* Hillsdale, NJ: Lawrence Erlbaum Associates.

Gagne, R. M. (1979). Learnable aspects of human thinking. In A. E. Lawson (Ed.), *The psychology of thinking and creativity* (pp. 1–27). Columbus, OH: ERIC.

Ginsburg, H. P. (Ed.). (1983). *The development of mathematical thinking.* New York: Academic Press.

Greeno, J. G. (1978). A study of problem solving. In R. Glaser (Ed.), *Advances in instructional psychology Vol. 1* (pp. 13–75). Hillsdale, NJ: Lawrence Erlbaum Associates.

Greeno, J. G. (1980). Some examples of cognitive task analysis with instructional implications. In R. E. Snow, P. Federico, & W. E. Montague (Eds.), *Aptitude, learning, and instruction* (Vol. 2, pp. 1–21). Hillsdale, NJ: Lawrence Erlbaum Associates.

Groen, G. J., & Parkman, J. M. (1972). A chronometric analysis of simple addition. *Psychological Review, 97,* 329–343.

Hinsley, D., Hayes, J. R., & Simon, H. A. (1977). From words to equations. In P. Carpenter & M. Just (Eds.), *Cognitive processes in comprehensions.* Hillsdale, NJ: Lawrence Elrbaum Associates.

Mansfield, R. S., Busse, T. V., & Krepelka, E. J. (1978). The effectiveness of creativity training. *Review of Educational Research, 48,* 517–536.

Mayer, R. E. (1981a). Frequency norms and structural anlaysis of algebraic story problems into families, categories, and templates. *Instructional Science, 10,* 135–175.

Mayer, R. E. (1981b). *The promise of cognitive psychology.* New York: Freeman.

Mayer, R. E. (1982a). Different problem solving categories for algebra word and equation problems. *Journal of Experimental Psychology: Learning, Memory and Cognition, 8,* 448–462.

Mayer, R. E. (1982b). Memory for algebra story problems. *Journal of Educational Psychology, 74,* 199–216.

Mayer, R. E. (1983). *Thinking, problem solving, and cognition.* San Francisco: Freeman.

Mayer, R. E. (in press). The elusive search for learnable aspects of problem solving. In R. Ronning & J. Glover (Eds.), *Historical foundations of educational psychology.* New York: Plenum.

Mayer, R. E., Larkin, J. H., & Kadane, J. (1984). A cognitive analysis of mathematical problem solving ability. In R. Sternberg (Ed.), *Advances in the psychology of human intelligence* (pp. 231–273). Hillsdale, NJ: Lawrence Erlbaum Associates.

Newell, E., & Simon, H. A. (1972). *Human problem solving.* Englewood Cliffs, NJ: Prentice-Hall.

Owen, E., & Sweller, J. (1985). What do students learn while solving mathematics problems? *Journal of Educational Psychology, 77,* 272–284.

Paige, J. M., & Simon, H. A. (1966). Cognitive processes in solving algebra word problems. In B. Kleinmentz (Ed.), *Problem solving: Research, method, and theory* (pp. 51–119). New York: Wiley.

Polya, G. (1957). *How to solve it.* Garden City, NY: Doubleday Anchor.

Polya, G. (1968). *Mathematical discovery.* New York: Wiley.

Reed, S. K. (1985). Effect of computer graphics on improving estimates to algebra word problems. *Journal of Educational Psychology, 77,* 285–298.

Reed, S. K., Dempster, A., & Ettinger, M. (1985). Usefulness of analogous solutions for solving algebra word problems. *Journal of Experimental Psychology: Learning, Memory and Cognition, 11,* 106–125.

Resnick, L. B., & Ford, W. (1981). *The psychology of mathematics for instruction.* Hillsdale, NJ: Lawrence Erlbaum Associates.

Riley, M., Greeno, J. G., & Heller, J. (1982). The development of children's problem solving ability to arithmetic. In H. Ginsburg (Ed.), *The development of mathematical thinking* (pp. 153–196). New York: Academic Press.

Rubinstein, M. F. (1975). *Patterns of problem solving.* Englewood Cliffs, NJ: Prentice-Hall.

Schoenfeld, A. H. (1979). Explicit heuristic training as a variable in problem solving performance. *Journal for Research in Mathematics Education, 10,* 173–187.

Siegler, R. S. (1978). The origins of scientific reasoning. In R. S. Siegler (Eds.), *Children's thinking: What develops?* (pp. 109–149). Hillsdale, NJ: Lawrence Erlbaum Associates.

Silver, E. (Ed.). (1979). Students perceptions of relatedness among mathematical verbal problems. *Journal of Research in Mathematics Education, 10,* 195–210.

Silver, E. (Ed.). (1985). *Teaching and learning mathematical problem solving: Multiple research perspectives.* Hillsdale, NJ: Lawrence Erlbaum Associates.

Simon, H. A. (1980). Problem solving and education. In D. T. Tuma & F. Reif (Eds.), *Problem solving and education* (pp. 81–96). Hillsdale, NJ: Lawrence Erlbaum Associates.

Soloway, E., Lochhead, J., & Clement, J. (1982). Does computer programming enhance problem solving ability? Some positive evidence on algebra word problems. In R. J. Sediel, R. E. Anderson, & B. Hunter (Eds.), *Computer literacy* (pp. 171–185). New York: Academic Press.

Thorndike, E. L. (1922). *The psychology of arithmetic*. New York: Macmillan.

Thornton, C. A. (1978). Emphasizing thinking strategies in basic fact instruction. *Journal for Research in Mathematics Education, 9,* 214–227.

Woods, S. S., Resnick, L. B., & Groen, G. J. (1975). An experimental test of five process models for subtraction. *Journal of Educational Psychology, 67,* 17–21.

10 A Task Analysis of Algebra Word Problems

Dale E. Berger
Jeffrey M. Wilde
The Claremont Graduate School

ABSTRACT

Algebra word problems have been a source of consternation to generations of students. Recent cognitive analyses of problem solving have provided a new perspective on the mental processes involved in solving problems. In the study reported in this chapter, a set of algebra word problems was analyzed in terms of the information integration tasks that are required to solve the problems. A comparison of beginning and advanced high school students on their strategies and skills with algebra word problems demonstrated the advantages experts have in recognizing and using the overall structure of problems to guide them to a solution. Instruction that focuses on the structure of the problems was successful in improving performance of a group of novices, although generalization to a related problem was limited. The current study and similar analyses of the cognitive operations involved in problem solving point the way to instructional strategies that can be applied by teachers and designers of instructional materials.

INTRODUCTION

If you have not repressed the memory, you may recall the sense of frustration and feeling of incompetence that probably accompanied your first encounter with algebra word problems. Although some students quickly overcome these feelings as they gain a degree of mastery over word problems, many other students continue to struggle with little success. Even students who are expert at solving algebraic equations are often baffled when the same problems are cloaked in a verbal cover story (Mayer, Larkin, & Kadane, 1984).

In recent years there has been a tremendous surge of interest in problem solving and instruction, providing a growing area of productive interaction between cognitive psychologists and educators (cf. Frederiksen, 1984; Lester, 1982; Lochhead & Clement, 1979; Segal, Chipman, & Glaser, 1985; Silver, 1985; Tuma & Reif, 1980). In this chapter we describe (a) a cognitive analysis of the tasks involved in solving algebra word problems, (b) a comparison of "novice" and "expert" high school problem solvers in terms of their strategies and their competence with these tasks, and (c) the impact of a brief training session focused on these tasks and strategies.

Stages in Problem Solving

Sixty years ago Wallas (1926) described four stages of problem solving: preparation, incubation, illumination, and verification. Over the years there have been many analyses that divide the problem-solving process into stages (e.g., Duncker, 1945; Greeno, 1973; Polya, 1957, 1968). A limitation of many such analyses is that they do not necessarily provide much insight into the mental processes that are involved in crucial stages, such as "illumination." One contribution of cognitive psychologists has been to generate a better understanding of the basic mental mechanisms that are used in the course of problem solving.

In a recent analysis of problem solving, Mayer (1982b) has identified two main stages: (a) forming a representation or understanding of a problem, and (b) searching the problem space in memory for a solution. Within the first stage, problem solvers need to access linguistic, factual, and schematic knowledge so that the problem is correctly encoded along with relationships of the problem to other problems. Within the second stage, problem solvers draw on algorithmic knowledge of how to perform well-defined procedures and strategic knowledge of useful approaches to problems (p. 3).

Gaining Expertise with Algebra Word Problems

Typical classroom instruction in algebra word problems focuses on algorithmic skills, whereas strategies and schemata that can be used to organize principles are not taught directly. Greeno (1980) has suggested that current methods for teaching problem solving are akin to teaching swimming by tossing the student into the water, a method that may be "successful for some students, but it has obvious negative consequences for others" (p. 6). Unfortunately, even if algebra teachers could be persuaded to devote significant instructional effort to teaching organizing principles, we do not have much information on how students learn to use schemata and strategies nor how organizing principles can best be taught.

One useful approach has been to compare the problem-solving performance of *experts* to that of *novices* (e.g., Chi, Feltovich, & Glaser, 1981; Kintsch &

Greeno, 1985; Larkin, McDermott, Simon, & Simon, 1980; Simon & Simon, 1978). A general finding is that persons skilled in a problem domain have a sizable body of domain-specific knowledge, including patterns or schema for types of problems. Recognition of a familiar pattern provides quick access to relevant procedures. Larkin et al. (1980) found that persons expert with physics problems were able to work problems from the *bottom up,* proceeding to combine basic information in a sequence of steps that led to the goal. The experts apparently had a mental model or schema of the structure of the entire problem, which allowed them to take a direct path toward the solution. On the other hand, novices were more likely to apply a *means-ends* strategy, working backwards from the goal by defining subgoals successively farther from the goal and closer to the basic information that was given in the problem. There is recent evidence that when students use means-ends analysis, this strategy may actually interfere with the acquisition of schema and awareness of the structure of the entire problem (Owen & Sweller, 1985) and hence impede the progress from novice to expert status.

Analysis of Algebra Word Problems

Our understanding of the domains within algebra word problems was greatly advanced by Mayer (1981) when he compiled and categorized 1,097 word problems from 10 major algebra texts used in California public schools. On the basis of underlying source formulas (e.g., rate × time = distance), he identified 25 families, such as time-rate and unit-cost problems. Families were divided into categories that share variables, formulas, and methods of derivations. For example, the time-rate family was divided into 13 categories, such as motion, current, and work problems. Each category was further divided into templates, defined by the propositional structure of the problems. Motion problems, for example, have at least 12 templates, including vehicles converging, one overtaking another, and one vehicle making a round trip. Problems within a template differ only in the values that are used, and in details of the wording of the problem.

Mayer (1981) found that the relevant information in nearly all problems could be described using four types of propositions:

1. assignments (e.g., A cup holds 8 ounces.)
2. relations (e.g., A bottle holds four times as much as a cup.)
3. relevant facts (e.g., John will sell cups of soda.)
4. questions (e.g., How much money will John earn?)

In a series of studies with college freshmen, Mayer (1982a) found that recall was poorer for relational propositions than for assignment propositions, and when students were asked to construct their own word problems they rarely made use of relational propositions. Reed, Dempster, and Ettinger (1985) found that college students also had special difficulty expressing relationships correctly in word problems.

These findings suggest that an analysis of the ways in which information is collected and combined in solving algebra word problems might provide a useful tool for characterizing problem structure and relationships between problems. We conducted such an analysis and used a coding system based on this analysis to examine the approach used by first-year algebra students (novices) compared to the approach taken by more experienced problem solvers (experts). We also examined the effects special training with problem tasks and structure had on task performance.

Information Integration Tasks in Algebra Word Problems

We analyzed the structure of 50 common word problems selected from Mayer's (1981) collection, and organized a list of the information integration tasks involved in solving these problems. The tasks were sorted into three levels of information integration: value assignment, value derivation, and equation construction. Each level contained three types of tasks. An example of each of these nine tasks is shown in Table 10.1.

The first level, Value Assignment, requires little more than direct translation of text into an equation. Value Assignments are established by equivalence assignment when a noun phrase from the problem is set equal to a numerical value, by unknown assignment when a noun phrase is set equal to a symbol representing an unknown value, or by relation assignment when a noun phrase is set equal to a simple relationship with another noun phrase, as Rate $2 = 2x$ (see Table 10.1).

The second level, Value Derivation, involves operating on assigned values to produce new values. Values may be derived through transformation by operating on a Level 1 value assignment, such as adding a constant to both sides of an equation. A second mode of value derivation is by construction, where Level 1 value assignments are combined, as by addition or subtraction, to produce a value for a noun phrase. Third, a value may be derived by using a source formula such as "rate × time = distance," where knowledge of any two values permits derivation of the third.

The third level of information integration is Equation Construction, which requires creation of a computational representation of the structural relationship between the variables in the problem. One way this may be accomplished is by applying a function rule provided in the statement of the problem (See Table 10.1). A second way is by applying a source formula not presented directly in the problem, such as "area = length × width." A third type of equation is formed by combining components, such as "area of garden = total area − area of walkway."

TABLE 10.1
Taxonomy of Information Integration Tasks

Sample Problems	Level of Information Integration		
	Level 1: Value Assignment	Level 2: Value Derivation	Level 3: Equation Construction
A man is now 40 years old and his son is 14. How many years will it be until the man is twice as old as his son?	Equivalence Assignment Man's age today = 40 Son's age today = 14	Transformation Man's age x years from now = 40 + x Son's age x years from now = 14 = x	Function Rule (40+x) = 2(14+x)
A framed mirror is 45 by 55 cm. 1911 square cm of the mirror shows. How wide is the frame?	Unknown Assignment Width of the frame = x	Construction L = 55 - 2x W = 45 - 2x	Source Formula A = (L)(W) A = (55-2x)(45-2x)
Two hikers start at the same time from towns 36 miles apart, and meet in 3 hours. One hiker walks twice as fast as the other. What is the rate of each hiker?	Relation Assignment [Rate 1 = x] Rate 2 = 2x	Source Formula (R)(T) = D (x)(3) = D_1 (2x)(3) = D_2	Combination D = D_1 + D_2 36 = 3x + 6x

There is a hierarchical relationship among the three levels of information integration. The value assignments from the first level are often operated upon in the second level to derive new values, which are then used in the third level for the construction of the equations. However, problem solving can begin at any of the three levels. Activities at each level place constraints on activities to be completed at each of the other levels. For example, if one can determine the form of the final equation, the range of possibly appropriate value assignments and derivations may be reduced.

THE CURRENT RESEARCH

The present research was designed to compare novice and expert problem solvers in terms of their facility with information integration tasks at each level, and in terms of their awareness and use of the structure of the problem. We expected the novice problem solvers to have relatively more difficulty with aspects of problem solving that require an appreciation for the structure of the problem. This would be reflected in greater difficulty with the information integration tasks at the second and third levels than for tasks at the first level, which require only assignment of values and unknowns. We also examined the effects of instruction on problem structure for novice problem solvers. We were hopeful that the training would improve the performance of novices on the higher levels of information integration.

Method

Three groups of high school students were recruited for this study. Volunteers from first-semester algebra classes were assigned to one of two groups of novice problem solvers: an instruction group and a control group. A third group of experienced problem solvers was composed of volunteers from analytic geometry classes. Each student was paid $2.00 for participating. A detailed description of the study is available as an unpublished dissertation (Wilde, 1984).

The initial task for all groups was a set of six word problems, followed by a vocabulary test. About a month later half of the novices were given special instruction on word problems (described in a later section) while the other half served as a control group. A posttest followed for both groups. A test of ability to identify the structure of word problems was given to the control group of novices at the end of the second session and to the experts at the end of their first and only session.

The six word problems in the initial test were two problems each from Mayer's (1981) motion, age, and rectangle families. All students had been exposed to these three categories of problems in their classrooms. Students were tested individually. The problems were presented in a booklet, with each problem written on the top of a separate page, leaving space for calculations below. Students were asked to write down each step, and to report their thoughts as they worked. The experimenter recorded all comments. Students who were unable to get started on a problem were prompted with the hint that they should first determine what the problem's unknown was. If this failed, they were told to go on to the next problem. No problem could be returned to once the page was turned.

Results and Discussion

On the six problems, the combined novice groups solved only 9% of the problems compared to 85% for the experts. The problem protocols were analyzed for each group to determine the proportion of tasks completed at each level of information integration. The results of this analysis are shown in Table 10.2.

Here, and in other analyses where the dependent variable was a proportion, we used an arc sine transformation to reduce potential effects of skew in the data prior to conducting an analysis of variance. The two main effects and the interaction were all highly significant in this table, all in the expected direction. Experts

TABLE 10.2
Mean Proportion of Information Integration Tasks Completed

| Group | n | Level of Information Integration | | |
		1	2	3
Novice	35	.73	.27	.09
Expert	13	1.00	.92	.85

outperformed the novices, and performance for both groups was progressively poorer as the integration tasks required more structure-specific integrations. Value assignments (Level 1) were easiest whereas formula constructions (Level 3) were the most difficult. The interaction indicated that the effect of integration level was greater for novices than for experts. Novices were reasonably competent at setting up givens but very poor at applying procedures that depended on the problem structure. Details of the results, including statistical tests of significance, are available in Wilde (1984).

Problem Solving and Verbal Abilities. One might expect verbal comprehension to be a good predictor of algebra word problem solving success, since translation of problems depends on verbal comprehension. To evaluate this notion, we gave all students the first part of Vocabulary Test II from the ETS Kit of Factor Referenced Cognitive Tests (Ekstrom, French, Harman, & Derman, 1976). The correlation between the proportion of information integration tasks completed and verbal comprehension for the entire sample was a highly significant .75. This high correlation was the result of large differences between the groups on both measures. The average score on the 18-item vocabulary test was 14.3 for the experts, and only 8.2 for the novices. The correlation between problem solving and vocabulary for the experts alone was .17 and for the notives .01, both nonsignificant. A high level of verbal ability may be required to become established in the high-math-performance group, but verbal ability does not account for the variability of math performance found within a group. These data also indicate that the experts were a select group. It seems unlikely that all of the novices could be expected eventually to make the transition to expert status.

Comparison of Novices and Experts on Information Integration Tasks. We next examined performance of the experts and novices on specific tasks. Table 10.3 shows the mean proportion of success for each type of task at each of the three levels. Split-plot analyses of variance were computed on the proportion of tasks successfully completed at each level by the two groups. ANOVAs were followed by a posteriori Tukey's HSD tests for individual comparisons.

Following Mayer (1982a), we expected performance on Value Assignments (Level 1) to be poorer for relation assignments than for equivalence and unknown assignments. The ANOVA showed both of the main effects and the interaction to be highly significant. The experts performed better than the novices on each task. For the novices, performance on unknown assignments and relation assignments did not differ significantly, but both were easier than equivalence assignments. This was surprising since equivalence assignments seem so straightforward. A closer look at equivalence assignments uncovered an important distinction: Some assignments describe individual objects or actors (e.g., in the Hikers problem in Table 10.1, Rate 1 = x) and some assignments are used to connect parts of the problem (e.g., in the Hikers problem, the distance between two towns = 36 miles). The mean proportion of correct Equivalence Assignments was .77 for the individual objects, but only .45 for the connections.

At Level 2 were the Value Derivation tasks using transformations, construction, and source formulas. Transformations were completely specified by the problem in that the initial value, the transforming value, and the transforming operation were all stated explicitly. Constructions and source formulas, however, involve combining information based on ideas about the problem structure that were not stated explicitly in the problem. This led to the prediction that for novices transformations would be easier than constructions and source formulas.

The analyses showed that novices found the construction tasks significantly more difficult than either the source formula or the transformation tasks, which did not differ significantly from each other. No differences between tasks were reliable for the experts.

One might suspect that the poor performance of the novices in using source formulas might be because they do not know the formulas. However, when they were asked to recall the formulas at the end of the experiment, 83% of the novices correctly recalled the area formula and 71% recalled the rate formula. It is the application of the formulas that is not well understood.

Performance of the novices on value derivation by construction was abysmal. An inability to construct variables by combining components of the problem is consistent with the hypothesis that novices do not have a good understanding of the structure of the word problems.

The Level 3 integration tasks of Equation Construction involved the use of a function rule, source formula, or combination of variables to produce a summary equation reflecting the structure of the problem. We expected the performance of novices to be especially poor at Level 3 because these tasks are most dependent on a good understanding of the structure of the problem. (In the six problems used here, no source formulas were needed at Level 3.)

Expectations were confirmed in that novices had little success with the Level 3 tasks (see Table 10.3). Both groups were more likely to obtain the final equation when a function rule was required than when a combination of variables was needed.

It is important to note that although novices were usually successful at translating the problem text into equations, this skill did not guarantee that they would be able to solve the problem. The inability of novices to combine information at the higher levels resulted in very low solution rates.

TABLE 10.3
Mean Proportion of Information Integration Tasks Completed

Level of Information Integration	Novices (n=35)	Experts (n=13)
1. Value Assignment Tasks:		
Unknown Assignment	.81	1.00
Relation Assignment	.75	1.00
Equivalence Assignment	.64	.99
2. Value Derivation Tasks:		
Transformation	.45	.98
Source Formula	.20	.89
Construction	.03	.83
3. Formula Construction:		
Function	.19	.92
Combination	.04	.81

These results should be interpreted with some caution since there were only six problems in the test set. Generalization to a wider range of problems has not been established.

Perceptions of Problem Structure. To assess more directly the students' ability to detect and compare the structure of algebra word problems, we developed a simple test for this purpose. The test consisted of five triads of problems, where each triad was constructed of three problems from the same category, with two from one template and the third from a different template. Students were asked to determine, for each triad, which two problems were most alike. An example of a problem triad is shown in Fig. 10.1. The first two problems here are isomorphs that differ only in values of the variables. The third problem presents the second proposition in a form different from the first two problems.

STRUCTURE TASK

Which two of the following three problems are most alike?

(a) Problem 1 and Problem 2.   ( )
(b) Problem 1 and Problem 3.   ( )
(c) Problem 2 and Problem 3.   ( )

1. Dana is five times as old as his dog, Texas. In 9 years Dana will be twice as old as Texas. What are their ages now?

2. Roger is four times as old as his sister. In 6 years he will be twice as old as she. How old are they now?

3. Pam is twice as old as her brother. In 5 years their ages will total 22 years. How old are they now?

FIG. 10.1. Sample Problem from the Structure Task.

Chance performance on the structure task was 33% correct. The novices performed right at chance, 33% correct, whereas the experts were correct on 88% of the triads. This is convincing evidence that the novices had little appreciation for the structure of the problems, in contrast to the experts who were able to identify the structure quite consistently.

Analysis of Problem Protocols.   A third source of data was the problem protocols. All students were asked to write down each step of their solution attempt, and to "think out loud" as they proceeded. These protocols showed striking differences between the novices and the experts in terms of their use of the problem structure.

Strategies that led to solution are listed first in Table 10.4. Just over half of the problems solved by experts showed a "working-down" strategy that started with the Level 3 integration, demonstrating an understanding of the structure of the problem, which in turn provided the solver with a relatively clear indication of a path to the goal. The novices never started with the Level 3 integration. On the 18 problems solved by novices, 17 showed a working-up strategy where the protocols gave all Level 1 integrations first, then the Level 2 integrations, and

TABLE 10.4
Strategies Used by Novice and Expert Problem Solvers

	Number of Problems	
Strategy Type	Novices	Experts
1. Successful Strategies	18 (9%)	66 (85%)
(a) work up	17	25
(b) work from the middle	0	4
(c) work down	0	31
(d) diagram a familiar procedure	0	5
(e) ideosyncratic arithmetic model	1	1
2. List Variables	108 (51%)	4 (5%)
3. Memory for a Similar Problem	20 (10%)	6 (8%)
(a) generate a formula table	20	1
(b) diagram a familiar procedure	0	5
4. Oversimplify Structure	36 (17%)	2 (3%)
(a) simplify formula	4	0
(b) simplify diagram	32	2
5. Structure Insensitive	28 (13%)	0 (0%)
(a) incorrect direct translation	10	0
(b) incorrect arithmetic relations	14	0
(c) no apparent strategy	4	0
Total number of problems	210	78

Note. This table is based on six problems given to 35 novices and 13 experts. The numbers indicate a count of instances where each strategy or type of strategy was used.

finally the Level 3 equation. These data are consistent with the conclusions of Larkin et al. (1980) that experts make greater use of knowledge of the problem structure in their approach to problems.

The most common strategy for the novices, shown on 51% of the problems, was a simple listing of some or all of the Level 1 value assignments, with little else.

Another common strategy was to draw on memory for similar problems. This strategy was reflected in errors where a familiar formula or procedure was applied inappropriately. Novices were likely to show formulas, whereas experts tended to show diagrams. The novices also were likely to oversimplify the structure of the problems, usually resulting in simple diagrams that did not reflect the structure of the problem. Finally, a small proportion of the protocols from novices showed inappropriate direct translation of variables (e.g., for the Hikers problem in Table 10.1, the student might simply write: Hiker = 3) or inappropriate combinations of the values presented in the problem, such as simply adding values together.

Consistent with other information, the protocol data show that the novices generally made little use of the structure of the problems in determining their approach to the problems. The experts, on the other hand, made extensive use of their knowledge of the problem structure to find their path to the solution.

These data suggest that if we wish to train novices to approach problems more like experts, it may help to teach students how to make value assignments and derivations, but it is likely to be more effective to concentrate on helping students learn how to generate a representation of the structure of the problems. Specifically, we would expect training on the three levels of information integration and diagram construction to facilitate problem solving. We designed a short training program to test this notion.

Effects of Instruction.   The novice problem solvers were paired on the basis of their performance on the six word problems, and then were randomly split into two groups, instruction ($n = 16$) and control ($n = 17$). Four weeks after the initial testing, the instruction group received about 30 minutes of individual training.

Students were first given the Hikers problem (third example in Table 10.1) and were asked to list the variables, defined as things named in the problem that have a numerical value. Examples were given, and the students were helped to produce a list of the rates and times for the two hikers and the initial distance between them. Students were next asked to determine the values for each variable on the list. Particular note was made of the facts that x can represent an unknown value and that the value of one variable may be defined in terms of another. Next, the students were asked to find the equality and find the values that must be derived to complete the equality. Figure 10.2 was provided to aid students.

	R	☼	T	=	D
Trip made by Hiker 1					
Trip made by Hiker 2					
	Distance covered by H_1	Distance covered by H_2	Total distance Covered		
Relation Between Trips					

FIG. 10.2.   Diagram used to demonstrate the structure of the rate problems used for instruction.

The same procedure was repeated for a second motion problem, two cyclists riding toward each other. The final step was to have the students compare the two problems using the figure. The similarity of variables, value derivation, and equation construction was pointed out.

The control group of novices were given the same two motion problems and asked to set them up, but no special instruction was provided. A posttest for both groups consisted of four problems, three of which were isomorphs of the training problems sharing category and template features. The fourth was a generalization problem which was a motion problem from a different category. The isomorphs involved combining two subdistances to equal a known total, whereas the generalization problem involved comparing two subdistances to find an unknown total.

We expected performance of the Instruction group to be improved for the problems isomorphic to the training problems. Expectations for the generalization problem were not as clear, since others have found little improvement on generalization problems following training (e.g., Gick & Holyoak, 1980; Reed et al., 1985).

The Instruction group outperformed the Control group on both the isomorphs and on the generalization problem. The Instruction group solved .87 of the isomorphic problems, and the Control group solved .47. For the generalization problem the corresponding proportions were .79 and .40, respectively.

An examination of performance at each of the three levels of information integration showed that the Instruction group did better than the Control group at all three levels on the isomorphic problems, and also at the first level (Value

Assignment) on the generalization problem. Differences between the groups on the second and third levels of information integration were in the direction of an advantage for the training group, although they did not attain statistical significance.

These results are encouraging in that they demonstrate an apparently effective approach to teaching students how to solve algebra word problems. Obviously our special instruction involved training on numerous skills, including the assignment of variables, the use of diagrams, and comparisons of the structure of similar problems. Although it may be interesting to attempt to separate the contribution of factors such as these, we believe it will be more productive to study how these components interact. For example, value assignment skills are crucial, and students must be able to translate equivalencies expressed in words into equations; yet training on value assignment skills alone will produce no more than marginal effects for many students, since the relationships among the variables must also be understood if the problem is to be solved. On the other hand, it may be futile to teach students about the structure of problems if they have not mastered the skill of translating basic equivalencies into algebraic expressions.

CONCLUSIONS

Overall, the clearest lesson to be drawn from our study is that an appreciation of problem structure is a crucial part of expertise in problem solving. Experts are quickly able to identify the form of the equation to be solved and they use this information to guide them on the path to solution. Novices are much more likely to stop after they have generated a list of value assignments, unable to see relationships inherent in the structure of the problem. A key advantage that experts hold is that they are familiar with a large number of problem forms. If the structure of a problem is recognized, the problem becomes a mere exercise in applying familiar algorithms. A likely reason that algebra word problems are so difficult for many people is because there are so many different patterns of word problems to be learned.

We still do not know much about how expertise with word problems is developed. Cross-sectional studies that compare good and poor solvers provide a somewhat distorted view of the development of expertise, because novices and experts may not be from comparable populations. Most novices will never reach expert status, and we have no way of knowing which novices will.

There is little information on how some novices do acquire expertise, and how instruction can facilitate the process. A common educational strategy is simply to present students with a large number of problems to solve, presumably in the hopes that expertise with a domain of problems will develop through an inductive process. There is ample evidence that solvers do not necessarily see the connection between problems unless these relationships are made explicit (e.g., Gick & Holyoak, 1980; Mawer & Sweller, 1982; Reed, Ernst, & Banerji, 1974).

An implication of the current study is that instruction on word problems should give explicit attention to helping students build schemata for the general structure of word problems and the specific structures found within problem categories. Our data on the use of diagrams by novices and experts indicate that diagrams can play an important role in helping students to organize information about a problem and to generate a structural representation of the problem. Our small training study suggests that detailed side-by-side comparisons of the structure of problems from the same category may be a useful technique for teaching students how to draw figures and create schematic representations of problems.

We are encouraged by the potential for cognitive analyses to provide new insights into the mental processes that are involved in problem solving, and we are hopeful that teachers and designers of instructional materials will be able to put the new information to good use.

ACKNOWLEDGMENTS

The study reported in this paper is based on a dissertation completed by J. Wilde under the supervision of D. Berger. We would like to thank Rich Ede and Ronnie Hardie, mathematics teachers at Claremont High School, for their help in this project.

REFERENCES

Chi, M., Feltovich, P., & Glaser, R. (1981). Categorization and representation of physics problems by experts and novices. *Cognitive Science, 5,* 121–152.

Duncker, K. (1945). On problem solving. *Psychological Monographs, 58:5,* Whole No. 270.

Ekstrom, R. B., French, J. W., Harman, H. H., & Derman, D. (1976). *Manual for kit of factor-referenced cognitive tests.* Princeton, NJ: Educational Testing Service.

Frederiksen, N. (1984). Implications of cognitive theory for instruction in problem solving. *Review of Educational Research, 54,* 363–407.

Gick, N. L., & Holyoak, K. J. (1980). Analogical problem solving. *Cognitive Psychology, 12,* 306–355.

Greeno, J. G. (1973). The structure of memory and the process of solving problems. In R. Solso (Ed.), *Contemporary issues in cognitive psychology. The Loyola Symposium* (pp. 103–133). Washington, DC: Winston.

Greeno, J. G. (1980). Some examples of cognitive task analysis with instructional implications. In R. Snow, P. Frederico, & W. Montague (Eds.), *Aptitude, learning, and instruction: Vol. 2. Cognitive process analysis of learning and problem solving* (pp. 1–21). Hillsdale, NJ: Lawrence Erlbaum Associates.

Kintsch, W., & Greeno, J. G. (1985). Understanding and solving word arithmetic problems. *Psychological Review, 92,* 109–129.

Larkin, J. H., McDermott, J., Simon, D. P., & Simon, H. A. (1980). Expert and novice performance in solving physics problems. *Science, 208,* 1335–1342.

Lester, F. K. (1982). Building bridges between psychological and mathematical education research on problem solving. In F. W. Lester & J. Garofalo (Eds.), *Mathematical problem solving: Issues in research* (pp. 55–58). Philadelphia: Franklin Institute Press.

Lochhead, J., & Clement, J. (1979). *Cognitive process instruction.* Philadelphia: Franklin Institute Press.

Mawer, R., & Sweller, J. (1982). The effects of subgoal density and location on learning during problem solving. *Journal of Experimental Psychology: Learning, Memory, and Cognition, 8,* 252–259.

Mayer, R. E. (1981). Frequency norms and structural analysis of algebra story problems into families, categories, and templates. *Instructional Science, 10,* 135–175.

Mayer, R. E. (1982a). Memory for algebra story problems. *Journal of Educational Psychology, 74,* 199–216.

Mayer, R. E. (1982b). The psychology of mathematical problem solving. In F. K. Lester & J. Garofalo (Eds.), *Mathematical problem solving: Issues in research* (pp. 1–13). Philadelphia: Franklin Institute Press.

Mayer, R. E., Larkin, J. H., & Kadane, J. (1984). A cognitive analysis of mathematical problem solving ability. In R. Sternberg (Ed.), *Advances in the psychology of human intelligence* (pp. 231–273). Hillsdale, NJ: Lawrence Erlbaum Associates.

Owen, E., & Sweller, J. (1985). What do students learn while solving mathematics problems? *Journal of Educational Psychology, 77,* 272–284.

Polya, G. (1957). *How to solve it.* Garden City, NY: Doubleday Anchor.

Polya, G. (1968). *Mathematical discovery. Volume II: On understanding, learning and teaching problem solving.* New York: Wiley.

Reed, S. K., Dempster, A., & Ettinger, M. (1985). Usefulness of analogous solutions for solving algebra word problems. *Journal of Experimental Psychology: Learning, Memory, and Cognition, 11,* 106–125.

Reed, S. K., Ernst, G. W., & Banerji, R. (1974). The role of analogy in transfer between similar problem states. *Cognitive Psychology, 6,* 436–450.

Segal, J. W., Chipman, S. F., & Glaser, R. (Eds.). (1985). *Thinking and learning skills: Vol. 1. Relating instruction to research.* Hillsdale, NJ: Lawrence Erlbaum Associates.

Silver, E. A. (Ed.). (1985). *Teaching and learning mathematical problem solving: Multiple research perspectives.* Hillsdale, NJ: Lawrence Erlbaum Associates.

Simon, D. P., & Simon, H. A. (1978). Individual differences in solving physics problems. In R. Siegler (Ed.), *Children's thinking: What develops?* Hillsdale, NJ: Lawrence Erlbaum Associates.

Tuma, D. T., & Reif, F. (Eds.). (1980). *Problem solving and education: Issues in teaching and research.* Hillsdale, NJ: Lawrence Erlbaum Associates.

Wallas, G. (1926). *The art of thought.* New York: Harcourt Brace Jovanovich.

Wilde, J. M. (1984). Setting up algebra word problems: A task analytic approach to problem difficulty (Doctoral dissertation, The Claremont Graduate School, 1984). *Dissertation Abstracts International, 44(8-B),* 2544–2545.

TRADEOFFS IN THE DESIGN OF HUMAN-COMPUTER INTERFACES

Perhaps the most significant development in our ongoing computer revolution is the rather recent one in which computers have been placed on users' desks in the form of time-sharing terminals or, even more recently, microcomputers. The significance of this development is that now the majority of users are able to use the computer in such a way that it becomes quite literally integrated into their thought processes: The potential of the computer as a truly cognitive machine is finally being realized. The integration is made possible by the easy availability of computing when it is on one's desk, by the fast response now possible, and by interactive software written to exploit these properties of modern computing. Sitting at a terminal, one can begin to think ''in'' the computer language—it becomes the language of thought—and can use the computer as an extension of one's thought processes. By contrast, when users had to take their jobs to a computer center and wait up to a day for a response, computing could have little impact on the way people thought about problems. The computer was simply a powerful tool that was applied to a problem as an external agent.

Given the nature of modern computing, it is no surprise that users are demanding ever more flexibility and speed, and looking for software that will, in effect, give them more thought power. Any decision in developing a computer system involves trade-offs, and it is difficult to determine in advance what trade-offs should be made. For example, is it better to make a computer language as much like English as possible (and thus assure initial compatibility for English-speakers) or is it better to require users to learn a wholly new syntax and set of symbols (and thus possibly create a more efficient, powerful language)? For another example, is it better to have a few powerful symbols in a computer language or is it better to have an abundance of symbols and add still more as new functions are needed? The former strategy is reminiscent of LISP, the latter of APL. Decisions in this domain involve consideration of tradeoffs, not simply selection of the ''best'' choice.

A central theme of the chapters in this section is precisely the question of how to deal with these tradeoffs using design principles to guide the choices. Donald Norman's chapter, "Design Principles for Human-Computer Interface," presents four strategies for generating design principles, and he illustrates some principles with an analysis of tradeoffs between costs and benefits of design decisions in two areas: menu size and workspace size. The approach he takes is to define a user satisfaction function for each component of the tradeoff. By assuming fairly simple and reasonable functions for each component and having user satisfaction for a system be the weighted sum of the user satisfaction values of the components, he shows how the effects of tradeoffs can be specified quantitatively. Norman's analysis provides an important design tool, one that allows designers in many cases to move from intuitive assessments of tradeoffs to quantitative measures of them.

In their chapter, "Some Tools for Redesigning System-Operator Interfaces," Arthur Graesser, Kathy Lang, and C. Scott Elofson concentrate on design principles for the interface between the operator and the system. This is the area that Norman singled out as being the most critical. Four complementary approaches to interface design are discussed and applied to a case study. This chapter presents the reader with tools for establishing a computer interface system. Graesser and his colleagues suggest that cognitive psychologists who want to redefine themselves as cognitive engineers will need some new ways of thinking, and will need tools of the sort presented in this chapter. Furthermore, the term *cognitive engineer* is seen in their treatment to define a new and important branch of engineering.

David McArthur's chapter, "Developing Computer Tools to Support Performing and Learning Complex Cognitive Skills," makes the case for an important design principle for teaching programs: Software should be designed around the mental processes and structures that are involved in learning. Further, such software, if intelligently conceived, can be based on relatively simple components. McArthur proposes a number of software tools that are designed around the learner's needs, tools that facilitate learning by conforming to these needs. He presents evidence to show that this approach can be as effective as more complex intelligent computer tutors.

Sheng-Ping Fang and Ovid Tzeng offer a set of design principles in a domain that presents a formidable problem for design: Creation of a system for communicating with a computer in Chinese. In their chapter, "An Evaluation Model for the Chinese Computer," they outline the nature of the problem, present a number of systems that have been used, discuss the various tradeoffs that must be considered, and propose nine measures to be used in evaluation of systems. This is clearly an unsolved design problem. Fang and Tzeng's evaluation criteria could aid progress in this area by helping designers to know whether a proposed change would be a real improvement. This problem area represents an interesting case study.

Morton Friedman's chapter presents "WANDAH—A Computerized Writer's Aid," a highly intelligent word processor. WANDAH apparently answers the complaint McArthur voices in his article, namely that "Text editors . . . do not provide significant tools to help the processes of writing papers or *turning thoughts into words*" (italics his). Indeed, the whole purpose of WANDAH is to add an author's helper (and, to some extent, tutor) to the resources of a word processor. WANDAH is the first program of its kind and has attracted a good deal of interest. This chapter describes its features and design strategies. By the time this book appears, WANDAH will be on the market, and we will soon be able to see how it works in practice. Meanwhile, it seems very promising and it appears to represent the start of a new generation of word processors.

11
Design Principles for Human-Computer Interfaces*

Donald A. Norman
University of California, San Diego

ABSTRACT

If the field of Human Factors in Computer Systems is to be a success it must develop design principles that are useful, principles that apply across a wide range of technologies. In the first part of this paper I discuss some of the properties that useful principles should have. While I am at it, I warn of the dangers of the tar pits and the sirens of technology. We cannot avoid these dangers entirely, for were we to do so, we would fail to cope with the real problems and hazards of the field.

The second part of the paper is intended to illustrate the first part through the example of tradeoff analysis. Any single design technique is apt to have its virtues along one dimension compensated by deficiencies along another. Tradeoff analysis provides a quantitative method of assessing tradeoff relations for two attributes x_i and x_j by first determining the *User Satisfaction* function for each, $U(x)$, then showing how $U(x_i)$ trades off against $U(x_j)$. In general, the *User Satisfaction* for a system is given by the weighted sum of the *User Satisfaction* values for the attributes. The analysis is used to examine two different tradeoffs of information versus time and editor workspace versus menu size. Tradeoffs involving command languages versus menu-based systems, choices of names, and handheld computers versus workstations are examined briefly.

*Published in A. Janda (Ed.), *Proceedings of the CHI '83 Conference on Human Factors in Computing Systems*, 1983, New York: ACM. Copyright 1983, Association for Computing Machinery, Inc., reprinted by permission.

If we intend a science of human-computer interaction, it is essential that we have principles from which to derive the manner of the interaction between person and computer. It is easy to devise experiments to test this idea or that, to compare and contrast alternatives, or to evaluate the quality of the latest technological offering. But we must aspire to more than responsiveness to the current need. The technology upon which the human-computer interface is built changes rapidly relative to the time with which psychological experimentation yields answers. If we do not take care, today's answers apply only to yesterday's concerns.

Our design principles must be of sufficient generality that they will outlast the technological demands of the moment. But there is a second and more important criterion: the principles must yield sufficiently precise answers that they can actually be of use: Statements that proclaim "Consider the user" are valid, but worthless. We need more precise principles.

This new field—Human Factors in Computer Systems—contains an unruly mixture of theoretical issues and practical problems. Just as it is important that our theoretical concerns have breadth, generality, and usability, so too is it important that we understand the practical problems. We are blessed with an exciting, rapidly developing technology that is controlled through the time-consuming and addictive procedure called programming. There are traps for the unwary: let me tell you about them.

Tar Pits and Sirens of Technology

As with most unexplored territories, dangers await: tar pits and sirens. The former lie hidden in the path, ready to trap the unwary. The latter stand openly, luring their prey to destruction with bewitching sweetness. I see too many of you trapped by one or the other.

To program or not to program, that is the question. Whether it is nobler to build systems or to remain pure, arguing for abstract principles independent of the technology. Build systems and you face the tar pits, writing programs whose sole justification is to support the writing of programs, eating up work-years, eating up resources, forever making "one last improvement." When you finish, others may look and nod, saying, "yes, how clever." But will anything general be learned? Will the next technological leap pass it by? Programming can be a pit that grabs the unwary and holds them down. While in the pit they may struggle and attract attention. Afterwards, there may be no visible trace of their passing.

Alternatively, you may be seduced by the sirens of technology. High resolution screens, color, three-dimensions, mice, eye-movement detectors, voice-in, voice-out, touch-in, feelers-out; you name it, it will happen. Superficial pleasure, but not necessarily any lasting result. What general lessons will have been learned?

Damned if you do, damned if you don't. The pure in heart will avoid the struggles, detour the tar pits, blind their eyes to the sirens. "We want general principles that are independent of technology,'' they proclaim. But then what should they study? If the studies are truly independent of the technology, they are apt to have little applicability. How can you develop useful principles unless you understand the powers and weaknesses of the technology, the pressures and constraints of real design? Study a general problem such as the choice of editor commands and someone will develop a new philosophy of editing, or a new technological device that makes the old work irrelevant. The problem is that in avoiding the paths that contain the tar, you may never reach any destination; in avoiding temptation, you remain pure, but irrelevant. Life is tar pits and sirens. Real design of real systems is filled with the messy constraints of life: time pressures, budget limitations, a lack of information, abilities, and energy. We are apt not to be useful unless we understand these constraints and provide tools that can succeed despite them, or better, that can help alleviate them. Experimental psychology is not noted for its contributions to life; the study of human-computer interface should be.

Four Strategies for Providing Design Principles

What can we accomplish? One thing that is needed is a way of introducing good design principles into the design stage. How can we do this? Let me mention four ways.

1. Try to impress upon the designer the seriousness of the matter, to develop an awareness that users of systems have special needs that must be taken account of. The problem with this approach is that although such awareness is essential, good intentions do not necessarily lead to good design. Designers need to know what to do and how to do it.
2. Provide methods and guidelines. Quantitative methods are better than qualitative ones, but all are better than none at all. These methods and guidelines must be usable, they must be justifiable, they must have face validity. The designer is apt to be suspicious of many of our intentions. Moreover, unless we have worked out these guidelines with skill, they will be useless when confronted with the realities of design pressures. The rules must not only be justified by reasonable criteria, they must also appear to be reasonable: designers are not apt to care about the discussions in the theoretical journals.
3. Provide software tools for interface design. This can be a major positive force. Consider the problem of enforcing consistent procedures across all components of a system. With appropriate software tools, consistency can be enforced, if only because it will be easier to use the tools rather than to do without them. We can ensure reasonable design by building the principles into the tools.

4. Separate the interface design from other programming tasks. Make the interface a separate data module, communicating with programs and the operating system through a standardized communication channel and language. Interface design should be its own discipline, for it requires sophistication in both programming and human behavior. If we had the proper modularization, then the interface designer could modify the interface independently of the rest of the system. Similarly, many system changes would not require modification of the interface. The ideal method would be for software tools to be developed that can be used in the interface design by non-programmers. I imagine the day when I can self-tailor my own interface, carrying the specification around on a micro-chip embedded in a plastic card. Walk up to any computer terminal in the world, insert my card, and *voila,* it is my personalized terminal.

I recommend that we move toward all of these things. I have ordered the list in terms of my preferences: last being most favored; first being easiest and most likely today. Each is difficult, each requires work.

There has been progress towards the development of appropriate design methods. One approach is demonstrated through the work of Card, Moran, and Newell (1983) who developed formal quantitative methods of assessing a design. Their techniques provide tools for the second of my suggested procedures. Card, Moran, and Newell emphasize the micro-processes of interaction with a computer—for example, analysis at the level of keystrokes. At UCSD, we are attempting to develop other procedures. In the end, the field will need many methods and guidelines, each complementing and supplementing the others. Let me now describe briefly the approach that we are following, then present one of our techniques—the tradeoff analysis—in detail.

THE UCSD USER CENTERED SYSTEM DESIGN PROJECT

At UCSD we have a large and active group attempting to put our philosophy into practice. Our goal is to have pure heart and clear mind, even while feet and loins are in tar and temptation.

The principles that we follow take the form of statements plus elaboration, the statements becoming slogans that guide the research. The primary principle is summarized by the slogan that has become the name of the project: *User Centered System Design.* The slogan emphasizes our belief that to develop design principles relevant to building human-machine interfaces, it is necessary to focus on the user of the system. This focus leads us naturally to a set of topics and methods. It means we must observe how people make use of computer systems.

It brings to the fore the study of the *mental models* that users form of the systems with which they interact. This, in turn, leads to three related concepts: the designer's view of the system—the *conceptual model;* the image that the system presents to the user—the *system image;* and third, the *mental model* the user develops of the system, mediated to a large extent by the system image. We believe that it is the task of the designer to establish a conceptual image of the system that is appropriate for the task and the class of users, then to construct the system so that the system image guides the user to acquire a mental model that matches the designer's conceptual model.

The Slogans

There are five major slogans that guide the work:

- There are no simple answers, only tradeoffs.
- There are no errors: all operations are iterations towards a goal.
- Low level protocols are critical.
- Activities are structured.
- Information retrieval dominates activity.

There are no simple answers, only tradeoffs.   A central theme of our work is that in design, there are no correct answers, only tradeoffs. Each application of a design principle has its strengths and weaknesses; each principle must be interpreted in a context. One of our goals is to make the tradeoffs explicit. This point will be the topic of the second half of the paper.

All operations are iterations towards a goal.   A second theme is that all actions of users should be considered as part of their attempt to accomplish their goals. Thus, even when there is an error, it should be viewed as an attempt by the user to get to the goal. Typing mistakes or illegal statements can be thought of as an approximation. The task for the designer, then, is to consider each input as a starting point and to provide appropriate assistance to allow efficient modification. In this way, we aid the user in rapid convergence to the desired goal. An important implication of this philosophy is that the users' intentions be knowable. In some cases we believe this can be done by having the users state intentions explicitly. Because many commands confound intentions and actions, intentions may substitute for commands.

Low level protocols are critical.   By "protocol," we mean the procedures to be followed during the conduct of a particular action or session, this meaning being derived from the traditional meaning of protocol as "a code of diplomatic or military etiquette or precedence." Low level protocols refer to the actual operations performed by the user—button pushes, keypresses, or mouse operation—and these permeate the entire use of the system. If these protocols can be made consistent, then a major standardization takes place across all systems.

Activities are structured. User actions have an implicit grouping corresponding to user goals; these goals may be interrelated in various ways. Thus, a subgoal of a task is related to the main task in a different way than is a diversion, although both may require temporary cessation of the main task, the starting up of new tasks, and eventual return to the main one. We believe the grouping of user goals should be made explicit, both to the user and to the system, and that doing so will provide many opportunities for improved management of the interaction. For example, the system could constrain interpretation of user inputs by the context defined by the current activity, the system could remind users of where they are as they progress through a collection of tasks, or, upon request, it could provide suggestions of how to accomplish the current task by suggesting possible sequences of actions. The philosophy is to structure activities and actions so that the users perceive themselves as selecting among a set of related, structured operations, with the set understood and supported intelligently by the system (see Bannon, Cypher, Greenspan, & Monty, 1983).

Information retrieval dominates activity. Using a computer system involves stages of activities that include forming an intention, choosing an action, specifying that action to the system, and evaluating the outcome. These activities depend heavily upon the strengths and weaknesses of human short- and long-term memory. This means that we place emphasis upon appropriate design of file and directory structures, command "workbenches," and the ability to get information, instruction, and help on the different aspects of the system. We are studying various representational structures, including semantic networks, schema structures of both conventional and "additive memory" form, browsers, hyper-text structures, and other retrieval aids (see O'Malley et al., 1983).

A Demonstration System

This is where we traverse the tar pits. We feel it essential that our ideas be tested within a working system, not only because we feel that the real constraints of developing a full, usable system are important design considerations that must be faced, but also because we believe that full evaluation can only take place within the bounds of a complete, working environment. Therefore, we intend to construct a test and demonstration system based around a modern workstation using the UNIX operating system. UNIX was chosen because it provides a rich, powerful operating environment. However, because UNIX was designed for the professional programmer, unsophisticated users have great trouble with it, providing a rich set of opportunities for our research.

Although we intend that our design principles will be applicable to any system regardless of the particular hardware being used, many of the concepts are effective only on high-resolution displays that allow multiple windows on the screen and that use simple pointing devices. These displays allow for a considerable improvement in the design of human-computer interfaces. We see no choice but to brave the sirens of technology. The capabilities of the hardware factor into the tradeoff relationships. We intend the demonstration systems to show how the tradeoffs in design choices interact with the technology.

TRADEOFFS IN DESIGN

Now let us examine one of our proposals—tradeoffs—as a prototype of a quantitative design rule. It is well known that different tasks and classes of users have different needs and requirements. No single interface method can satisfy all. Any single design technique is apt to have its virtues along one dimension compensated by deficiencies along another. Each technique provides a set of tradeoffs. The design choices depend upon the technology being used, the class of users, the goals of the design, and which aspects of interface should gain, which should lose. This focus on the tradeoffs emphasizes that the design problem must be looked at as a whole, not in isolated pieces, for the optimal choice for one part of the problem will probably not be optimal for another. According to this view, there are no correct answers, only tradeoffs among alternatives.

The Prototypical Tradeoff: Information Versus Time

One basic tradeoff pervades many design issues:

> *Factors that increase informativeness tend to decrease the amount of available workspace and system responsiveness.*

On the one hand, the more informative and complete the display, the more useful when the user has doubts or lacks understanding. On the other hand, the more complete the display, the longer it takes to be displayed and the more space it must occupy physically. This tradeoff of amount of information versus space and time appears in many guises and is one of the major interface issues that must be handled. To appreciate its importance, one has only to examine a few recent commercial offerings, highly touted for their innovative (and impressive) human factors design that were intended to make the system easy and pleasurable to use, but which so degraded system response time that serious user complaints resulted.

It is often stated that current computer systems do not provide beginning users with sufficient information. However, the long, informative displays or sequence of questions, options, or menus that may make a system usable by the beginner are disruptive to the expert who knows exactly what action is to be specified and wishes to minimize the time and mental effort required to do the specification. We pit the expert's requirement for ease of specification against the beginner's requirement for knowledge.

I approach this problem by tackling the following questions:

- How can we specify the gain in user satisfaction that results from increasing the size of a menu;
- How do we specify the user satisfaction for the size of the workspace in a text editor;
- How can we specify the loss in user satisfaction from the increase in time to generate the display and decrease in available workspace;
- How can we select menu size, workspace, and response time, when each variable affects the others?

I propose that we answer the question by use of a psychological measure of *User Satisfaction*. This allows us to determine the impact of changing *physical* parameters upon the *psychological* variable of user satisfaction. Once we know how each dimension of choice affects user satisfaction, then we can directly assess the tradeoffs among the dimensions.

Example: Menu Size and Display Time

Let $U(x)$, the user satisfaction for attribute x, be given by a power function, $U(x) = kx^p$. (In Norman, 1983, I give more details of the method. See Stevens, 1974, for a review of the power function in Psychology.) For the examples in this paper I used the method of magnitude production to estimate parameters.

User preference for menu size.   The preferred amount of information must vary with the task, but informal experiments with a variety of menus and tasks suggest that for many situations, about 300 characters is reasonable: I assigned it a satisfaction value of 50. This is the size menu that can be requested for our laboratory's computer mail program ("msg"). It serves as a reminder for 26 single-letter mnemonic commands. To do the power function estimates, I examined a variety of menus of different sizes for the message system (thereby keeping the task the same). I estimated that the menu size would have to increase to half the normal video terminal screen (1000 characters) in order to double my satisfaction. This is a typical result of psychological scaling; a substantial increase of the current value is required to make the increase worthwhile. If $U(300) = 50$ and $U(1000) = 100$, then the parameters of the power function are $k = 1.9$ and $p = 0.6$: $U(S) = 1.9S^{0.6}$.

User preference for response time.   There already exists some literature on user satisfaction for response time: the judgments of "acceptable" response times given by Shneiderman (1980, p. 228: The times are taken from Miller, 1968). The times depend upon the task being performed. For highly interactive tasks, where the system has just changed state and the users are about to do a new action, 2.0 seconds seems appropriate. I determined that I would be twice as satisfied with a response time of 1 second. Therefore, $U(2\ sec) = 50$ and $U(1\ sec) = 100$. For these values, the power function becomes $U(T) = 100/T$ ($k = 100$, $p = -1$).

Size of menu and display time.   We need one more thing to complete the tradeoff analysis: the relationship between menu size (S) and the time to present the information (T). In general, time to present a display is a linear function of S: $\tau = \sigma + S/\beta$, where S is measured in characters, β is the display rate in characters per second (cps) and σ is system response time.

The tradeoff of menu size for display time.   Knowledge of $U(S)$, $U(T)$, and the relationship between S and T, lets us determine the tradeoff between User Satisfaction for size of the menu and for time to display the information: $U(S)$ versus $U(T)$. If $\sigma << S/\beta$, then we can probably ignore σ, letting $T = S/\beta$. This lets us solve the tradeoff exactly.[1] If the two power functions are given by $U(S) = aS^p$ and $U(T) = bT^q$, then $U(S) = kU(T)^{p/q}$, where $k = \dfrac{a}{b^{p/q}}\beta^p$. The tradeoff relationship using the parameters estimated for menus is shown in Fig. 11.1.

Maximizing Total User Satisfaction

Let overall satisfaction for the system, $U(system)$, be given by the weighted sum of the $U(x_i)$ values for each of its attributes, x_i: $U(system) = \Sigma\omega_i U(x_i)$, where ω_i is the weight for the i-th attribute. When there are only two attributes, x_1 and x_2, if we hold $U(system)$ constant at some value C, we can determine the *iso-satisfaction* line: $U(x_1) = \dfrac{C}{\omega_1} - \dfrac{\omega_2}{\omega_1} U(x_2)$. Thus, the iso-satisfaction functions appear on the tradeoff graphs as straight lines with a slope of $-\omega_2/\omega_1$, with higher lines representing higher values of $U(system)$.

If the tradeoff functions are concave downward (as are some in later figures), the maximum satisfaction occurs where the slope of the tradeoff function is tangent to the iso-satisfaction function: that is, when the slope of the tradeoff function $= -\omega_2/\omega_1$. In this case, maximum satisfaction occurs at some compromise between the two variables.

If the tradeoff functions are concave upward (as in Fig. 11.1), then the *minimum* satisfaction occurs where the iso-satisfaction curves are tangent to the

---

[1]Letting $\sigma = 0$ simplifies the tradeoff relations, but this is not a necessary assumption. If system response time is slow, then σ should be reinstated: the tradeoff can still be determined quite simply.

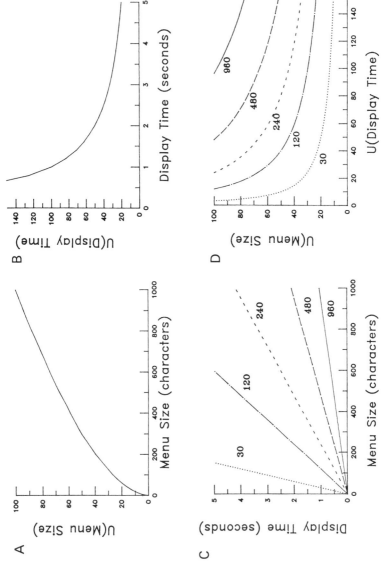

Fig. 11.1. Tradeoff of menu size for display time. Panels A and B show User Satisfaction for menu size, $U(S) = 1.9S^{0.6}$, and display time, $U(T) = 100T^{-1}$, respectively. Panel C shows display time as a function of menu size, $T = S/\beta$, for different values of display rate, β (specified in *characters/second*). Panel D shows the tradeoff between $U(S)$ and $U(T)$ for different values of display rate (β).

tradeoff functions. Maximum satisfaction occurs by maximizing one of the two attributes. The expert, for whom $\omega_T/\omega_S >> 1$, will not sacrifice time for a menu. The beginner, for whom $\omega_T/\omega_S << 1$, will sacrifice display time in order to get as big a menu as possible. For intermediate cases between that of the extreme expert or beginner, the optimum solution is still either to maximize menu size or to minimize display time, but the user might be indifferent as to which of these two was preferred. These conclusions apply to the tradeoff functions of Fig. 11.1D regardless of display rate, as long as the curves are concave upward.[2]

These analyses say that the tradeoff solution that one tends to think of first—to compromise between time and menu size by presenting a small menu at some medium amount of workspace—actually provides the least amount of total satisfaction. Satisfaction is maximized by an all or none solution. The all-or-none preference applies only to tradeoff functions that are concave upward, such as that between menu size and display time. Later we shall see that when time is not relevant, the analysis of the tradeoff between menu size and workspace predicts that even experts will sacrifice some workspace for a menu.

Workspace

Available workspace refers to the amount of room left on the screen after the menu (or other information) is displayed. This is especially important where the menu stays on the screen while normal work continues. The tradeoff is sensitive to screen size. If we had a screen which could display 60 lines of text, using 6 lines to show the current state of the system and a small menu of choices would not decrease usability much. But if the screen could only display 8 lines at a time, then using 6 of them for this purpose would be quite detrimental.

User preference function for workspace.   The user preference function for workspace clearly depends upon the nature of the task: some tasks—such as issuing a command—may only require a workspace of 1 line, others—such as file or text editing—could use unlimited workspace. Let us consider the workspace preferences for text editing of manuscripts. The most common editors can only show 24 lines, each of 80 characters: 1920 character positions. I let $U(1920)$

---

[2]Whether a tradeoff function exhibits upward or downward concavity depends upon the choice of user satisfaction function. If both functions are power functions with one exponent positive and the other negative, the tradeoff functions are always concave upward. When both exponents are positive, the tradeoff functions are always concave downward. When the two functions are logarithmic, the tradeoff functions are always concave downward, and when they are both logistic, the tradeoff functions are both concave upward and downward, switching from one to the other as a function of the other variables (e.g., display rate). These conclusions hold whenever the two variables x_1 and x_2, are linearly related.

= 50. To estimate the workspace that would double the value, I imagined working with screen editors of the sizes shown in Table 11.1. I concluded that I would need the size given by the two page journal spread. That is, $U(6400) = 100$. The power function parameters are $k = 0.64$ and $p = 0.6$, so that $U(w) = 0.64w^{0.6}$: the same exponent used for menu size but with a different scale factor, k. This function is shown in Fig. 11.2.

Trading workspace for display time.   One penalty for increasing the size of the workspace is increased time to display the workspace. If we use the same User Satisfaction function for time as in Fig. 11.1B, we get the tradeoff functions shown in Fig. 11.2B. Large workspaces require very high display rates before they are satisfactory. Because these tradeoff functions are concave upward (and are very similar to the functions of Fig. 11.1D), the same conclusions apply here as to those earlier functions: the optimum operating point is an all-or-none solution. Thus, the user either prefers a large workspace, regardless of the time penalty, or a very fast display, regardless of the workspace penalty. Here, however, the relative weights are apt to be determined by the task rather than by the user's level of skill.

Suppose the task were one in which the display changes relatively infrequently. In this case we would expect $\omega_{\text{workspace}} >> \omega_{\text{display time}}$, so that the optimum solution is to have as big a workspace as possible. If the task were one that requires frequent changes in the display, then we would expect the reverse

TABLE 11.1
Size of Common Texts and Devices (in characters)

Text or Device	Approximate Number of Character Positions
Portable Computer (Radio Shack Model 100)	320
Home Microprocessor (Apple 11)	960
Standard Video Display Unit	1,920
One typed manuscript page (double spaced)	2,600
One typed manuscript page (single spaced)	4,000
Journal page (Cognitive Science)	3,200
Double page spread	6,400
Page of Proceedings (Gaithersberg Human Factors in Computer Systems)	5,500
Double page spread	11,000
Newspaper page (Los Angeles Times)	30,000
Double page spread	60,000

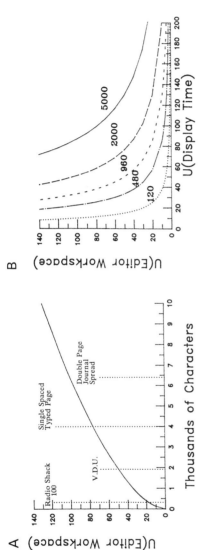

Fig. 11.2. Panel A. User Satisfaction function for editor workspace, w: $U(w) = 0.64w^{0.6}$. Typical character sizes for various displays are also shown. Panel B shows the tradeoff function of workspace against time. $U(w)$ versus $U(T)$, for different display rates, β (*characters/second*). $U(T)$ is shown in Fig. 11.3: $U(T) = 100T^{-1}$.

153

result: $\omega_{workspace} \ll \omega_{display\ time}$, so the optimum solution is to shrink the workspace to the smallest size at which the task can still be carried out, thereby minimizing display time.

Trading workspace for menu size. Adding a menu to the display decreases the amount of available workspace. Let W be the total size of the workspace that is available for use, w the workspace allocated to the text editor, and m the space allocated for a menu: $w = W-m$. We know that $U(m) = am^p$ and $U(w) = b(W-m)^q$, where $a = 2$, $b = 0.6$, and $p = q = 0.6$. This leads to the tradeoff functions shown in Fig. 11.3.

Note that $U(editor\ workspace)$ is relatively insensitive to $U(menu\ size)$. This is because a relatively small sized display makes a satisfactory menu, whereas it requires a large display to make a satisfactory editor workspace. As a result, changing the size of the menu by only a few lines can make a large change in User Satisfaction, whereas the same change in workspace is usually of little consequence.

In some commercially available editors, the menu of commands can occupy approximately half the screen (usually 24 lines). Fig. 11.1 indicates that for a menu of 12 lines (960 characters), $U(menu) = 100$. However, from Figs. 11.2 and 11.3 we see that with a workspace of only 1920 characters, a menu of around 1000 characters (or of $U(menu) = 100$) reduces $U(editor\ workspace)$ from its value of 50 with no menu to 34: a reduction of almost one third. From Fig. 11.3 we see that we would be much less impaired by the same size menu were the workspace considerably greater. In such cases, we have a clear tradeoff between the need for the menu information and the desire to have a reasonable workspace.

Maximizing total user satisfaction for menu and workspace. When tradeoff functions are concave downward (as in Fig. 11.3), maximum satisfaction occurs where the slope of the tradeoff function is tangent to the iso-satisfaction function. For the user who values workspace and menu equally (so that the preferred slope is -1), the optimum solution is to operate at the right-hand side of Fig. 11.3.

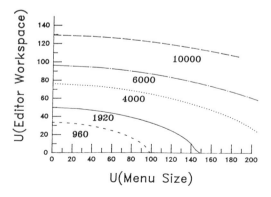

Fig. 11.3. The tradeoff of User Satisfaction for menu size against User Satisfaction for editor workspace, for different values of total workspace, W. Horizontal lines represent constant values of $U(m)$ and, therefore, of m: the values of m can be determined from panel A of Fig. 11.1. Similarly, vertical lines represent constant values of w: the values of w can be determined from panel A of Fig. 11.2.

This makes for a relatively high value of user satisfaction for the menu (which means a large menu—the exact sizes can be determined from Fig. 11.1A)—but with little sacrifice in user satisfaction for workspace. The more expert user will have an iso-satisfaction function with a much smaller slope, and so will sacrifice menu for workspace. Similarly, the beginner will have an iso-satisfaction curve with high slope which will maximize menu size at the expense of workspace. These results are quite unlike the tradeoffs that involved time in which an all-or-none solution was optimal: here, the optimum values are compromises between workspace and editor size. Display rate and amount of total available workspace alter the point of optimum operation. The analysis provides exact numerical determination of how the optimal operating point is affected by these variables.

A CRITIQUE OF THE TRADEOFF ANALYSIS

There are a number of problems with the tradeoff analyses presented in this paper. There are two major criticisms, one minor one. Let me start with the minor one, for it represents a misunderstanding that would be good to clear up. I illustrate the misunderstanding for the variable of menu size, but the discussion applies to other variables as well:

- The functions must be wrong: $U(menu\ size)$ continually increases as a function of *menu size*, yet when the size gets too large, the menu becomes less useful: $U(menu\ size)$ should also decrease.

User Satisfaction for the System Is the Sum of Its Parts

This misunderstanding derives from confusing *User Satisfaction* for a single attribute with *User Satisfaction* for a system. A major philosophy of the tradeoffs analysis is that a system can be decomposed into its underlying component attributes and *User Satisfaction* for each assessed individually. The *User Satisfaction* for the entire system can only be determined from the combination of the *User Satisfaction* values for each of its components. The satisfaction for the amount of information conveyed by the menu continues to increase with size, but the ability to find something (captured by ''search time'') decreases with increasing size of a menu. The overall satisfaction for the menu is given by the sum of the increasing satisfaction for the information and the decreasing satisfaction for search effort: the result is a U-shaped curve that decreases as size gets too big.
    Now let me address the two major critiques:

- The tradeoff functions are arbitrary;
- How do we determine the functions when we design? It would be more useful were there a set of standards (perhaps in handbook form);

These two issues point to unsolved problems with the method. My defense is to argue that this procedure is new. The goal is to introduce the philosophy and to encourage others to help in the collection of the relevant data and in the development of the method. However, the numbers and the particular functions used here may be useful for the tasks for which they were derived: they do mesh well with my intuitions.

The Tradeoff Functions Are Arbitrary

Although the functions used here are indeed arbitrary, three things need to be noted. First, power functions have a long tradition of satisfactory use in psychology and so are apt to be good approximations. Second, I have actually computed User Satisfaction functions using the logistic, power, and logarithmic functions; over much of the range of interest, the results differed suprisingly little, while at high data rates, the concave upward tradeoff functions became concave downward when the logistic was used for size and time, although at low data rates they were still concave upward (see footnote 2). Third, I agree that the preferred thing would be to have an experimental program to determine the exact forms and parameters of the functions. In particular, the all-or-none prediction is sensitive to the form of the User Satisfaction functions.

How Do We Determine the Functions When We Design?

Here, again, empirical work is needed. I suspect the functions will be found to vary only for a reasonably small number of classes of users, classes of tasks, and design attributes, so that it would be possible to collect typical values in a handbook. Alternatively, quick data collection methods might be devised: the magnitude estimation procedures are especially easy to apply. A handbook might be quite valuable. Before this can be done, of course, it is necessary to determine that the hypothesis is correct—that there are a relatively small number of tasks, user classes, and tradeoff variables that need be considered. Moreover, one must extend the analysis to a larger domain of problems and demonstrate its usefulness in actual design.

SOME OTHER EXAMPLES OF TRADEOFFS

There are numerous other tradeoff analyses in addition to the ones presented here. Three other situations seem important enough to warrant consideration here, even though they are not yet ready for quantitative treatment. These are: (1) the comparison between command languages and menu-driven systems; (2) how to choose names for commands and files; and (3) the tradeoffs that result when moving among computer systems of widely varying capabilities, as in the differences between hand held computers and powerful, networked workstations.

Command Languages Versus Menus

The relative merits of menu-based systems and *command language* systems are often debated, seldom with any firm conclusion. It is useful to compare their tradeoffs, but before we do, it is necessary to be clear about what is meant by each alternative. In this context a command language system is one in which no aids are presented to the user during the intention or choice stages, and the action specification is performed by typing a command, using the syntax required by the operating system. (The distinctions among the intention, choice, and specification stages come from Norman, 1985.) Command languages are the most frequent method of implementing operating systems. Similarly, in this context a menu-based system is one in which all commands are presented via menus, where a command cannot be specified unless it is currently being shown on the active menu, and where the commands are specified either through short names or single characters (as indicated by the menu items) or by pointing at the relevant menu item (or perhaps at a switch or mark indicated by the item). These are restricted interpretations of the two alternatives, confounding issues about the format for information presentation and action specification. Still, because they represent common design alternatives, it is useful to compare them.

Command languages offer experts great versatility. Because of their large amount of knowledge and experience with the system, experts tend to know exactly what operations they wish performed. With a command language they can specify their operations directly simply by typing the names of the commands, as well as any parameters, files, or other system options that are required. Command languages make it easy to specify parameters (or "flags") to commands, something that may be difficult with menu-based systems.

Menus offer the beginner or the casual user considerable assistance. At any stage, information is available. Even abbreviated menus serve as a reminder of the alternatives. Experts often complain about menu-based systems because of the time penalty in requesting a menu, waiting for it to be displayed, and then searching for the desired item. Moreover, systems with large numbers of commands require multiple menus that slow up the expert. The problem is that the system is designed to give help, whether or not the user wishes it.

Two of the difficulties with menus are the delay in waiting for them to be plotted and the amount of space they occupy. Fig. 11.1D shows that the tradeoff between amount of information and time delay is especially sensitive to information transmission rate. When transmission time becomes fast enough, there is little penalty for menus, whereas at slow rates of data transmission, the penalty is high. In similar fashion, Fig. 11.3 shows that the tradeoff between menu size and workspace is especially sensitive to the amount of total workspace available.

When sufficient workspace is available, there is little penalty for menus. Thus, slow transmission rates and small workspaces bias the design choice toward command language systems; high data rates and large workspaces bias the system toward menu-based systems.

The two systems also differ in the kinds of errors they lead to and ease of error correction. In a command language system, an error in command specification usually leads to an illegal command: no action gets performed. This error is usually easy to detect and to correct. In a menu-based system, an error in specification is almost always a legal command. This error can be very difficult to correct. If the action was subtle, the user may not even be aware it was performed. If the action was dramatic, the user will often have no idea of what precipitated it, since the action specification was unintentional.

Some of the tradeoffs associated with menu-based systems and command language systems are summarized in Table 11.2. Command languages tend to be virtuous for the expert, but difficult for the novice; they are difficult to learn and there are no on-line reminders of the set of possible actions. Menus are easy to use and they provide a constant reminder. On the other hand, menus tend to be

TABLE 11.2
Tradeoffs Between Menu-Based Systems and Command Systems

Attribute	Menu-Based	Command Language
Speed of use:	Slow, especially if large or if has hierarchical structure.	Fast, for experts; operation can be specified exactly, regardless of system state.
Prior knowledge required:	Very little--can be self-explanatory.	Considerable--user is expected to have learned set of alternative actions and command language that specifies them.
Ease of learning:	High. Uses recognition memory: easier and more accurate than recall memory. Easy to explore system and discover options.	Low. Users must learn names and syntax of language. If alternatives are numerous, learning may take considerable time. No simple way to explore system and discover options not already known.
Errors:	Specification error leads to inappropriate action: difficult to determine what happened and to correct.	Specification error usually leads to illegal command: easy to detect, easy to correct.
Most useful for:	Beginner or infrequent user.	Expert or frequent user.

slow—for some purposes, the expert finds them tedious and unwieldy—and not as flexible as command languages.

This analysis is brief and restricted to the particular formats of command language and menu-based systems that were described. There do exist techniques for mitigating the deficiencies of each system. Nonetheless, the analysis is useful, both for pointing out the nature of the issues and for being reasonably faithful to some existing systems. In the argument over which system is best, the answer must be that neither is: each has it virtues and its deficiencies.

The Choice of Names for Commands and Files

Another example of a common tradeoff is in the choice of name for a command or a file. The problem occurs because the name must serve two different purposes: as a *description* of the item and also as the string of characters that must be typed to invoke it, that is, as the *specification;* these two uses pose conflicting requirements.

Consider the properties of names when used as descriptions. The more complete the description, the more useful it can be, especially when the user is unsure of the options or is selecting from an unfamiliar set of alternatives. However, the longer the description, the more space it occupies and the more difficult to read or scan the material. In addition, there are often system limitations on the length and format of names. For these reasons, one usually settles for a partial description, counting on context or prior knowledge to allow the full description to be regenerated by the user.

Once the appropriate name has been determined, the user enters the specification stage of operation; the user must specify to the computer system which name is desired. Most users are not expert typists, and so it is desirable to simplify the specification stage. As a result, there is pressure toward the use of short names, oftentimes to the limit of single character command names.[3]

The desirability for short names is primarily a factor when specification must be done by naming. When the specification can be done by pointing, then ease of typing is no longer a factor. Nonetheless, there are still constraints on the name choice: the longer the name, the easier to find and point at the desired item. but at the cost of using a larger percentage of the available workspace, of increasing display time, and the ease of reading and search. Now names might wish to be chosen so they are visually distinct, or so that they occupy appropriate spatial

---

[3]A number of systems allow for shortcuts in specification, so that one need only use sufficient characters (plus some 'escape' or 'wild-card' character) to make the name unique. This option poses its own naming constraints; now a name is chosen not only to be descriptive, but with the added requirement that one or two letters be sufficient to distinguish it uniquely from all other names. The typing aid introduces its own form of naming constraint.

locations on the display, in all cases adding more constraints to the naming problem. In general the descriptive requirements tend to push toward longer names, names that provide as much information as possible. The specification requirements tend to push toward shorter names, names that are easy to type.

Handheld Computers Versus Workstations

New developments in technology are moving computer systems in several conflicting directions simultaneously. Workstations are getting more powerful, with large memories, large, high resolution screens, and with very high communication bandwidths. These developments move us toward the ability to present as much information as is needed by the user with little penalty in time, workspace, or even memory space. At the same time, some machines are getting smaller, providing us with briefcase-sized and handheld computers. These machines have great virtue because of their portability, but severe limitations in communications speed, memory capacity, and amount of display screen or workspace.

Just as workstations are starting to move toward displays capable of 1,000 line resolution, showing several entire pages of text, handheld computers move us back toward only a few short lines—perhaps 8 lines of 40 characters each—and communication rates of 30 cps (300 baud). The major differences between workstations and handheld computers relevant to the tradeoffs discussion are in the amount of memory, processor speed and power, communication abilities, availability of extra peripherals, and screen size: in all cases, the handheld machine has sacrificed power for portability. Because the same people may wish to use both handheld machines and workstations (one while at home or traveling, the other at work), the person may wish the same programs to operate on the two machines. However, the interface design must be different, as the tradeoff analyses of this paper show.

SUMMARY AND CONCLUSIONS

The tradeoff analysis is intended to serve as an example of a quantitative design tool. In some cases it may not be possible to select an optimum design, not even for a restricted class of activities and users. In these cases, knowledge of the tradeoffs allows the designer to choose intelligently, knowing exactly what benefits and limits the system design will provide. Finally, the analyses show that some design decisions are heavily affected by technology, others are not. Thus, answers to design questions are heavily context dependent, being affected by the classes of users for whom the system is intended, the types of applications being performed, which stages of user activities are thought to be of most importance, and the level of technology being employed.

The work presented here is just the beginning. In the ideal case, the tradeoff relationships will be known exactly, perhaps with the relevant quantitative parameters provided in handbooks. This paper has limited itself to demonstrating the basic principles. Considerable development must still be done on this issue and on the other major parameters and issues that affect the quality of the human-machine interaction. Much work remains to be done.

A second point of the paper is to argue for more fundamental approaches to the study of human-machine interaction. All too often we are presented with minor studies that do not lead to general application, or studies that are restricted to a particular technology. All too often we are trapped in the tar pits of the field or seduced by the sirens of technology. If we are to have a science of design that can be of use beyond today's local problems, we must learn to broaden our views, sharpen our methods, and avoid temptation.

A major moral of this paper is that it is essential to analyze separately the different aspects of human-computer interaction. Detailed analyses of each aspect of the human-computer interface are essential, of course, but because design decisions interact across stages and classes of users, we must also develop tools that allow us to ask for what purpose the system is to be used, then to determine how best to accomplish that goal. Only after the global decisions have been made should the details of the interface design be determined.

ACKNOWLEDGMENTS

This research was supported by Contract N00014-79-C-0323, NR 667-437 with the Personnel and Training Research Programs of the Office of Naval Research and by a grant from the System Development Foundation.

These ideas have benefited greatly by interactions with the UCSD Human-Machine Interaction project, especially Liam Bannon, Allen Cypher, Steve Draper, Dave Owen, Mary Riley, and Paul Smolensky. Comments on a draft of the paper by Danny Bobrow, Jonathan Grudin, Peter Jackson, Allen Munro, and Julie Norman resulted in major improvements of the ideas and exposition.

REFERENCES

Bannon, L., Cypher, A., Greenspan, S., & Monty, M. L. (1983). Evaluation and analysis of users' activity organization. In A. Janda (Ed.), *Proceedings of the CHI '83 Conference on Human Factors in Computing Systems.* New York: ACM.
Card, S., Moran, T., & Newell, A. (1983). *The psychology of human-computer interaction.* Hillsdale, NJ: Lawrence Erlbaum Associates.
Miller, R. B. (1968). Response time in man-computer conversational transactions. *Proceedings of the Spring Joint Computer Conference, 33,* 267–277.
Norman, D. A. (1983). *Tradeoffs in the design of human-computer interfaces.* Unpublished manuscript.

Norman, D. A. (1985). Four stages of user activities. In B. Shakel (Ed.), *INTERACT '84: First conference on human-computer interaction.* Amsterdam: North-Holland.

O'Malley, C., Smolensky, P., Bannon, L., Conway, E., Graham, J., Sokolov, J., & Monty, M. L. (1983). A proposal for user centered documentation. In A. Janda (Ed.), *Proceedings of the CHI '83 Conference on Human Factors in Computing Systems.* New York: ACM

Shneiderman, B. (1980). *Software psychology: Human factors in computer and information systems.* Cambridge, MA: Winthrop.

Stevens, S. S. (1974). Perceptual magnitude and its measurement. In E. C. Carterette & M. P. Friedman (Eds.), *Handbook of perception* (Vol. 2, pp. 361–389). New York: Academic Press.

12

Some Tools for Redesigning System-Operator Interfaces

Arthur C. Graesser
Memphis State University

Kathy L. Lang
Memphis State University

C. Scott Elofson
California State University, Fullerton

ABSTRACT

Individuals prefer to purchase computer systems that are easy to learn, easy to operate, and that solve their problems. Consequently, designers of computer software and hardware recognize the importance of catering to the human side of computer-human interfaces. Corporations are hiring an increasing number of cognitive engineers and human factors engineers to improve the quality of these interfaces. The cognitive engineers evaluate existing interfaces and recommend engineering changes for future designs.

Engineering change proposals should not be based entirely on the intuitions of the cognitive engineer. Intuition-based proposals do not usually convince the managers, programmers, and system designers in a corporate setting. The proposals must have some defensible foundation. If the cognitive engineer is lucky, the recommendations are based on established guidelines or published research. However, there are no standards, guidelines, and published studies to motivate most design decisions on a specific computer system. The field of computer-human interaction has not yet matured to the point of generating design standards (although discussions of standards for software design have started to emerge). In most cases, the cognitive engineer must collect data from operators of the specific computer system before effective design changes can be proposed. When data need to be collected, there is the open-ended problem of deciding what data to collect and how to analyze them. This chapter presents some methods of data collection and analysis that are particularly useful for improving the interface between a computer system and human operators.

This chapter begins with a brief review of four different approaches to studying system-operator interfaces. We argue that all four approaches must be seriously considered when the cognitive engineer conducts an empirical study and proposes design changes for a specific interface. In order to illustrate an effective methodology for data collection and analysis, we discuss a project that we conducted on a Communication Control System (CCS) that was developed by the Singer Corporation.

FOUR APPROACHES TO INVESTIGATING A SYSTEM-OPERATOR INTERFACE

This section presents four different approaches to investigating and improving interface design. These approaches include (1) guidelines and standards, (2) psychological models of system-operator interaction, (3) analysis of troublesome errors, and (4) assessment of operators' background knowledge and mental models. Effective engineering change proposals emerge after the cognitive engineer investigates a specific interface from the perspective of these four approaches.

Guidelines and Standards

Human factors researchers have documented several guidelines for system-operator interface design (Morland, 1983; Wickens & Kramer, 1985; Woodson, 1981). These guidelines can be adopted when a cognitive engineer recommends design changes on a specific interface. For example, one guideline states that the overall density of information on a computer display should not exceed 25% (Kruk & Muter, 1983; Monk, 1984; Tullis, 1983). Thus, when averaging over all of the potential character locations on a computer screen, only 25% or less of the locations should be filled with characters. The display is cluttered and more difficult to scan and read when the overall density exceeds 25%. In addition to overall density, there are also guidelines for local density (Kruk & Muter, 1983).

Guidelines and standards provide quick solutions for design decisions, but it is important to acknowledge that there are tradeoffs associated with most of these guidelines (Norman, 1983). A particular design feature might be beneficial to the operator in some ways, but problematic in other ways. For example, suppose that the cognitive engineer embraces the 25% density guideline and recommends that fewer prompts, messages, and data fields be presented on the computer screen. Some drawbacks to this recommendation are that (a) the prompts might be less distinctive, because they end up being shorter, (b) the messages might be more difficult to comprehend, in an effort to save words, and (c) the operator might lose a global perspective on the data presented on the screen.

There are several guidelines and published studies that are helpful for proposing design changes at the perceptual level, involving "lower-level" cognitive processes. There are guidelines for the proper angle of the keyboard and computer screen (Miller & Suther, 1983), the size of display windows (Duchnicky & Kolers, 1983; Neal & Darnell, 1984), the optimal response time of the computer (Morland, 1983; Williges & Williges, 1982), the optimal layout of letters on a keypad (Norman & Fisher, 1982), and the optimal layout of numbers on a keypad (Long, Whitefield, & Dennett, 1984). There is an extensive literature on guidelines for generating computer command names and abbreviations for words (Benbasat & Wand, 1984; Ehrenreich & Porcu, 1982; Landauer, Galotti, & Hartwell, 1983; Rogers & Moeller, 1984). The scope of some of these guidelines is quite fine-tuned and specific. For example. when the operator scans the material on the screen, it is best to print words in capital letters (al-caps) rather than mixed, upper and lower case; when the operator reads and comprehends the material, it is better to print the verbal material in upper and lower case than in al-caps (Tullis, 1983).

There are substantially fewer guidelines for facilitating cognitive processing at deeper levels of analysis. This deficit has encouraged researchers to devote more attention to problems involving software organization, computer languages, command and query formats, and other dimensions of the interface that are primarily conceptual (i.e., not directly tied to the perceptual input). There are some guidelines for designing computer prompts and error messages (Morland, 1983; Shneiderman, 1982), for designing "on-line" help facilities (Houghton, 1984; Morland, 1983), and for designing menu-based interfaces (Reid, 1984). However, research and guidelines are comparatively scarce at the deeper, more conceptual levels of cognitive processing.

Psychological Models of System-Operator Interaction

Some psychologists have developed models that simulate certain aspects of system-operator interactions. The most ambitious psychological model developed so far is the GOMS model (Card, Moran, & Newell, 1983). The GOMS model accounts for strategies, actions, and keystrokes that operators execute during text editing.

GOMS is an acronym for the four major components of the model: *Goals, operators, methods,* and *selection rules.* The user has a hierarchy of goals that are eventually achieved during a successful text-editing session. Some goals are comparatively superordinate in the hierarchy (e.g., editing a manuscript, saving a file) whereas others are comparatively subordinate (inserting, deleting, replacing, and moving text). "Operators" are very subordinate behavioral units, such as entering a command, attending to a portion of the screen, and executing a keystroke. Goals are fulfilled by selecting and executing operators. "Methods" are sequences or chunks of operators that ordinarily fulfill a goal when executed.

The user constructs these methods through experience and interactions with the text editor. "Selection rules" determine what methods are selected to fulfill goals when there are two or more methods to achieve the goals. Selection rules are represented as "IF<state>—THEN<method/operator>" productions; a specific method or operator is applied if a specific state exists.

The GOMS model explains many of the performance characteristics when individuals use text editors. The model accounts for the sequences of operators and methods that are executed during a task. The model accounts for the duration of executing the methods and operators at different grain sizes (i.e., global plans versus keystrokes). The model accounts for errors committed by experienced users of a text editor. The model also provides a framework for evaluating and designing text editors (Roberts & Moran, 1982), so it is a practical tool in addition to a theoretical model.

The GOMS model was developed to explain computer-human interaction during text editing. However, the model provides a useful foundation for investigating system-operator interactions that do not involve text editing per se. There are at least three aspects of the GOMS model that would generalize to most or all computer system-operator interfaces. First, many of the components and tasks in text editing also occur in tasks other than text editing. Computer interfaces frequently involve accessing files, saving files, entering commands, searching the screen for information, and choosing an alternative on a menu. Second, the basic architecture of the GOMS model (e.g., goal structures, methods, production systems, etc.) generalizes to other interfaces. Third, the model is grounded in psychological theory and research that should generalize to several tasks and interfaces. For example, the GOMS model could estimate the task completion times for specific tasks by integrating their model with well-established psychological laws (e.g., the law of practice, Fitts law, Hicks law). These laws would apply to all tasks and interfaces.

Troublesome Errors

Troublesome errors occur when the interface has a design flaw or when the operator lacks some critical knowledge about the system. When troublesome errors occur, there are extremely long pauses and the operator may face a permanent barrier. Troublesome errors demand serious attention because operators spend several minutes trying to interpret and recover from barriers in the interaction. According to Embley and Nagy (1981), 25% to 50% of the time that a novice spends interacting with a computer system consists of committing, recovering, and agonizing over errors. In very complex systems the novice faces a negative feedback loop in which "things get worse before they get better." Some operators eventually give up after trying to cope with these time-consuming errors.

In order to investigate troublesome errors, the cognitive engineer must apply methods that expose the errors and the operators' interpretations of the errors. We recommend that three steps be pursued when investigating troublesome errors. First, the cognitive engineer should select *benchmark tasks* that have a high likelihood of manifesting the troublesome errors. Benchmark tasks are tasks that the operators perform in empirical studies. Second, the operators should supply verbal protocols that expose their conception of (a) the cause of a particular error, (b) methods of correcting or recovering from the error, and (c) consequences of not correcting the error. For example, researchers have collected *think aloud* protocols (Mack, Lewis, & Carroll, 1983) or *question-answering* protocols (Graesser & Murray, in press) from the operators while they complete benchmark tasks; the operators' verbal protocols reflect their cognitive representations of the troublesome errors. Third, there should be a theoretical or analytical system for classifying the troublesome errors (Norman, 1981; Rouse & Rouse, 1983).

Carroll and Carrithers (1984) introduced the notion of a "training wheels" interface for minimizing troublesome errors that beginning operators experience. The training wheels interface is a simplified version of the target interface, but it preserves the major design features of the target interface (e.g., *menus, spatial layout, messages, prompts,* etc.). The training wheels interface makes troublesome errors unreachable to beginning operators by cutting out problematic response options. For example, a novice sometimes pursues unusual alternatives on a menu interface, such as system diagnostics or "house cleaning" routines that reorganize files in external storage. As a consequence, the novice ends up expending several minutes trying to understand esoteric alternatives on the menu that are unrelated to the task the novice wants to complete. The novice also expends several minutes trying to restore the main menu. The training wheels system would block the operator from pursuing these problematic alternatives on the menu. When such alternatives are selected, the computer would return the message "XXX is not available on this training system." Carroll and Carrithers conducted some experiments that demonstrated that the training wheels interface provides a very effective training method. When the operators were eventually transferred from the training wheels system to the target system, they completed tasks faster, they committed fewer errors, and they liked the target system better than did operators who had alternative training methods.

Background Knowledge and Mental Models

Operators must have a sufficient amount of background knowledge before they can solve novel problems and make complex decisions while interacting with a computer system. It is therefore important to assess what the operator knows about different domains of world knowledge (which we will call *topics*) that are relevant to the system-operator interaction. For example, suppose that a software company wanted to develop a program that keeps inventory for parts in a small automobile business. The relevant topics would include (a) data base management systems, (b) automobiles and their parts, and (c) the operation and organization of small businesses. All of these topics would probably contribute information when the operator performs a difficult inventory task on the computer.

It would be impractical to assess all of the operators' knowledge about the relevant topics. However, it is quite feasible to sample some of the key concepts associated with the topics. For example, a question-answering methodology could be adopted for probing an individual's knowledge of critical terms and topics (Graesser & Clark, 1985; Graesser & Murray, in press). After a systematic analysis of the question-answering protocols, the investigator has some idea of *what* the operators know in addition to *how much* they know.

More sophisticated analyses would address how the background knowledge is represented and organized in the human mind. It is beyond the scope of this chapter, however, to discuss the problem of how knowledge is organized and represented. According to one contemporary view, an individual's knowledge about a technical topic (e.g., physics or electronics) consists of a set of *mental models* (Gentner & Stevens, 1983). A mental model is a simplified knowledge structure that explains certain aspects of the topic in question. As a person becomes an expert on a particular topic, the person acquires more and more mental models, and explains more aspects of the topic. An individual's understanding of a topic substantially improves after the individual acquires some critical mental models that explain major properties of the topic (Mayer, 1975).

BACKGROUND AND GOALS OF PROJECT: INVESTIGATING THE COMMUNICATION CONTROL SYSTEM

We recently completed a 4-month project that investigated the system-operator interface on a communication control system (CCS). The CCS was developed by the Librascope division of the Singer Corporation. The CCS provides communications control and management for all Army-automated communications media that are targeted to last through the year 2010.

There are two primary tasks of the CCS operator. First, the operator creates and edits communication networks by entering data in the CCS. Second, the operator responds to system alerts that signify malfunctions in hardware and software. Figure 12.1 shows an example communication network. When the operator creates and edits this communication network, the operator enters information about the following components.

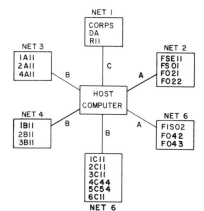

FIG. 12.1.   An example communication network that the operator enters on the communication control module (CCM).

1. There is a set of *subscribers,* the basic nodes in the communication network. There is a subscriber corresponding to each identification code in Fig. 12.1 (e.g., 1B11, 2B11, 3B11 in Net 4).

2. For each subscriber, there are a set of *fields* that are filled with *values.* For example, one field assigns an identification code to the subscriber, another field assigns a network number to the subscriber, and another field specifies the subscriber's security classification. For each subscriber there are 1–2 dozen unique fields that must be filled with values.

3. The network has connectivity properties, including *channels* of communication (e.g., nets 1 through 6 in Fig. 12.1) and *communications media* associated with each channel. The links in Fig. 12.1 contain a letter code that would declare the type of communications media. When channels and communications media are created, the operator enters data that assign specific values to fields.

Communication networks have other components and properties, but the above description is satisfactory for this chapter.

When communication networks are created and edited, the operator interacts directly with a communication control module (CCM). In the existing "testbed" CCM, the operator interacts directly with three hardware components, which are presented in Fig. 12.2a. First, there is a touch panel screen that displays information and response options. The operator presses the touch panel screen in order to declare certain response options. Second, there is a teletype keyboard for entering alphanumeric code. Third, there is an auxiliary keyboard that contains 16 fixed-function keys. Singer-Librascope is planning on revising the CCM, as illustrated in Fig. 12.2b. The revised CCM will have a larger touch panel screen than the testbed CCM. The revised CCM will also eliminate the

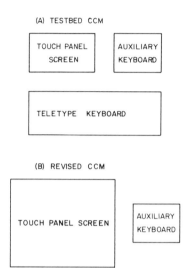

(A) TESTBED CCM

TOUCH PANEL
SCREEN

AUXILIARY
KEYBOARD

TELETYPE   KEYBOARD

(B) REVISED CCM

TOUCH PANEL SCREEN

AUXILIARY
KEYBOARD

FIG. 12.2.   Major hardware components on (A) the testbed communication control module and (B) the
revised   communication   control
module.

teletype keyboard by incorporating a "soft keypad" on the enlarged touch panel
screen. Consequently, the touch panel screen will be the center of most CCM-
operator interactions during data entry.

Project Goals, Constraints, and Responsibilities

Our role in the project was to identify problems with the testbed CCM, to
propose engineering changes for the revised CCM, and to evaluate the impact of
the planned CCM modifications (e.g., the enlarged touch panel screen and the
elimination of the keyboard). These project objectives were intentionally open-
ended. We were expected to collect data that analyze the operators' knowledge,
the operators' tasks, and the system constraints at several different levels. Focusing on one or a few aspects of the system-operator interaction would be entirely
inappropriate. In essence, we needed a methodology for data collection and
analysis that approached the CCM-operator interface from many different perspectives and at many different levels.

There were some practical constraints and responsibilities in this project.
There was a deadline; we had only 4 months to conduct the project. There were
limited funds for the project; only two part-time cognitive engineers and two
research assistants were funded on this 4-month project. During the 4 months,
we were expected to learn about the communications control system, to plan a
study and collect data from 12 CCM operators, and to write two documents (an
operator task analysis and the engineering change proposals). Therefore, Singer-
Librascope expected us to produce a large amount of data analyses, insights, and
documents in a very short amount of time. In retrospect, a more realistic timeta-

ble would have been a minimum of 6 months for a team of six cognitive engineers and research assistants.

Additional Features of the CCM-operator Interface

The CCM operator interface was designed to facilitate the ease of data entry and to minimize data entry errors. The interface imposed minimal demands on the operator by emphasizing decoding processes (i.e., recognizing desired responses on the touch panel screen) rather than production processes (i.e., generating commands and strategies from memory). This subsection summarizes some of the major features of the CCM-operator interface that were implemented to achieve these design objectives.

Hierarchical Software Organization.   The CCS has a hierarchical organization of major tasks and screen displays. Design decisions needed to be made about how to segment screen displays, subgoals, and operations into self-contained tasks. Decisions needed to be made about the organization of the tasks in the hierarchy, i.e., when should one task be embedded in another task, and how should the tasks be ordered?

Menus.   A menu-directed interface was adopted because it is the easiest (but often not the fastest) interface for operators to use. The menu is used for moving "downward" to deeper levels of the software organization and for moving "laterally" within a major task. The operator selects items on the menu by pressing response alternatives on the touch panel screen. Design decisions needed to be made about the selection, labeling, and spatial layout of the response alternatives.

Fixed Function Keys.   The auxiliary keyboard contains some fixed function keys for moving "upward" in the hierarchical software organization. For example, when a MENU key is pressed, the computer jumps to the main menu display (the root node in the screen display hierarchy). A RETURN key moves the operator up one level in the hierarchy.

Windows.   The touch panel screen is divided into separate windows containing information, indicators, or response options that have a common function. The revised CCM has four windows. The *display window* presents the database that the operator is working on. The database includes lists of subscribers, channels, communication media, or fields. The *operator input window* displays the operator's response options. On some displays, this window contains an alphabet keypad or a number keypad. The *control window* presents control functions that are available to the operator. Examples of these control functions are advancing to the next page of data, moving a cursor, or deleting a particular field. The *alert windows* display system alerts and alerts that result from erroneous actions of the operator. Design decisions needed to be made about the spatial layout and the information displayed in these windows.

Pages, Entries, and Fields.   Portions of the communication network are presented within the display window on the touch panel screen. The database is presented in "page" increments. A page may contain a list of "entries" (e.g., subscribers, channels). Alternatively, a page may contain a list of fields and field values associated with a single entry. When the operator creates a network, the operator creates new entries and fills in field values for each entry. During editing, the values of fields are modified and entries get added or deleted. For some fields, the operator enters alphanumeric code on soft keypads within the operator input window. For other fields, the operator presses a labeled response option on the touch panel screen. Design decisions needed to be made about the formatting, content, and spatial layout of approximately 200 touch panel screens. Decisions also needed to be made about the method of entering the data (e.g., entering alphanumeric code on a keypad versus pressing a labeled response alternative).

Defaults.   The values of many fields in the database are automatically filled by default while the operator enters network data. Consequently, the operator does not need to actively declare all of the information in the communication network. It is well acknowledged that default facilities speed up data entry substantially. Design decisions needed to be made about the default values assigned to specific fields and methods of conveying these default values to the operator.

On-line Help Facility.   In the revised CCM the operator can receive help in an on-line capacity. The auxiliary keyboard has a HELP key that provides help messages for alerts, control functions, response alternatives, and display items. When the operator needs help, the operator presses the HELP key and then presses the touch panel display where help is needed. The operator presses the RETURN key to remove the help messages. Design decisions needed to be made about the content and format of the help messages.

METHODS OF DATA COLLECTION

We collected data from 12 operators of the testbed CCM. We planned the study so that informative data would be available for different levels and aspects of the CCM-operator interface. We collected three sources of data: display-response data, troublesome error data, and background knowledge data.

Display-response Data

These data consist of the responses that operators produce for specific displays when they perform benchmark tasks. The operators executed a series of benchmark tasks. These tasks would normally be performed when an operator creates a communication network, edits the network, and responds to alerts that are presented on the touch panel screen. The operator was handed some sheets of paper depicting a communication network and were instructed to initialize the network on the CCM. After the network was created, the operator performed tasks that reviewed the network and modified the network. Alerts periodically occurred throughout the benchmark tasks. The operator was videotaped during the entire session.

When the videotapes were analyzed, we collected several measures for specific screen displays. These measures included (1) the operators' responses to the specific display, (2) response times, (3) the likelihood of committing a data entry error, (4) the likelihood of correcting a data entry error, and (5) the time to recover from data entry errors.

Troublesome Errors

There were a number of troublesome errors distributed throughout the benchmark tasks. As discussed earlier, troublesome errors occur when the operator is stuck and there are long pauses. We anticipated that certain troublesome errors would occur at specific points in the benchmark task, whereas other troublesome errors were not expected. An alert appeared on the screen when the operator encountered most of these troublesome points during the interaction; the computer would diagnose an erroneous response and pass down an alert message. It should be noted that the alert messages in the testbed CCM were usually uninformative (e.g., INVALID ENTRY, TRY AGAIN).

A question-answering methodology was used to uncover the operator's interpretation of the troublesome errors and the corresponding alerts. The operator was questioned about the meaning of the alert ("what does that mean?"), about the operator's rationale for executing a response ("why did you do that?"), about the cause of the alert ("why did that alert occur?"), about appropriate responses to the alert ("what should you do about that?"), and about thoughts that the operator has during long pauses ("what are you thinking about now?"). The answers to these questions were transcribed, segmented into basic idea units, and classified for further analyses. Graesser and Clark (1985) discuss in detail how these verbal protocols would be segmented and categorized.

Background Knowledge

We assessed the background knowledge that the operators had about the communication control system and other relevant topics. This knowledge ranged from global knowledge about the CCS to specific knowledge about particular communication devices. We assessed the background knowledge in two ways. Regarding the first method, we prepared a list of 120 terms and expressions that are associated with the CCS, with particular communications media, with the Army, or with the CCM interface. For each of these terms, we questioned the operator about the meaning of the term and tape-recorded the answers. The answers were transcribed, segmented into idea units, and categorized. The terms themselves were also segregated according to topic (e.g., the CCS, communications media, the Army, the CCM interface).

Regarding the second method of tapping the operators' background knowledge, the operators were probed with why-questions when they performed a sample of actions during the benchmark tasks. The answers to these why-questions expose the goals and goal structures that guide the operators' organized behavior (Graesser & Clark, 1985; Graesser & Murachver, 1985: Graesser & Murray, in press).

DATA ANALYSES AND ENGINEERING CHANGE PROPOSALS

It is beyond the scope of this section to discuss all of the analyses and recommendations for engineering changes. We performed hundreds of analyses on the data we collected from the operators. We recommended approximately 100 design changes, based on (a) published guidelines and research and (b) the data collected from the 12 CCM operators. This section presents some analyses that illustrate how informative data can be extracted from our methodology and how these data support recommendations for design changes.

State Transition Networks

State transition networks have been used to represent system-operator interactions (Jacob, 1983). In the context of the communication control system, the specific displays on the touch panel screen constitute the "states" in the state transition network (STN). There are approximately 200 states in the entire system. The operators' alternative responses for a specific display constitute the "transitions" in the STN. Each transition has a set of conditions that must be satisfied in order for the operator to execute the transition.

Figure 12.3 and Table 12.1 present an example of STN for a task on the CCM. The example is simplified substantially. A typical STN for a task involves dozens of states and transitions whereas the example has only four states and five transitions. There is only one transition associated with the first touch panel screen display. When the operator executes this transition, the operator types in an ID on the touch panel screen and then presses ENTER. There is more than one transition associated with displays 2 and 3. One of the transitions is a default transition, in

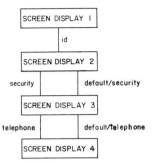

FIG. 12.3. An example state transition network (STN).

TABLE 12.1
Transition in the State Transition Network in Figure 12.3

Transition	Specification of Transition
id	Condition: Display 1 is presented Action: Operator type in ID on touch panel screen &THEN Operator press ENTER on touch panel screen
security	Condition: Display 2 is presented Action: Operator press (security) option on touch panel screen
default/security	Condition: Display 2 is presented & Operator knows default value & default value is consistent with network Action: Operator press DEFAULT on touch panel screen
telephone	Condition: Display 3 is presented Action: Operator type in telephone number &THEN Operator press ENTER on touch panel screen
default/telephone	Condition: Display 3 is presented & There is no telephone number specified in network & Operator knows that default value is "none" Action: Operator press DEFAULT on touch panel screen

which the operator accepts the default value for the field associated with the display. For example, the default value for security clearance might be ''unclassified'' and the default value for the telephone number would be ''none.'' It should be noted that executing the default transition is easier than typing in alphanumeric code or choosing a response option among several alternatives.

An STN was prepared for each benchmark task that the 12 operators performed on the testbed CCM. As discussed in the previous section, we collected data on each screen display, including operators' responses, response times, error rates, and so on. Consequently, there were data available for most of the transitions in the STN.

An analysis of the STNs and benchmark task data are useful to the cognitive engineer in four major ways. First, it is easy to identify troublesome points in the CCM-operator interaction by inspecting the STN. The troublesome transitions have extremely long response times and high error rates. Second, an analysis of the response times and errors provide information about the speed and accuracy of data entry on the device that is being tested. We should point out that speed and accuracy can be simulated for communication networks and situations that were not directly tested in the benchmark tasks; a different communication network would simply involve a different sequence of states and transitions. Third, the speed and accuracy of data entry can be simulated for hypothetical devices and designs that have not yet been manufactured. An STN can be constructed for a hypothetical design, with response times estimated for each transition. Fourth, by inspecting the entire STN and transition data, it is easy to identify general trends and patterns in the empirical data.

We should elaborate a bit on simulating speed and accuracy data for hypothetical designs and devices. For purposes of illustration, consider the response times associated with specific transitions on the CCM, and the time to complete an entire task. Response times can be estimated for specific transitions on the hypothetical CCM based on (a) the data collected on similar transitions on the testbed CCM and (b) adjustments in the response times based on available research and psychological laws. For example, we were able to use Fitts law (see Card, Moran, & Newell, 1983) to estimate the savings in time when fingers are moved between locations on the revised CCM versus the testbed CCM (see Fig. 12.2). It should be noted that the distance that the finger moves between successive responses is often much greater on the testbed CCM; the operator often alternates between responses on the touch panel screen and data entry on the keyboard (which was approximately 18 inches from the touch panel screen). Both minimum and maximum values may be computed when estimating the adjusted response times. For example, a maximum value would correspond to a slow operator who enters data ''cold'' (i.e., without any practice) whereas the minimum value would correspond to a fast operator entering data after extended practice.

Task completion times can be simulated for a hypothetical design under different conditions. When we simulated task completion times on the revised CCM, we compared conditions in which maximum values versus minimum values were assigned to the transitions. We compared conditions where the operator accepted default values (whenever appropriate) with conditions in which none of the fields would be filled with default values. After we performed simulations on the testbed CCM and the revised CCM under different conditions, we found that the task completion times were between 26% and 38% faster on the revised CCM (according to conservative estimates).

Of course, it is possible to generate several hypothetical CCM designs and to simulate task completion times for each design. This simulation methodology allows us to evaluate the impact of specific changes in the interface. For example, we can assess the impact of combining displays, reordering displays, and adding additional control functions to the interface. In some cases, it would be feasible to converge on an optimal interface design that minimizes task completion times and/or error rates.

As we pointed out earlier, it is easy to identify trends and patterns in the data when the data are summarized in the form of an STN. For example, when we inspected the STN for the testbed CCM, we discovered a speed-accuracy tradeoff in the default facility. The operator saved a considerable amount of time in data entry by accepting default values for fields (approximately a 40% savings in speed). However, the error rate was very high (5%) whenever a "non-default" response was appropriate for a field that was normally assigned a default value; in comparison, the error rates for other transitions were very low, less than 1%. This speed-accuracy tradeoff in the default facility inspired some engineering change proposals that would decrease the error rate.

Troublesome Errors and Transitions

One class of troublesome errors occurred when the operator did not know how to execute a procedure that was required in the benchmark task. Consequently, the operator confronted a serious, if not permanent, barrier. When these troublesome errors occurred, the operator was probed with questions. The operators' answers to these questions provided valuable information for designing the revised CCM. In particular, we proposed that the on-line help facility present messages that specify (a) the goals of a given task, (b) the procedures for executing the task, and (c) suggestions about what tasks to perform next during the CCM-operator interaction. The operators' knowledge and misconceptions, which were exposed in the question-answering protocols, provided some guidance in writing effective help messages.

We intentionally planted some errors in the communication network that the operators were asked to enter during the benchmark tasks. Thus, there were some incompatibilities between the network sheets (handed to the operators) and the CCS constraints. These errors produced alerts during data entry so the operators were probed with questions at these points during the session. The answers uncovered the operators' knowledge and misconceptions about the causes of the alerts, the prevention of the alerts, effective actions to perform in response to the alerts, and the consequences of failing to act on the alerts. It should be noted that an experienced operator should have been able to prevent the alert by correcting the erroneous network data prior to data entry. At the very least, a knowledgeable operator would be able to identify the cause of the alert and to execute a procedure for correcting the problem.

Once again, the question-answering protocols provided some guidance in writing effective help messages. The protocols also furnished useful clues on how to modify other aspects of the CCM-operator interface. Indeed, the protocols either directly or indirectly had an impact on our recommendations for several types of design changes. At the local level, we needed to design screen displays with informative prompts, labels,and spatial layouts. At the global level, major tasks needed to be segmented into natural, self-contained subtasks.

After analyzing the question-answering protocols, we were convinced that certain misconceptions would persist, even after substantial training on the system; we needed to reorganize and reorder the tasks so that these misconceptions would not lead to troublesome consequences. However, it is beyond the scope of this chapter to specify exactly how the question-answering protocols furnish insights for design changes.

Background Knowledge of Operators

The operators needed to have an adequate background knowledge about the CCS, the Army, communications media, and the interface in order to correct network errors and solve network problems. We tried to uncover the operators' background knowledge by having them answer questions about the meaning of 120 terms and expressions. We also probed the operators with why-questions when they performed certain actions during the benchmark tasks. In this subsection we illustrate how an analysis of this background knowledge led to recommendations for engineering changes.

Lacking Some Critical Mental Models.   The operators' technical knowledge of specific communication media and devices was adequate, for the most part. In contrast, they did not have a well-developed set of mental models for networks. As a consequence of this deficit in background knowledge, most operators were unable to correct the network errors that occurred during the benchmark tasks.

One way of educating the operator about communication networks is to develop graphic displays of the networks on the touch panel screen. Therefore, we recommended that the revised CCM have a graphics generator that summarizes the subscriber nodes, channels, and connectivity of the communication network. The operator could view the entire network as a whole, thereby furnishing a global perspective. The operator could also review subsections of the network by pressing one of the subscriber nodes or channels on the touch panel screen; the CCM would subsequently present the node or channel and the elements that are directly connected to it. The graphics generator would eventually educate the operator about the important mental models and constraints that underly communication networks.

Goal Structures.   Goals and goal structures guide the operators' interaction with the CCM. The operator needs to know what the important goals are, how they are structurally related, and how the tasks map onto the goals. Stated somewhat differently, the operators must know the functional significance of the tasks they perform.

The operators' goal structures were manifested in their answers to why-questions when they performed specific actions during the benchmark tasks. As we discussed earlier, why-questions are well suited to exposing the goal hierarchies that underlie organized behavior. We discovered that the goal structures of some of the operators were inadequate. Sometimes critical goals were missing. Alternatively, the goals were not adequately structured so the operator did not understand how certain tasks were interrelated.

The help facilities could be designed to educate the operator on the critical goals and goal organization. At the global level, the touch panel screen could present a tree structure diagram with the major goals and tasks. At the local level, a goal structure could be presented when the operator seeks help on a specific task. Information about the goals could also be transmitted through the prompts and banners on the touch panel screen during normal operation.

FINAL COMMENTS

We are convinced that cognitive engineers have a wealth of powerful and practical tools for serious participation in the design of system-operator interfaces. However, many of the important tools at our disposal do not bear a close resemblance to the standard experimental methods that cognitive psychologists have embraced in the past. The typical cognitive psychologist does not construct state transition networks and simulate performance characteristics of alternative design configurations. The typical cognitive psychologist does not videotape human performance in naturalistic or quasi-naturalistic situations, occasionally probing the subjects with question-answering protocols and think-aloud protocols. Cognitive psychologists do not normally try to uncover the subjects' background knowledge about the topics that are relevant to the phenomenon under investigation. However, these are some of the methodological tools that are useful in applied research, at least in the context of interface design. Some psychologists will need to purchase a new set of tools when they move from cognitive psychology to cognitive engineering.

ACKNOWLEDGMENTS

The research reported in this chapter was funded by the Librascope Division of the Singer Corporation. We thank Richard Haugene, Patti Hopkinson, Tona Meyers, Keith Millis, David Shapiro, and Barbara Throckmorton for their assistance in transcribing and analyzing the data collected in this study. We also thank Robert Lang and John Good at Singer-Librascope for their guidance when we learned about the communication control system.

REFERENCES

Benbasat, I., & Wand, Y. (1984). Command abbreviation behavior in human-computer interaction. *Communications of the Association for Computing Machinery, 27,* 376–383.
Card, S. K., Moran, T. P., & Newell, A. (1983). *The psychology of human-computer interaction.* Hillsdale, NJ: Lawrence Erlbaum Associates.

Carroll, J. M., & Carrithers, C. (1984). Blocking learning error states in a training wheels system. *Human Factors, 26,* 377–391.

Duchnicky, R. L., & Kolers, P. A. (1983). Readability of text scrolled on visual display terminals as a function of window size. *Human Factors, 25,* 683–692.

Ehrenreich, S., & Porcu, T. A. (1982). Abbreviations for automated systems: Teaching operators the rules. In A. N. Badre & B. Schneiderman (Eds.), *Directions in human/computer interaction* (pp. 111–136). Norwood, NJ: Ablex.

Embley, D. W., & Nagy, G. (1981). Behavioral aspects of text editors. *ACM Computing Surveys, 13.*

Gentner, D., & Stevens, A. L. (Eds.) (1983). *Mental models.* Hillsdale, NJ: Lawrence Erlbaum Associates.

Graesser, A. C., & Clark, L. F. (1985). *Structures and procedures of implicit knowledge.* Norwood, NJ: Ablex.

Graesser, A. C., & Murachver, T. (1985). Symbolic procedures of question answering. In A. C. Graesser & J. B. Black (Eds.), *The psychology of questions* (pp. 15–88). Hillsdale, NJ: Lawrence Erlbaum Associates.

Graesser, A. C., & Murray, K. (in press). A question answering methodology for exploring a user's acquisition and knowledge of a computer environment. In S. P. Robertson & J. B. Black (Eds.), *Cognition, computing, and interaction.* Norwood, NJ: Ablex.

Houghton, R. C. (1984). On-line help systems: A conspectus. *Proceedings of the Association for Computing Machinery, 27,* 126–133.

Jacob, R. J. K. (1983). Using formal specifications in the design of human-computer interface. *Communications of the Association for Computing Machinery, 26,* 259–264.

Kruk, R. S., & Muter, P. (1983). Reading of continuous text on video screens. *Human Factors, 26,* 339–346.

Landauer, T. K., Galotti, K. M., & Hartwell, S. (1983). Natural command names and initial learning: A study of text-editing terms. *Communications of the ACM, 26,* 495–503.

Long, J., Whitefield, A., & Dennett, J. (1984). The effect of display format on the direct entry of numerical information by pointing. *Human Factors, 26,* 3–17.

Mack, R. L., Lewis, C. H., & Carroll, J. M. (1983). Learning to use word processors: Problems and prospects. *ACM Transaction on Office Information Processing, 1,* 254–271.

Mayer, R. E. (1975). Different problem solving competencies established in learning computer programming with and without meaningful models. *Journal of Educational Psychology, 67,* 725–734.

Miller, W., & Suther, T. W. (1983). Display station anthropometrics: Preferred height and angle settings of the CRT and Keyboard. *Human Factors, 25,* 401–408.

Monk, A. (Ed.) (1984). *Fundamentals of human-computer interaction.* New York: Academic Press.

Morland, D. V. (1983). Human factors guidelines for the terminal interface design. *Communications of the ACM, 26,* 284–294.

Neal, A. S., & Darnell, M. J. (1984). Text-editing performance with partial-line, partial-page, and full-page displays. *Human Factors, 26,* 431–442.

Norman, D. A. (1981). Categorization of action slips. *Psychological Review, 88,* 1–15.

Norman, D. A. (1983). Design rules based on analyses of human error. *Communications of the ACM, 26,* 254–258.

Norman, D. A., & Fisher, D. (1982). Why alphabet keyboards are not easy to use: Keyboard layout doesn't much matter. *Human Factors, 24,* 509–519.

Reid, P. (1984). Work station design, activities, and display techniques. In A. Monk (Ed.), *Fundamentals of human-computer interaction* (pp. 107–126). New York: Academic Press.

Roberts, T. L., & Moran, T. P. (1982). Evaluation of text editors. *Proceedings of the Conference on Human Factors in Computer Systems,* Gaithersburg, MD.

Rogers, W. H., & Moeller, G. (1984). Comparison of abbreviation methods: Measures of preferences and decoding performance. *Human Factors, 26,* 49–59.

Rouse, W. B., & Rouse, S. H. (1983). Analysis and classification of human error. *IEEE Transactions on System-Man Cybernetics, 13,* 539–549.

Shneiderman, B. (1982). System message design: Guidelines and experimental results. In A. Badre & B. Shneiderman (Eds.), *Directions in human-computer interaction* (pp. 55–78). Norwood, NJ: Ablex.

Tullis, T. S. (1983). The formatting of alphanumeric displays: A review and an analysis. *Human Factors, 25,* 657–682.

Wickens, C. D., & Kramer, A. (1985). Engineering psychology. *Annual Review of Psychology, 36,* 307–349.

Williges, R. C., & Williges, B. H. (1982). Modeling the human operator in computer-based data entry. *Human Factors, 24,* 285–300.

Woodson, W. E. (1981). *Human factors design handbook.* New York: McGraw-Hill.

13

Developing Computer Tools to Support Performing and Learning Complex Cognitive Skills

David McArthur
Rand Corporation

ABSTRACT

The main aim of this paper is to demonstrate that new and highly effective computer-based learning tools can be designed by adhering to a simple principle: Good learning tools conform to and support the processes and structures that comprise learning. I first discuss the processes involved in learning cognitive skills, then describe several software tools that support and facilitate these skills. The examples I discuss are drawn from learning problem-solving skills in high school algebra, and learning how to play the strategic board game of Go. Although some of the tools described embed considerable complex intelligence, many are relatively simple to implement and are easily within the current state of the art of computer hardware and software.

INTRODUCTION

The computer is a demanding tool. Unlike most pieces of technology it has no single purpose, and because it can be used in so many ways, it can be badly misused. Educational applications of computers are a good case in point. Most educational software does a poor job of helping us learn, and many of the programs that do have educational value do not effectively exploit the computer medium. They embed teaching techniques developed in and for a pencil-and-paper educational environment. The mindless translation of educational materials from traditional media to the computer is especially unfortunate because computers have the potential to be much better learning tools than pencil and paper. To begin to develop outstanding educational software we must stop using past techniques as a guide, and having thrown away the old guides, we must find new principles to follow.

The main aim of this paper is to indicate some new guiding principles, and to show that, using them, it is now possible to design very useful and novel learning tools that exploit unique properties of the computer medium. The paper discusses examples of how computers can provide *interactive practice tools* for the development of complex cognitive skills. The examples illustrate that many practice environments are easily within the current state of the art of hardware and software. The tools described obtain their leverage not only through complex, intelligent software, but also through simple software intelligently conforming to, and guided by, the *processes* and *structure* behind *cognitive skills.*

LEARNING THROUGH PRACTICE

Cognitive skills, like how to speak, play chess, or solve algebra problems, can only be learned well by practicing them. To improve our speech we make utterances, to improve our chess we play games, to improve our algebra we solve problems. Clearly, to aid in the learning of cognitive skills we need effective practice environments. Unfortunately, most traditional and computer-based environments do not promote rapid learning through practice. The main reason we possess few good learning aids is that we have few principles to guide us in the development of educational aids. The wisdom of hindsight, more than foresight, tells us why some educational experiments failed (e.g., the "new math"). We need principles that will act as criteria for the design of educational tools and that will allow us to understand *in advance* why one kind of aid would be more effective than another.

One principle I suggest is that the design of learning aids should be based on an understanding of how people perform cognitive skills and how they learn from practice. This principle should not be controversial. It is accepted that tools aiding the performance of a mechanical skill (e.g., building a table) facilitate the specific component activities or processes of the skill (e.g., T-squares make it easier to get right-angled corners). Once we accept the idea that cognitive skills, analogous to mechanical skills, comprise specific information processing steps, then referring to educational aids as tools ceases to be an idle metaphor. Educational materials should be viewed as tools that aid the performance of cognitive skills precisely because, to be successful, they should facilitate the component activities that make up the skill.

Learning through practice is itself a cognitive skill. Consequently, learning tools should not just be designed to help practice as an undifferentiated whole; they should facilitate the particular information processing activities that we know contribute to learning cognitive skills. Brown (1984) has also noted the importance of tailoring software aids to the cognitive processes of the user, and

Shavelson (1981), among others, has pointed out several contributions of cognitive research to the teaching and learning of mathematics.

Until recently we have not been able to put this principle into operation because the processes behind the practice and learning of cognitive skills have been a mystery. In the past decade, however, work in cognitive psychology and artificial intelligence on *learning-by-doing* has produced parts of a formal theory of how students might learn through practice (Anderson, 1982; Brown & Burton, 1978; Brown & Van Lehn, 1980). This theory is still fragmentary, and developing a more complete theory of learning through practice remains a high priority task in designing an environment for learning cognitive skills. But it is not necessary to wait for a fully mature theory before beginning to develop useful tools to support learning. A modest consensus picture of learning through practice is beginning to emerge. I believe that keeping in mind just a few of these consensus, "commonsense," notions of learning through practice will enable us to design some surprisingly powerful educational aids.

These notions should assist in creating and evaluating educational tools developed for any medium; however, they should be especially useful in helping us to develop educational software. Because the computer is potentially a reactive and interactive medium, it is in a unique position to support the processes associated with learning and performing cognitive skills. In the next section I describe the basic processes of learning through practice, mentioning especially where they become difficult and go astray. The following sections discuss a variety of computer-based education tools that students can use to simplify learning processes.

A Commonsense View of Learning Through Practice

Common sense tells us that learning a complex skill through practice is a cyclic process that begins when the student is given a *task* or *problem,* and uses his or her formative *knowledge* of the skill to produce a line of *reasoning* that gives an observable result or *answer.* Knowledge that contributes to an answer falls into one of two broad types. *Factual* knowledge encodes declarative information specific to the problem domain. *Planning knowledge* encodes information about how to use the factual truths of the domain in actually reasoning toward a task goal. Planning knowledge can include both general, domain-independent, problem-solving methods (e.g., heuristic search), and highly domain-specific reasoning techniques. Typically students already know general methods when they are first exposed to a domain, and initially use them to accomplish tasks. However, although these methods are general, they are also often weak and inefficient at producing solutions. This inefficiency motivates students to acquire less generally applicable methods that make problem solving much more rapid.

The student often selects and applies knowledge repeatedly to a task, each iteration yielding one or more reasoning steps. Once the student has exercised his formative skills and has given an answer (or a partial answer; he need not actually complete his reasoning before deciding he is on the wrong track), he needs to collect information that will allow him to *diagnose* success or failure. Diagnosis goes well beyond simply determining whether the student is wrong or right. If students cannot quickly determine *why* they were wrong (or inefficient) they have little chance to improve their knowledge. Therefore, the process of diagnosis involves *detecting* the specific reasoning step(s) in error, and thus the piece(s) of knowledge that caused an overt mistake, amongst all the knowledge used in reasoning. If the student's answer is correct, diagnosis, if done at all, takes on the character of a review of the formative knowledge that has contributed to the answer.

The idealized steps the student takes up to this point are preparation for learning, but they do not accomplish it. These steps are the "practice" part of "learning through practice." The student would execute all, or most, of these steps even if she were only performing the skill (problem solving) and not attempting to learn at all. In the actual learning step, the student uses diagnostic information to attempt to *fix* parts of the knowledge that were used to generate an answer. If the student answers incorrectly, she usually focuses on trying to modify those *misconceptions* in factual or planning knowledge believed responsible for failure, so that on the next problem she will succeed. A variety of generalization or discrimination techniques may be used to effect the modifications (see e.g., Anderson, 1982; Dietterich & Michalski, 1981). A student who answers correctly may still use available diagnostic information to make her planning knowledge more efficient. Lines of reasoning that lead to dead ends can be examined for misconceptions, as can redundancies in the main solution line. Even an ideal solution line can yield improvements in knowledge, not by provoking misconceptions to be fixed so much as by helping *formative conceptions* to be solidified. For example, the student may compose sequences of rules (Anderson, 1982) into macro-operators, or may simply change the "strength" associated with rules or methods, so they are more likely to be chosen on future similar occasions.

As a concrete example of this abstract cycle, consider the student learning algebra by doing homework problems. The student's task is to solve the next problem in the book. His formative knowledge of algebra includes an understanding of algebra transformation rules (e.g., axioms such as $x + y = y + x$) and algebra planning methods, beliefs about how to manipulate expressions in order to achieve algebra problem solving goals (e.g., "If there is more than one instance of the unknown in the equation, consider using transformation rules that collect" (Bundy & Welham, 1980). For each question, the student must decide which planning methods and transformation rules are relevant to the current expression, and apply that knowledge to produce one or several steps of mathematical reasoning. This process repeats until the reasoning chain produces an answer.

Once the student has exercised her algebra skills in this fashion, she may learn from the process. If the student sees the answer is incorrect, can isolate the faulty reasoning step, and can determine the specific misconception underneath the faulty step (e.g., a factual error might be the belief that $\sqrt{a + b} = \sqrt{a} + \sqrt{b}$), then she is in a position to modify the relevant algebra knowledge in a principled way. If the answer is correct, the student may still improve her algebra planning knowledge. The answer may contain extraneous steps that can be eliminated by more refined planning methods (e.g., One may refine the above selection heuristic, creating "If there is more than one instance of the unknown in the equation and the equation is of the form a $<$ variable $>$ + b $<$ variable $>$ . . . then consider using the Distributive rule for addition and multiplication"). An answer without such wasted steps can also result in improvements to knowledge. For example, students often learn to compose rules in algebra. Well-practiced axioms, like the commutativity of addition, become composed with other axioms; you rarely see two successive steps in a proof that differ only through the application of $x + y = y + x$.

Why Learning Through Practice with Existing Tools is Often Ineffective

I think it is fair to say that people currently learn very slowly and inefficiently through practice. With even our modest characterization of learning we can begin to understand *why* it is so difficult. It is possible to isolate several specific points at which each of the major learning processes can go awry, and many reasons why a student may fail to learn from a particular practice task using existing educational tools. In turn, this understanding provides a basis for designing educational tools that better support those specific learning processes.

Consider the algebra student again. Both standard textbooks and programmed-learning systems may not elicit a high volume of student misconceptions or formative conceptions because they pose questions in a fixed sequence. It is haphazard, therefore, whether a given question will cause the student to *exercise* any mistaken or weak beliefs. Questions that only elicit well-practiced knowledge rarely lead to significant learning.

Even if a question elicits suspect conceptions, the student may fail to perform an adequate *diagnosis*, or *detect* the conception causing an incorrect response. For example, a question can elicit a mistaken belief that accidentally produces the correct answer; or it may cause multiple suspect misconceptions to be exercised, obscuring the actual mistaken one. Students may also fail to detect errors because traditional teaching methods delay information critical for diagnosis. Diagnostic processes work most effectively when critical information is available at the time of reasoning. If the student does a question one day, and is not told the answer is wrong until the next day (i.e., the teacher grades and returns the homework), he may have forgotten the reasoning that led to the mistake. Unless the student is now able and willing to painstakingly reconstruct his reasoning, he will have lost any chance to detect reasoning errors. Finally, questions that do expose misconceptions may do so inefficiently. One observes, for example, that much of the time students spend answering many questions is actually spent making slips, losing track of where they are, regaining a line of thought, or practicing well-learned operations, not focusing on weak ones.

Once the student has invested the time to detect a mistaken belief, his effort may still be wasted because the sparse feedback provided by a textbook (usually they only give the correct answer) often fails to provide the required support to help the student correctly *fix* mistaken beliefs. Telling the student he is incorrect when he says $\sqrt{16 + 4} = 6$ may be enough to cause him to discard the belief $\sqrt{a + b} = \sqrt{a} + \sqrt{b}$. However, often the correct modification is not to throw out a belief, but to alter it slightly, or add a new transformation rule. For example, assume the student has the following mistaken belief about "cross multiplication": $\frac{e_1}{e_2} + \frac{e_3}{e_4} = e_5 \equiv e_1 e_4 + e_3 e_2 = e_5$ (where e_1 denotes any expression). If a question exposes this error to the student we would like a tutor to ensure that he does not simply eliminate the belief, but instead modifies it slightly to: $\frac{e_1}{e_2} + \frac{e_3}{e_4} = e_5 \equiv e_1 e_4 + e_3 e_2 = e_5 e_2 e_4$. Simply telling the student his answer is correct or incorrect is rarely adequate support to successfully accomplish this change. Such sparse feedback is even less useful in the case where a student makes an error because he does not believe a certain valid transformation rule, rather than because he does believe an invalid rule. If a student does not know trigonometric identities such as $\sin(x) = y \equiv \text{ARCSIN}(y) = x$, saying he is wrong on questions requiring the use of these tautologies gives no information. The student will repeatedly make the same mistake.

Goals of Tools for Learning Through Practice

Our analysis indicates that learning through practice comprises several major processes that are difficult for students to complete successfully by themselves. Further, if any of the component processes fail, students are unlikely to learn anything from the task or question at hand. This analysis, coupled with insight into how existing educational aids fail to facilitate learning processes, suggests many goals for designing new tools. A few of them are:

- Maximizing the student's opportunity to exercise formative and flawed conceptions.
- Helping the student detect and diagnose the misconceptions that contribute to any sub-optimal performance, especially by providing immediate feedback information. The misconceptions include both flaws and omissions in planning knowledge, and flaws and omissions in knowledge of domain facts.
- Helping the student fix misconceptions, once they have been detected and characterized.

- Helping the student strengthen and make more efficient (e.g., by composing operations) correct but formative conceptions that have been exercised.

In the following sections I discuss examples of tools that fulfill some of these goals. The examples are by no means exhaustive; instead, they are meant to suggest the wide range of relatively simple solutions that are possible.

LEARNING TOOLS THAT HELP EXERCISE FORMATIVE AND FLAWED CONCEPTIONS

A first obvious step is to develop facilities to elicit and exercise more misconceptions and formative conceptions. Each question or task provides an opportunity to improve a facet of a complex cognitive skill only if we use that facet in arriving at an answer, and only if that facet has some weakness or flaw. One technique, therefore, would be to consistently provide tasks that are challenging for the student, ones that are likely to elicit flawed or formative conceptions. All good human tutors, whether in chess or algebra, try to pick problems at the student's level, for just this reason.

This sort of tailoring, however, is difficult for humans to do, and even more difficult to build into an automated tutoring environment. It requires the tutor to maintain a *student model,* a structure that represents the tutor's idea of formative knowledge of the student at a point in time. Although recent research in artificial intelligence has improved our ability to build student models (Burton & Brown, 1982; London & Clancey, 1982; Sleeman, 1982; Sleeman & Smith, 1981), there is currently no strong theory of how to rapidly and accurately induce such models from the student's overt performances. This research should be continued to the point where we can build tutors that are highly skilled at building student models. However, while pursuing this goal, we should not lose sight of the fact that it now is possible to design useful learning aids that are within the current state of the art.

Although it is difficult to elicit misconceptions by intelligently guiding students through questions that will exercise weaknesses in their formative knowledge, it is relatively easy to help them by making their own self-guided search more efficient. Specifically, a simpler approach to eliciting a higher volume of student misconceptions is to increase the rate at which students do questions or, more accurately, the speed with which they perform the reasoning steps that lead to an answer. If students can reason more conveniently, they can do more tasks in a given time, and should thus encounter more of their formative and erroneous conceptions.

One way to make reasoning more convenient and rapid is to provide the student with an assistant who can take care of the more mundane details of solving a problem, letting the student focus on the harder parts—the parts from

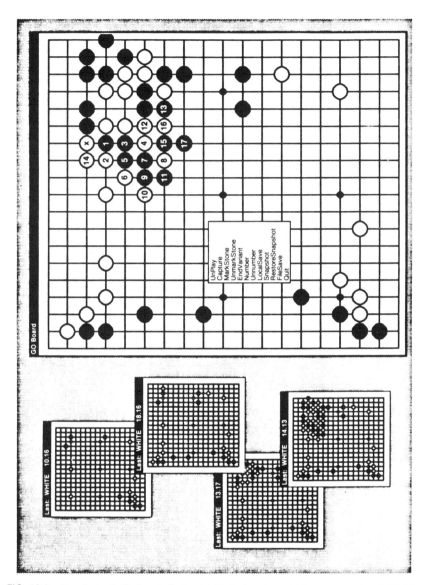

FIG. 13.1. The electronic Go board. To the right is the board on which games are played. Clicking the left mouse button on a location puts a black stone there; clicking the middle button puts a white stone at the location. The right mouse button brings up the menu shown in the center. Many of the options in the menu are explained in the text. To the left are several game icons. The positions they contain can be restored to the main board at any time.

which he or she could potentially learn. In algebra, again, a student solving for w in $2(3w + 55) + 2w = 870$ might go through the following reasoning steps: do the algebraic multiplication $[2(3w) + 2(55) + 2w = 870]$; do the numeric multiplication $[6w + 110 + 2w = 870]$; do the additions $[8w + 110 = 870]$; do the movement of terms $[8w = 760]$; and, finally, do the division $[w = 95]$. If the student is already an expert in numeric computations and is now practicing symbolic multiplication skills, only the first and second of these steps are germane to the *point* of the question. He or she can only exercise formative knowledge and acquire new knowledge on these steps. The rest of the steps exercise well-practiced skills; hence, much of the time spent answering the question does not contribute to learning. Worse still, if the student makes a slip in these well-learned steps, it may obscure a mistake in the first steps, thus taking away any chance at all of learning from the question. An automated assistant could alleviate these problems by doing the unimportant details of problem solving. A student interacting with a computerized algebra environment could construct the first steps of the solution, then select a mouse button, or menu item, to tell the assistant to "do the rest," or even "do until the next interesting step."

Although such an assistant would not have to maintain a complete model of the student, it would need to be an "algebra expert system." The assistant would need to know how to solve algebra problems from any point at which the student might want to stop. Fortunately, this technology, unlike student modeling, is within reach today. There are several programs (e.g., REDUCE and MAC-SYMA) that are very competent algebraists. It is relatively simple to interface them to a simple assistant who would pass them the equation left by the student and possibly some instructions about the form of the required result. GED is a graphical algebra editor that provides such a capability (McArthur, 1985). It is part of our ongoing project to develop an intelligent tutor for algebra, some aspects of which I discuss below.

Learning Tools with Limited Intelligence

Even a tool with no particular general or domain-specific expertise can provide significant learning aids. Consider an electronic Go board like the one shown in Fig. 13.1. Go is a complex game of strategy like chess. One player is black, the other white, and they alternate placing circular "stones" on the intersections of a 19×19 board. The electronic Go environment is not a Go playing program; it knows nothing about Go, or about students of Go. It only provides a way of allowing users to play stones (users select the intersection they want to play on by pointing and touching a mouse button) and a menu of options. The options, however, make the electronic Go board a much more powerful learning environment than a traditional Go board.

The LOCALSAVE and FILESAVE menu options allow the Go student to record and recall any game he or she wishes. The student therefore does not need to waste time setting up game situations to learn from. More important, the MARKSTONE, NUMBER and ENDVARIANT options provide the student with a simple but powerful facility for exploring alternate lines of play. At any time, the student can number the stones in the order played, market one of the stones, then request that all stones played after the marked one be removed. He or she can therefore rapidly back up and try another alternative. The SNAPSHOT and RESTORESNAPSHOT options provide similar functionality. Using them, the student can take a "picture" of any interesting game situation, like the ones on the left side of Fig. 13.1, then recall these alternatives at any future time by simply pointing.

In the traditional gaming environment, this sort of learning by exploring alternatives is almost impossible. In the electronic Go environment, however, trying out many alternative hypotheses and exercising many pieces of formative Go knowledge is both low-cost (it takes almost no time) and high-safety (by trying new lines the student does not risk losing old, perhaps better, lines; they can be recalled at any time). The simple electronic Go board *encourages* the student to rapidly try out a wide range of skills, both well learned and formative.

The ability to explore a wide range of hypotheses is an important way to exercise misconceptions and learn in many areas. In most cases, creating an environment that encourages this activity is no more difficult than it was for Go. For example, a simple graphical interface, called GED (McArthur, 1985), provides this functionality for algebra. Figure 13.2 shows a student interacting with GED.

GED consists of several windows. The middle-left window is a workspace in which the student transforms algebraic expressions that represent problems he or she has been given. The lower-left window contains menus that effect the transformations. All transformations are done by pointing at and marking pieces of expressions in the workspace, then selecting an operation in the menu. To the right of the workspace is a commentspace window that displays textual feedback from the tutor to the student. We attempt to keep its use to a minimum. More important for our present purposes is the top window, or displayspace. This window contains a *reasoning tree*, recording all the reasoning steps the student has taken in attempting to solve a problem. The empty box at the bottom of one of the lines or branches represents the current *problem focus*. When the student completes the current reasoning step, by modifying the equation in the workspace, he or she will select NEW STEP on the lower-right options menu. This option will cause the current workspace expression to fill the empty box, and a new box will sprout below. The options menu contains a number of items that allow the student to effectively manipulate expressions and to communicate with the tutor. Not all the options are yet functional, but we discuss several of the working items below.

The reasoning tree is analogous to the linear list of equations the student traditionally writes in a notebook. However, together with the options menu, the reasoning tree provides a much more powerful tool for supporting algebraic learning than the traditional pencil-and-paper medium. If the student decides the current solution line is not profitable, or just wants to investigate a new line of attack on the problem, he or she selects GO BACK on the options menu. GED will then ask which solution expression in the displayspace the student wants to now be the problem focus. The student responds by using a mouse to point to any expression in the reasoning tree and selects it by clicking one of the mouse buttons. This expression then becomes the current expression in the workspace, and in the

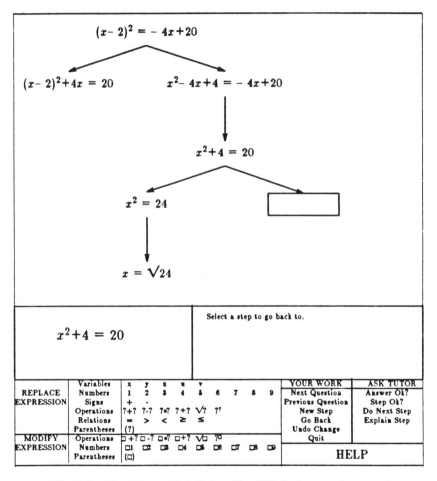

FIG. 13.2. The GED graphical display. The GED display comprises several windows. The top window, or displayspace, records the student's problem solving in the form of a reasoning tree. Below the displayspace is the workspace, where the student actually transforms the current expression to arrive at a new one, and a commentspace for textual feedback. The lower band of windows are menus. The student uses the selections from the left menu to edit or transform his current expression in the workplace. The options menu to the right allows the student and tutor to communicate about the problem.

displayspace it becomes the problem focus. A new empty box branches below the selected expression, creating a new solution line for the student to investigate. For example, in Fig. 13.2, having been told the answer ($x = \sqrt{24}$) is wrong, the student has just clicked on GO BACK, then selected the equation $x^2 + 4 = 20$. GED then rearranged the reasoning tree, adding a new branch, with an empty expression, at this point.

GED'S GO BACK option is just one of the ways it facilitates learning algebra. It provides a way for the student to try out problem-solving strategies efficiently. The traditional pencil-and-paper medium does not encourage this exploration and learning because it exacts a high cost to trying multiple solution lines. To try a new line, students must erase the old one, which they are reluctant to do because it is slow, and because they may forget the line, if they wish to return to it. Thus the traditional pencil-and-paper medium tacitly encourages the students to think of such changes as *mistakes to be avoided.* On the contrary, the ability to try out hypotheses rapidly, especially incorrect ones, is central to learning.

Although many aspects of GED, and our algebra tutor in which it is embedded, will contain sophisticated expertise, the previous facilities require only a bitmapped-display terminal and a generous amount of cheap memory. The tools obtain their leverage not through intelligent software, but through simple software intelligently conforming to the processes behind cognitive skills. The above tools try to simplify the processes of mathematical reasoning, in order to promote the use of formative and flawed algebraic knowledge. The process of mathematical reasoning has two important features for our purposes: It is a branching search through a space of possible mathematical transformations, and it is *nonlinear* in nature. Students will often want to change the focus of problem solving by pursuing one line of reasoning, suspending it, pursuing another, then returning to the first line. The GED editor obtains most of its strength as a learning tool by simply providing an external medium that reflects these properties. GED supplies a representation of reasoning steps that explicitly captures the tree-like results of the reasoning process and provides a mechanism that allows the student to externally change the focus of problem solving. GED is actually a medium in which you can *do* reasoning, unlike pencil-and-paper, which merely *records* reasoning.

LEARNING TOOLS THAT HELP DETECT AND FIX MISCONCEPTIONS

A student who makes a mistake is in a position to learn, but still has a long way to go before he or she can acquire knowledge from the current task. Providing supports that help students isolate and fix flawed and formative conceptions, or add an omitted conception to their knowledge, is just as important as providing tools to help elicit the misconception in the first place. As I have noted, the diagnosis and fixing of conceptual errors are the most difficult processes in learning through practice. Fortunately, although traditional educational media often do not aid these processes, interactive computer tools show great promise in doing so.

Again, many such tools would require the development of a highly intelligent, complex, system software, not only able to model the student, but also embedding a great deal of pedagogical expertise. Such expertise is necessary to decide when to intervene to help the student. You don't always interrupt students with advice when they make a mistake, or *only* when they make a mistake. Further, if you do interrupt the student, you must decide whether to do it immediately, or defer the interruption for a while. Finally, pedagogical expertise is necessary to determine what to say, once an interruption has occurred. As with student-modeling software, promising research has begun to formalize and test good pedagogical strategies (Brown, Burton, & de Kleer, 1982; Burton & Brown, 1982; Clancey, 1979); however, the development of a reliable tutor with such expertise is a long-term, not short-term goal. But, again, a variety of useful tools can be developed in the short term. Broadly, these tools take the form of *debugging* aids. They largely obviate the need for a sophisticated theory of when to stop the student and what to say, by leaving such decisions up to the student. Students are simply made aware of tools and invoke them at their discretion when they make a mistake or need help.

Consider again the task of the algebra student in Fig. 13.2 who has just answered the question incorrectly $(x = \sqrt{24})$. GED has encouraged the student to exercise much formative knowledge of algebra, but now, to learn from the task, she has to wade through all this easily generated reasoning to find the one step that hides a misconception. GED's options menu provides several tools that will help simplify this search. First, the STEP OK? menu item allows the student to ask the tutor if any step in the reasoning tree constitutes an appropriate mathematical transformation in the current context. The student selects STEP OK?, then points to any node in the reasoning tree. The REDUCE algebra expert system, which interfaces with GED, then says whether the step from the previous node to the selected one is acceptable. In critiquing the student's step, the tutor makes a distinction between steps that are mathematically invalid, and steps that are inappropriate. For example, in Fig. 13.2, the step from $(x - 2)^2 = -4x + 20$ to $(x - 2)^2 + 4x = 20$ is valid, but is inappropriate. It is not the one the algebra expert would choose, because it does not move the student closer to a solution. Thus, the student not only succeeds in isolating a faulty reasoning step, but also obtains a characterization of the misconception underlying the error. Invalid steps imply errors in knowledge of algebra transformation rules; inappropriate steps imply errors in algebra planning methods.

The student can use the STEP OK? operation any time he chooses. This freedom allows him to follow several problem-solving modes. For example, the student can proceed in "careful" mode, checking the appropriateness of each step as it is made, or at the other extreme, he can operate in "reckless" mode, creating reasoning steps until an answer is obtained that is obviously incorrect. The student then studies the reasoning tree, regarding it somewhat like an engineer regards a malfunctioning electronic circuit. The engineer may take voltage or current measurements at any point to isolate the fault; the algebra student uses STEP OK? to take "appropriateness" measurements, to isolate the misconception.

DO NEXT STEP is similar to STEP OK?. Although STEP OK? lets the student confirm the validity and appropriateness of a step, DO NEXT STEP lets the student ask the tutor to generate the next step that an expert algebra problem solver would take from the current problem focus. I have already discussed this option as a means of providing an assistant that could help the student exercise more formative knowledge of algebra by supplying the mundane steps of a solution, leaving only the hard ones for the student. However, it is useful in helping the student to detect misconceptions, as well as to exercise them. The most obvious way to help a student understand an error is to tell him about it, as STEP OK? does. This method is not the only one, nor necessarily the best one. For example, instead of telling the student about the error, one might show the *logical consequences* of continuing this line of reasoning, letting the student draw the appropriate conclusions, if the consequences appear absurd. By repeatedly applying DO NEXT STEP, the student can ask the tutor to provide such consequences at any point in the reasoning tree.

The immediate utility of STEP OK? and DO NEXT STEP are that they quickly allow the student to pinpoint a single reasoning error in a large tree of possibilities, and to characterize the misconception behind the faulty step. More generally, and perhaps more importantly, these activities teach the student that an important part of learning a cognitive skill is *learning to study your own reasoning processes*. A surprisingly few students understand that reasoning can be explicitly examined, let alone that it can be debugged or improved. For example, when students are asked why they do poorly on a mathematics test in grade school, common answers are "I'm dumb in math" (girls usually say this), or "I had a bad test," or "The test was unfair" (mainly coming from the boys). Very few identified specific knowledge that they might have lacked, or even understood that their correctable lack of knowledge might have been responsible for failure!

The ability to show students that their reasoning can be studied derives from GED's reasoning tree, which attempts to explicitly represent the process and structure of students' thinking. By externalizing students' reasoning process we impress upon them that it is a bona fide entity. Equally important, by providing students with ways of probing, querying, and commenting on the reasoning tree, we show them that the reasoning process is a manipulable, fixable entity. In addition, externalizing students' reasoning reduces memory load and makes it simpler for students to perform effective manipulations on their reasoning.

More Learning Tools with Limited Intelligence

Just as tools that do not rely on complex expertise can be developed to help students exercise misconceptions, similar simple tools can be developed to help students detect and fix those misconceptions. The electronic Go board, in Fig. 13.1, for example, provides the student with the ability to detect the logical consequences of moves without requiring a built-in Go "expert system." One of the best ways to learn Go, or any other complex game, is to replay experts' games, always trying to guess the next move. At each point where the student picks a wrong move (not the expert's) he or she should try to determine why the move was wrong and the expert's was right. This exercise provides the diagnostic information necessary for the student to fix the misconceptions responsible for deviations from the correct (expert's) line of play. Unless the expert is standing over the student's shoulder, the only reasonable way to understand the mistake is for the student to look at the consequences of a selection by playing out the line following from the move and to compare this result with the consequences following from the expert's move. Using a traditional Go board, this process is usually so tedious that most students rarely come to a good understanding of their mistakes. With the electronic Go board, on the other hand, it is so simple to play out lines and retract them that I personally find myself finally understanding 90% of experts' moves instead of less than 50%.

Similarly, we could easily extend GED to provide several sources of useful information about reasoning that do not rely on having access to algebra expertise. For example, we may implement a new menu option called SHOW ANSWER MATCHING, which will allow the student to access her solution tree for any past question, enabling her to visually compare the path previously taken, to the solution now being generated. A student solving a problem may transform an equation into a familiar form, but may forget how to deal with that form just now. For example, the current equation might be $(x + 8)(x + 2) = -10x$, and the student has done expansions before. If the student now selects the SHOW ANSWER MATCHING item, GED can search back as far as it needs in her past problem-solving history to find an expression of the form $(<variable> + <constant>)(<variable> + <constant>) = <constant>$. It will then display the reasoning tree that records how the student solved the matching problem. This example demonstrates that the student does not need to revert to an automated algebra expert to isolate a wrong step. She can do this isolation by comparing some past performance with the present buggy behavior.

The ability to rapidly recall previous performance and graphically compare it to present reasoning can have many diverse roles in learning. For example, the tutor should help strengthen formative conceptions as well as help fix misconceptions. One of the most important facets of such learning involves composing operations. It is well known that in many domains one of the main ways expert and novice problem solvers differ is that the former have *chunked* (Anderson, 1982; Chase & Simon, 1978) together operations that often follow one another in solving a problem. This composition results in complex schemas that the expert can automatically invoke when shown a new problem. This more structured knowledge not only lets the expert solve familiar problems more rapidly, but also allows the expert to identify and devote more time to reasoning about the non-standard aspects of more difficult problems. A major goal for a student learning a cognitive skill is, therefore, to identify which of the contiguous operations used in solving a problem should actually be composed, or remembered as a unit. The trouble is that not all contiguous operations can be usefully composed. The student needs to identify which operations have been *repeatedly* used together in correct solutions. An ideal way to simulate such learning would thus be to give the student a way of looking for *patterns of operations* in past problem solving. GED's complete record of the student's performance history and its graphical presentation of reasoning are ideal for this purpose. Not only is the student given all the information necessary to derive useful composition patterns, but the graphical presentation dramatically simplifies the student's job of searching the information and comparing lines. This tool, along with many other potentially useful ones, should be very simple to implement. All will rely on the complete audit trail of student editing activities that GED now retains. Such a record is trivial to maintain using an electronic algebra problem-solving medium, but impossible with the passive pencil-and-paper medium.

MOTIVATION AND LEARNING

Our discussion has ignored one important variable in learning. Obviously, techniques that increase the *motivation* of students will increase the rate at which cognitive skills are learned. Motivation seems to have a generally positive effect on all the important processes of learning cognitive skills. A highly motivated student works through more questions, and more rapidly, so will expose more of weak ideas and misconceptions. He will also spend more time doing the hard work of detecting and fixing misconceptions, even if no learning aids are available.

Considerable effort has recently gone into adding fantasy or "bells-and-whistles" features to educational software, in hope of heightening motivation. I have not emphasized these features for several reasons. First, although they certainly make learning more fun, these features have not been proved to make learning much better. Second, I believe that the sort of *responsive* and *reactive* learning tools outlined here themselves heighten motivation by appealing to important cognitive determinants of motivation.

Malone (1980) cites several such determinants of motivation, including a variable level of difficulty, multiple levels of goals, and the ability to control the environment. I believe another important cognitive determinant of motivation is *comprehensibility.* I feel a common classroom syndrome begins when otherwise average students miss key concepts in class and start to perform poorly. The students may not even be aware of why they are performing poorly, and rarely ask for help. Lack of success and failure to comprehend subsequent concepts cause the students to be less and less motivated to spend time solving problems, setting up a vicious circle. On the surface such students may appear simply not interested in mathematics. However, what they require is not merely to become more interested; they need an environment that will assist in identifying and overcoming their specific cognitive deficits and that will reduce their failure rates. In this respect, I believe the tools I have discussed can be highly motivating educational devices.

CONCLUSIONS

Computers have the potential to enhance the learning and doing of many cognitive skills, but have not yet lived up to that potential. Even the most successful computer software tools are not as useful as they could be. Text editors, for example, are just that; they provide aids for the processes of adding and moving text, but they do not provide significant tools to help the processes of writing papers or turning *thoughts into words.* (See Brown, 1984, for some ideas for tools along these lines.)

One line of thought, exemplified in artificial intelligence research, is that the way to make computers useful for learning is to develop computer tutors embedding vast amounts of human intelligence. Computer tutors are intended to capture much, if not all, of the functionality of human teachers, including the ability to inductively construct models of the student's reasoning processes, to guide the student through chosen questions and through the process of reasoning, and to carry out extensive natural-language dialogues with the student. Although this approach will ultimately lead to useful learning environments, I have argued that the development of simpler computer tools represents an equally effective approach. Unlike intelligent computer tutors, these computer tools do not actively guide the student through the large space of alternatives that must be considered. However, by conforming to the specific learning processes that students may have difficulty in completing successfully by themselves, these tools can make the student's self-guided search much more effective.

ACKNOWLEDGMENTS

The research reported here has been supported in part by the National Science Foundation (Applications of Advanced Technologies Program), Grant No. MDR-8470342.

REFERENCES

Anderson, J. R. (1982). Acquisition of cognitive skill. *Psychological Review, 89,* 369–406.

Brown, J. S. (1984). Process versus product: A perspective on tools for communal and information electronic learning. In *Education and the electronic age.* Proceedings of a conference sponsored by the Educational Broadcasting Company.

Brown, J. S., & Burton, R. R. (1978). Diagnostic models for procedural bugs in basic mathematical skills. *Cognitive Science, 2,* 155–192.

Brown, J. S., Burton, R. R., & de Kleer, J. (1982). Knowledge engineering and pedagogical techniques in SOPHIE I, II, and III. In D. H. Sleeman & J. S. Brown (Eds.), *Intelligent tutoring systems* (pp. 227–282). London: Academic Press.

Brown, J. S., & Van Lehn, K. (1980). Repair theory: A generative theory of bugs in procedural skills. *Cognitive Science, 4,* 379–426.

Bundy, A., & Welham, B. (1980). Using meta-level inference for selective application of multiple rewrite rule sets in algebraic manipulation. *Artificial Intelligence, 16,* 189–211.

Burton, R. R., & Brown, J. S. (1982). An investigation of computer coaching. In D. H. Sleeman & J. S. Brown (Eds.), *Intelligent tutoring systems* (pp. 79–98). London: Academic Press.

Chase, W. G., & Simon, H. A. (1978). Perception in chess. *Cognitive Psychology, 4,* 55–81.

Clancey, W. J. (1979). Tutoring rules for guiding a case method dialogue. *International Journal of Man-Machine Studies, 11,* 25–49.

Dietterich, T. G., & Michalski, R. S. (1981). Inductive learning of structural descriptions: Evaluation criteria and comparative review of selected methods. *Artificial Intelligence, 16,* 257–294.

London, B., & Clancey, W. J. (1982). Plan recognition strategies in student modeling: Prediction and description. In *Proceedings of the 1982 National Conference on Artificial Intelligence* (pp. 335–338).

Malone, T. W. (1980). *What makes things fun to learn? A study of intrinsically motivating computer games.* Xerox Cognitive And Instructional Series Report CIS-7 (SSL-80-11).

McArthur, D. (1985). GED: An easy-to-learn graphical editor for algebraic expressions. In preparation.

Shavelson, R. J. (1981). Teaching mathematics: Some contributions of cognitive research. *Educational Psychologist, 16,* 23–44.

Sleeman, D. H. (1982). Assessing aspects of competence in algebra. In D. H. Sleeman & J. S. Brown (Eds.), *Intelligent tutoring systems* (pp. 185–200). London: Academic Press.

Sleeman, D. H., & Smith, M. J. (1981). Modeling student's problem solving. *Artificial Intelligence, 16,* 171–187.

14

An Evaluation Model of Chinese Graphemic Input Systems

Sheng-Ping Fang
National Tsing Hua University, Taiwan

Ovid J. L. Tzeng
University of California, Riverside
The Salk Institute, San Diego

ABSTRACT

Due to its enormous number of distinctive logographs to be processed in a text, designing a "user friendly" system for the input of Chinese characters directly into computers is a challenge to both computer engineers and cognitive psychologists. This chapter examines problems encountered in the design of a graphemic input system for the Chinese writings. From knowledge accumulated over decades of research on human information processing, we tentatively propose a set of criteria to serve as an evaluation model for a graphemic input system. It is hoped that such a model can serve not only the function of evaluation but also that of diagnosis.

In their recent trip to Hong Kong, Drs. Ursula Bellugi and Edward Klima of the Salk Institute at San Diego made an interesting observation. They went to a local shop where hundreds of minicalculators were on display. They purchased several electronic items and were ready to pay. To their amazement, the owner of the shop was busy computing the total cost (i.e., adding up listed price on each item and subtracting the discount amount from the total) with a wooden abacus despite the modern electronic devices abundant in the shop.

Their experience is certainly not a unique one. In Taiwan where most of the world's computer chips are made, one can hardly find any large-scale application of the computer in everyday business. Even in the banking business, the use of computers is usually limited to number crunching, and word processing in Chinese is totally out of the question. It looks as if the wind of "the computer age" has never blown over the island where, ironically, millions of dollars worth of computer hardware boards and peripheral devices are exported daily. Why are the Chinese people immune to the computer fever that has been epidemic in other parts of the world? Many scholars and computer scientists blame it on the Chinese writing system in which thousands of distinctive logographs are required for printing everyday newspapers. Indeed, there is new urgency among the advocates of change to an alphabetical system (see Fang & Tzeng, in press, for a review).

However, there are other investigators who have decided to try an alternative approach in order to preserve the logographic system. Instead of alphabetizing the writing system, they are searching for a set of parsing rules that enable them to *alphabetize* or *digitize* each individual character. Such attempts have had some success as we shall see, but all such graphic recoding systems require the user to master a large set of usually arbitrary rules. The seemingly pure engineering research problems thus become psychological ones. It is now clear that for the sake of putting together a "user-friendly" machine, one has not only to look for a good hardware design for the graphic input system, but also, and probably much more important, to worry about a psychologically feasible program for the training of operators.

In this chapter, we first address the problems encountered in the design of a graphemic input system for the Chinese language and then review three major representative approaches to their solutions. Finally, from knowledge accumulated over decades of research on human information processing, we propose a set of criteria to serve as an evaluation model for a graphemic system for Chinese computers. It is hoped that such a model can serve not only the function of evaluation but also that of diagnosis. That is, we hope this model can help us determine the strong points and the weak points of a given input system in addition to its relative efficiency in comparison with other systems.

THE PROBLEM OF CHINESE INPUT SYSTEMS

Why do we need an evaluation model for Chinese graphemic input systems? Let us first examine briefly the problems of designing a Chinese input system, whether graphemic or phonetic, in general. A modern Chinese who tries to develop a computer input method for Chinese characters will encounter the same kind of difficulties as his ancestors did in designing an indexing system for a dictionary. The nature of the difficulties becomes clear when we consider the relationship between the structure of scripts and the efficiency of encoding. Take an alphabetic writing system such as English as an example. The formation of a word or a text is a linear arrangement of letters and blanks in a specific serial order. The code of any word is best defined by its spelling. The one-to-one relationship between a word of a text and its corresponding code is very obvious. Based upon this coding uniqueness and the well-established alphabetic order, the rule of lexicographical ordering for a dictionary is very natural and clear. The merit of the alphabetic ordering is further displayed in typewriting and computer operation. Anyone who knows how to spell can locate a word in a dictionary, can use a typewriter, and can create a file in the computer without further learning of coding methods.

However, this type of straightforward script-codes relation is lacking in Chinese. Simply knowing the pronunciation of a given character may not suffice for an unambiguous retrieval of that character, for there can be many homophones for a particular syllable. The problem of homophones can be and has been solved to a reasonable extent (e.g., Becker, 1983; Chang, Chiu, Yang, & Lin, 1973), allowing the phonetic systems to handle everyday typing. Nevertheless, the phonetic systems become useless in processing characters whose pronunciation is unknown to the user. Such characters might be rare in everyday writing, but are numerous in ancient writings, proper names, and geographical names. In order to gain computer aids in studies of Chinese classics and archaic Chinese, one must find means to encode the characters graphemically. However, the positioning of the constituent strokes of a character is so irregular that one has to learn encoding rules beyond one's existing graphemic knowledge to be able to encode graphemically. The nature of the encoding rules thus determines the efficiency of the coding method.

Although dozens of Chinese graphemic input systems have been developed by independent laboratories, the progress in such systems has been slowed by the lack of an adequate evaluation model. A major reason for this lack is that computer engineers tend to be unaware of the problems concerning human information processing, and they have not developed standard procedures for evaluating how well people can use their products. As a result, there is no empirical basis to support the common claim that any specific system is the most *efficient*. Often, new systems are presented that fail to use experience gained from earlier systems. There has consequently been a tremendous waste of time, money, and many other forms of resources. Occasionally, calls for an evaluation model have come from academic institutes (Shen & Sun, 1984; Yamada, 1983). Unfortunately, attempts to incorporate testing from a psychological perspective have had little impact on the computer industry.

Several recent developments promise to bring a change in attitude toward psychological research. First, a revival of research interest in visual information processing in reading produced some useful experimental results on basic processes in word or character perception (see Hung & Tzeng, 1981, for a review).

Second, a recent series of international conferences on the psychological studes of the Chinese language have resulted in publications (e.g., Kao & Cheng, 1982; Kao & Hoosain, 1984) that have caught the attention of professors of engineers interested in training programs for computer operators (Shen & Sun, 1984). Third and perhaps the most important, the growing availability of personal computers creates a demand for word processing software that could be used by nonspecialists. In the past, Chinese computers were assumed to be used solely by trained operators whose job was to input a text or program usually written by persons other than themselves. Now the demand for efficient word processing capability in a personal computer has put a high priority on development of an input system with a coding scheme that can be learned easily by everyone literate in Chinese.

These developments have forced the computer industry to take psychological studies on human information processing more seriously. A set of objective criteria must be established for the evaluation of graphemic input systems. But before we can consider such criteria, we need to know what approaches have been proposed to overcome the coding difficulties in designing a Chinese input system mentioned previously.

THREE GRAPHEMIC INPUT METHODS
FOR CHINESE CHARACTERS

Existing graphemic input systems can be classified into at least three categories (Fang & Tzeng, in press):

1. *The whole-character approach.* The keyboard contains thousands of characters, and the user inputs a character by directly pressing the corresponding key. This approach represents the first generation of Chinese typewriters and is apparently not suitable for the speedy input demanded by modern computers. It is mentioned here merely for the purpose of a historical note.

2. *The alphabetization approach.* According to Caldwell (1959), Chinese has an "alphabet" in the sense that all Chinese characters are written by selecting strokes from a small set of basic strokes. Chinese has a "spelling" in the sense that a sequence of strokes used in writing a given character is largely invariant. The alphabetization approach redefines the orthographical rules and arranges strokes in a serial form. In order to shorten the input string and to increase the input speed, the alphabetization systems usually *selectively* encode part of the character, instead of the complete character, and adopt common radicals, instead of basic strokes, as the spelling units.

A good example of alphabetization approach is the so-called *Cangjie* (倉頡) *system* originally developed by the Giantek Technology Corporation of Taiwan. The essence of the system is to distill all radical and phonetic components of Chinese characters into just 24 basic radicals, a number that can be easily handled by a conventional English typewriter keyboard. The user inputs a character by first decomposing it into between one and five basic radicals and then types these Cangjie codes on the keyboard to call up the appropriate character on screen. This system is currently very popular because it can be easily implemented in both IBM PC and APPLE II microcomputers. However, upon closer examination, the system is both cumbersome and arbitrary: It requires the user to know not only how to recognize variant forms of the 24 basic radicals, but also how to decide which components of the original character must be encoded with the basic radicals and which components of the character should be ignored and not encoded. As Bauer (1985), a Chinese linguist who has had a year's experience with the system, succinctly puts it, "In other words, one almost has to memorize the individual Cangjie code for every character in order to use this system efficiently" (p. 349).

3. *The digitalization approach.*   This approach is similar to the alphabetization approach except that it completely ignores the temporal relations between strokes and makes only a spatial analysis. The necessity of keyboard training is minimal in the digitalization approach since it requires only 10 numerical keys. One of the most advertised digitalization methods is the three-corner coding method (Hu, Chang, & Huang, 1978). Because this method exemplifies most of the characteristic operating stages involved in graphemic input systems, we will describe it in more detail for the sake of our later discussions.

The three-corner coding method requires analysis of features in the corners of a given character. The sequence of analysis is generally from the upper left to the upper right then from the lower left to the lower right. A maximum of three corners needs to be coded. Each corner is coded as two digits and each character is represented with six digits. This method is to provide a consistent means of digitalization that will reduce the problem of *coding collision* (i.e., assigning the same code to two or more different characters) to a minimum. The cost is that the difficulty of the input process has increased. Figure 14.1 shows 300 features grouped into 99 sets. Features in the same set share a two-digit code. The pairing between the features and the codes and between equivalent features is largely arbitrary, although the assignment of codes somewhat follows a mnemonic scheme. For example, features whose code starts with 0 (i.e., 01 to 09) usually have a⌐on the top, and features whose code starts with 6 (i.e., 60 to 69) usually contain a square. Seven principles of corner selection and eight principles of feature selection are adopted in this system.

基 本 符 號 總 表

	0	1	2	3	4	5	6	7	8	9
0	00 一	01 亠	02 卜	03 广 厂	04 文 夊夂	05 亦	06 言	07 方	08 立 产辛	09 穴 礻ネ宀
1	10 一	11 一	12 工	13 丁 雨	14 勹 刀頁	15 王 王王	16 石 阝卩	17 乙	18 西 覀西	19 示 礻示禾
2	20 丨	21 止	22 止	23 亻	24 隹	25 隹	26 牛 生生	27 厂 月	28 欠	29 禾 禾禾禾
3	30 丿	31 土	32 丶	33 冫	34 冫 水氷	35 灬 灬魚	36 馬	37 宀 宀尤无	38 之	39 彡 彡釆豕
4	40 十	41 十	42 ナ	43 ナ	44 大 犭犬	45 艹 艹	46 革	47 力	48 力	49 木
5	50 卄 廾	51 丰 丰申曲	52 曲	53 車	54 戈 戊戈	55 才 丁丬	56 中 虫	57 甲 申	58 夫	59 耒
6	60 口 山屮	61 口 日	62 日 日	63 田	64 田	65 田	66 口口 皿	67 易	68 貝 目	69 呈
7	70 匚 凵屮	71 凵	72 乚	73 フ ウ夕	74 弓 尸艮	75 ㄥ	76 匚	77 刀 刀犬殳	78 勹	79 乛
8	80 八	81 金	82 竹	83 竹	84 人 入	85 食	86 臼 日	87 生 宀气	88 骨 宀丹骨	89 門 門門
9	90 小	91 小 小氺	92 小	93 少	94 忄 小心	95 米	96 尸 尹彐	97 巳 巳巳	98 火	99 九 尤尢川

206

The Principles of Digitalization in Corner Coding

1. If a character is composed of four corners, only the first three corners are used for coding; the last one is ignored.

2. If a character can be completely coded using only one or two main features, the absent corners are coded as 00. For example, 又 (*again*) is coded as 880000.

3. If one feature occupies two corners of a character, those two corners should be treated as one corner. Such a character would have three corners to code. For example, 綠 (*green*) has three corner-features, 糹, 夕, and 水, and is coded as 747233.

4. If two features have completely occupied four corners, these features should be coded according to rule 3, resulting in the first four digits. Two more digits should be added by encoding the upper-left feature of the remaining parts of the character. For example, 樹 (*tree*) should be coded as 495441; 原 (*original*) should be coded as 129030.

5. If a main feature such as 囗, 匚, 門 has completely occupied four corners, it should be coded before the enclosed features, which then should be coded from top to bottom and from left to right. For example, 國 (*country*) is coded as 655330.

6. If an enclosing pattern such as 冂, 几, 戍 has only one opening on the bottom side, it should be coded before the enclosed features. The enclosed features then should be coded in a sequence opposite to the general sequence of corner selection; that is, from bottom to top and from right to left. For example, 風 (*wind*) is coded as 175630.

7. When a pattern such as 辶, 廴, and 走 occupies the upper-left, the lower-left, and the lower-right corners of a character, this pattern should be treated as occupying only the upper-left and the lower-left corners. The character should be coded according to rule 3. For example, 還 (*return*) should be coded as 386609.

8. An aspect of a pattern that has been coded should be completely disregarded during later steps of the coding process. For example, 我 (*I*) should be coded as 305320 rather than 305354. Since the stroke 一 is included in 戈, it cannot be used again in adjacent features.

9. If there is more than one candidate feature, select the one that consists of the most strokes. If two candidate features have an equal number of strokes, select the one with the greater numerical value. For example, 產 (*produce*) should be coded as 040225 rather than 040214.

FIG. 14.1.   Basic units and their equivalent features of the three-corner coding method. (See p. 206)

10. To allow the feature with the most strokes to be recognized, the vertical strokes | and 丿 can be split into parts at the contact point between | or 丿 and other strokes. For example, 串 (*bundle*) should be coded as 562066 rather than 565600.

11. Turning strokes, hook strokes, and 口 should not be decomposed. The character 至 (*arrive*), for example, should be coded as 104774 rather than 101431.

12. Both 十 and 亠 should be coded as 40 when they appear above 口, 四, or 冂. Both 十 and 亠 should be coded as 42 if they appear above 日 or 月. Therefore, 古 (*age-old*) is coded as 406000 and 南 (*south*) is coded as 407840. The character 真 (*true*) is coded as 428062 and 盾 (*shield*) is coded as 276242.

13. If the upper part of a character is symmetric and the central feature is taller than any adjacent features, the central feature should be treated as occupying the two upper corners. For example, 坐 (*sit*) should be coded as 418383 rather than 838341.

14. If the lower part of a character is symmetric, and the central feature is lower than any adjacent features, the central feature should be treated as occupying the two lower corners. For example, 幕 (*curtain*) should be coded as 442061 rather than 444261.

15. When two or more features overlap at a given corner, the one whose component strokes concentrate at that corner has the priority over the other. For example, the character 臾 (*transient*) should be coded as 858300 rather than 838500.

Mental Stages Involved in Coding Characters Graphemically

We have reviewed three different graphemic approaches to input Chinese Characters into a computer. The first one was listed only for historical reasons and it is no longer a viable approach. The remaining two approaches both involve the decomposition of characters into component parts. They differ in the resulting codes, one being a set of radical-alphabet and the other a set of digit symbols. On a closer analysis, the basic processes of encoding a Chinese character into either alphabetic or digital codes are very similar and can be broken down into at least three major stages:

Stage 1. Feature Extraction.   The analysis of a particular character, such as 扷 (*I*), into a set of features (e.g., ㇒, 戈, and 丨).

Stage 2. Feature-Code Transformation.   The conversion of the features into appropriate codes (e.g., ㇒ , 戈, and 丨 correspond to 30, 53, and 20, respectively).

Stage 3. Key-Striking Response.   The transformation of input codes into a series of motor responses.

This stage analysis is offered to aid exposition in the following discussion. We are not proposing a sequential stage model of processing for this domain.

Feature Extraction

Are all graphemic features embedded in a character equally easy to detect? Is there automatic visual-feature processing? According to a model dealing with the perception of visual arrays like pictures and words, pattern detection is the result of automatic unit integration: Small units are automatically integrated into higher order units. This model is called the *pattern-unit model* (Johnson, 1975, 1981).

Automatic Visual-Feature Unitization.   Let a pattern refer to a written symbol such as a word. The processing of a word begins with signals from the retinal receptors, which result in the detection of *simple features* such as curves, diagonal lines, and horizontal and vertical lines. The intersections of any two simple features will be represented by a *juncture feature.* For example, although an upper case *A* would have two diagonal lines and one horizontal line as simple features, it also would have three juncture features that represent the intersections of the three simple features. The juncture features fuse the simple features into a higher order unit that corresponds to a letter. There also would need to be a third type of feature to represent the position of one unit with respect to other units in the same visual array so that perceivers would be able to draw distinctions between items like *saw* and *was*.

If a display such as *word* is presented, the perceiver automatically assigns a single word-level encoding. The perceiver identifies a word by integrating small features into letters, then letter clusters, and finally a word. The word has to be moved from the perceptual system into memory in order to be subjected to attentional analysis. To put it another way, a word is successfully identified when it is moved into memory in a unitary form. However, it is unlikely that a perceiver has available a unitary encoding that could be used for display such as *SBJF*. After an initial attempt to assign a unitary encoding has failed, the perceiver would then have to fractionate the display and move it into memory on a letter-by-letter basis.

The main assumption of the pattern-unit model is that the process of feature unitization is involuntary. It cannot be intentionally discontinued before a unitary pattern is identified. In addition, only the unitary pattern, but not the features from which it is composed, would be immediately available to the perceiver. Small units are already unitized when they are first registered in human working memory and the initial contents of memory would be a single representation for the entire word. If the perceiver's task were to identify a component letter, he or she would have to decode or unpack the unitized representation to make the component information available. In other words, it requires more work and more time to identify a letter that is embedded in a word than to identify the word.

An experiment by Johnson (1975) confirmed the above prediction. A particular item (either a letter or a word) was designated as the target. The subject was then presented with displays containing either a single letter or a single word. When each display appeared, the subject was to indicate by pressing buttons whether it contained the target. The speed with which the subject could make the yes-versus-no decision was measured and compared. The results demonstrated that subjects indeed can identify a word faster than a letter within a word. This finding is taken as evidence that the unitization of visual features occurs automatically. It was also found that words and single letters in isolation are identified equally quickly. This finding illustrated the point that any small pattern that can be assigned a single unitary encoding should be treated no differently than any other such pattern. In a similar experiment, the word lengths employed were 3, 4, 6, and 8 letters. There appeared to be no effect of word length on either the time to identify a target or the time to reject a foil display (Johnson, 1977). Letters in isolation and words of any length can be identified equally quickly.

Although finding a component takes longer than finding the whole word, it appears that subjects are flexible and can decode the word immediately into letters or syllables depending on the task requirement. A study by Turner (1978) employed displays that consisted of compound words like *cupcake* and *lipstick*. The predesignated target for which observers were to search was either the compound word, the first syllable of the word, or the first letter of the word. The results showed that searching for a component was slower than searching for the word, but whether the component was a letter or a syllable seemed to make little difference.

Johnson (1981) demonstrated that not all features can be identified equally quickly. If they are fused into a single higher order pattern, they may be more difficult to detect. In this study, either two diagonals or two curves were presented. The two features either touched to form a unitary figure such as a circle, a *V* or an *X*, or they did not touch each other. When the features did not touch, the gaps between the closest points were either 8.5 mm or 4.0 mm. The subject's task was to determine whether the display contained the target feature (i.e., a diagonal or a curve). The results showed that if the features did not touch, the speed of response was about the same regardless of whether the gap was wide or narrow. If the features did touch, however, the time to respond to a *V* or an *X* was about the same, but it took subjects about 130 msec longer to make an affirmative response than it did when the features did not touch or intersect. The difference of 130 msec (0.13 sec) represnted an increase of about 20% and only an extremely small set of features was involved in obtaining this estimate. A greater difference would be expected when text is involved and a perceiver has to take into account all possible features in the written language.

Three major points have been laid out by the pattern-unit model: (1) Automatic visual-feature unitization: The process of feature integration is relatively involuntary and is not under the active control of the perceiver. The physical complexity of a pattern is irrelevant to the speed of unitization. (2) Decoding of the pattern-level representation: Only the unitary pattern is immediately available to the perceiver and component units become available only after some decomposition procedure has been applied. (3) Disjunction of contiguous features: A component unit that is contiguous to other units is more difficult to detect than a component unit that is not touched by other units.

Effortful Character Decomposition. The above discussion implies that regardless of the encoding method adopted, the visual configuration of a whole Chinese character will automatically and thus inevitably be available to the user. In addition, the number of strokes or feature assemblages should not affect the processing time. That is, a complex character like 杏 (*apricot*) should be identified as quickly as a simple character like 木 (*wood*). But it takes additional effort to identify the component strokes within a whole character.

Three types of graphemic decomposition can be identified in Chinese input methods:

1. *Isolating.* The pattern is divided into parts although each part is not physically contiguous to another. Take the character 茄 (*eggplant*) as an example. The top radical 艹 means grass. The remainder is a compound character 加 (*add*), which in turn is composed of two simple characters, 力 (*strength*), and 口 (*mouth*). According to the pattern-unit model, one should be able to identify the character 茄 as a whole faster than any of its component units. However, he should identify each component unit (艹 , 力 , 口 , and 加) with the same speed regardless of the fact that 力 can also be a component of 加 . The unit 力 embedded in 茄 is, although physically identical to, not necessarily functionally equivalent to the 力 embedded in 加. When the character 茄 is presented, searching for a 力 should take about the same time as searching for a 加.

2. *Disjunction.* One example would be to decode the character 且 (*for the time being*) into 月 and 一 . It should take longer than to decode the character 旦 (*dawn*) into 日 and 一 because the latter requires only isolating. Similarly, the feature | should be easier to identify when it is embedded in 引 (*lead*) rather than in 帚 (*condole*).

3. *Dissection.* This is to divide a single line into two or more parts as though it were cut up into portions with a razor blade. Human beings have a strong tendency to perceive the simplest and most stable figure of all possible alternatives. The pattern ◇ is seen as a diamond in the middle of two lines rather than a *W* on top of an *M*. Similarly, the pattern ⌒ is seen as a semicircle and a straight line rather than a curved line suddenly straightening or a straight line suddenly curving. This intrinsic tendency is described as the law of good continuation (Wertheimer, 1923/1958). One example of dissection is the decoding of 車 (*vehicle*) into 十, 田, and 十. This type of decomposition violates the law of good continuation and is expected to be more difficult than both isolation and disjunction.

Efficiency Measures of Feature Extraction.   An ongoing study at National Tsin Hua University shows that whole character identification (476 msec) is faster than isolating (699 msec), which in turn is faster than disjunction (808 msec) and dissection (869 msec). Although dissection does not differ from disjunction in terms of reaction times, it results in an error rate (.17) at least three times higher than other types of encoding.

Given a representative sample of 400 characters, it took the three-corner coding method 1007 counts of feature identification to encode these characters. Among the 1007 features identified, 46 were whole characters, 615 required isolation, 316 required disjunction, and 30 required dissection. Similar statistics can be obtained for other input systems. Since character-level features are consistently rare in alphabetization and digitalization systems, whole-character identification and isolating can be classified as one kind of decomposition (*simple decomposition*). Since disjunction and dissection do not differ in reaction times, they also can be classified as one kind of decomposition (*juncture decomposition*). The ratio of estimated frequency of simple decomposition to that of juncture decomposition thus might serve as a predictor of feature extraction speed. In the case of the three-corner coding method, the simple/juncture decomposition ratio is 1.91 (661:346). The estimated proportion of dissection (which is .03 or 30:1007 in the case of the three-corner coding method) might serve as a predictor of feature extraction error rates.

Feature-Code Transformation

Once the features suitable for a particular coding method are successfully identified, the user's next task is to make available the corresponding codes, which could be either digits, letters, or stroke-patterns, depending on the coding method. In order to perform this task, one has to learn a list of double items so that given one item of a pair he can provide the other member on his own. In the psychology literature, this type of learning is generally referred to as *Paired Associate Learning* (PAL).

Learning a single paired associate actually involves three components: (1) the stimulus learning, (2) the response integration, and (3) the hook-up or association between the first two.

The Stimulus Learning. The most critical aspect of the stimulus learning is distinctiveness. However, most existing graphemic systems tend to violate this principle. For example, although most input systems provide users with a table that lists all crucial features, the feature-code correspondence is often not on a one-to-one basis. Usually a particular feature is given one code, but the same code is often assigned to two or more features.

Another difficulty is learning to judge whether a particular stroke-pattern is crucial or irrelevant. A user's linguistic knowledge includes well-learned sets of radicals and basic strokes. An input system should take advantage of these natural sets by including all elements in a set as crucial features. However, not all stroke-patterns that the user is familiar with are used in a given input system.

Furthermore, perfect recall of listed features does not guarantee successful feature identification. After all, it is a whole character rather than an isolated feature that is actually presented in the text. The discrepancy between the learning activities (i.e., studying isolated features) and the retrieval requirements (i.e., recognizing features embedded in a character) may create difficulties. The efficiency of encoding performance, therefore, depends on the similarity between the task of stimulus learning and the task of feature extraction. When a feature is embedded in a character, it may be fundamentally altered by becoming a part of a new whole and result in an entirely different mental representation than when it is presented alone. Effective stimulus learning would have to include not only isolated features but also their appearance within characters.

In the discussion of feature extraction, it was pointed out that when a target feature is explicitly specified, identification speed is affected by the part-whole relationship and the presence of juncture features. Imagine identifying the pattern 力, embedded in the character 幼 (Li et al., 1973). Also, in an actual encoding situation, there is no explicitly specified target feature. The user is to recognize all likely features and select the most appropriate ones. As contiguity of strokes is expected to lower the ease of perception of features, violation of natural language habits such as order, position, and completeness of strokes should also be prime sources of difficulty for stimulus learning. This suggestion can be viewed as an expansion of Underwood and Postman's (1960) discussion on extra-experimental sources of interference.

The Response Integration. In most situations, the user needs only to recognize and discriminate the stimulus terms (the features). However, he or she has to recall the response terms (the codes). Most systems adopted frequently seen stroke-patterns, characters, or digits as codes. As in the case of stimulus learning, response recall is easier if codes form a natural set, provide concrete meanings, or are easy to pronounce (Underwood, 1966).

Associative Learning.   The ease of associative learning depends on both the number of features and codes and the quality of the feature-code relationship. The feature-code relationship is difficult to learn when it is randomly assigned or when it is inconsistent with natural language habits.

In summary, three major principles of feature-code transformation have been laid out by the above discussion:

1. *The principle of familiarity.*   The features, the codes, as well as the feature-code correspondence should be as familiar to the user as possible.

2. *The principle of natural set.*   The features as well as the codes should be made up with a complete natural set so that the difficulty of set differentiation can be avoided.

3. *The principle of context independence.*   There should be general rules describing the feature-code correspondence with a minimum of exceptions. When straightforward rules are not sufficient, exceptional rules can be added. However, the same cluster of features should never be provided with different codes that depend on the neighboring features (i.e., the context). Such context dependency will complicate the decision process and slow down the input rate. In an ideal system, the neighbors of a given feature should not bias its coding processes.

The above general principles should be followed on designing a system. In practical tests of the efficiency of the design, six measures might prove to be useful:

1. The total number of features.
2. The amount of practice required to master the feature-code relationship.
3. The speed with which a code is generated (e.g., the mean reaction time of code generation in response to a feature during the last perfect trial).
4. The speed with which a representative sample of Chinese characters is encoded.
5. The error rate of character encoding.
6. The total (or estimated) number of exceptional encodings.

The Key-Striking Response

A prominent efficiency measure of key striking is the number of codes or the size of the keyboard. If the keyboard is reasonably small, the association between a code and a series of finger movements can be formed as a result of motor paired associate learning. An individual can discriminate among the motor alternatives and select the appropriate response as quickly as possible. Visual search plays a minor role in this stage.

On the other hand, if the size of the response set is so large that fine discrimination between motor responses is impossible, visual search will become necessary. For example, a traditional Chinese typewriter has a keyboard containing approximately 3,000 characters. In order to touch-type, each finger would have to conduct over 200 discriminative responses. This would take a lifetime of training. Therefore, the traditional Chinese typewriting has been essentially a visual-search task. Literature has shown that search time increased regularly with increasing display density, which varied from 1 to 4,000 items (Smith, 1968). A smaller keyboard enhances the efficiency of a system in two ways: It increases the possibility of touch typing and it shortens the search time.

A TENTATIVE MODEL OF EVALUATION

For about 30 years researchers have struggled to make the Chinese language compatible with the computer. The problem is how to minimize needs for system-specific training as well as the occurrence of coding collisions. To achieve these goals, at least three graphemic approaches have been taken: whole-character, alphabetization, and digitalization. They all have achieved a reasonable success in reducing coding collisions. But for these systems, there exists a trade-off between the ease of character encoding and that of key striking. A system that is compatible with touch typing requires a great amount of encoding training and a system that is easy to learn requires a great amount of key searching.

In general, difficulties of graphemic encoding occur in at least five aspects: (1) the learning of a system-specific feature set, (2) effortful character decomposition, (3) unfamiliar feature-code association, (4) context-dependent feature selection, and (5) visual search for appropriate keys. However, it seems that the development of a Chinese input device has been very single-minded in that it considers only the fifth aspect, that is, the quantity of keys used. Across the three types of approaches, there are a decreasing number of codes but an increasing amount of coding difficulty. Future research should avoid this kind of one-sided "improvement" and take into consideration human factors involved in all five aspects.

In conclusion, we would like to propose nine measures that serve as possible predictors of the general efficiency of a graphemic system.

Two indicate the ease of feature extraction:

1. The simple-versus-juncture decomposition ratio, and
2. The estimated percentage of occurrence of dissection.

Six measures indicate the ease of code generation:

3. The total number of features,
4. The amount of training required to master the feature-code correspondence,
5. The speed of code generation,

6. The speed of character encoding,
7. The error rate of character encoding, and
8. The amount of exceptional encoding.

One measure indicates the ease of key-striking response:

9. The size of the keyboard.

Measures 1, 2, 3, 8, and 9 can be obtained by simply analyzing the design itself. Measures 4, 5, 6, and 7 would have to be collected by designing standard tests and actually testing a group of people. The system measures are therefore more economical to obtain than the behavioral measures. Further studies with multiple regression analysis can determine the relative predicting power of these measures. An ideal evaluation model should include predictors that are both powerful and economical.

ACKNOWLEDGMENT

Writing of this paper was supported in part by a grant from the National Science Council, Republic of China to Professor Kuang Mei (Grant No. NSC72-0301-H007-01), in part by a research grant from the University of California, Riverside to the second author, and in part by a National Institute of Health Grants #HD13249 awarded to the Salk Institute for Biological Studies.

REFERENCES

Bauer, R. (1985). Chinese character-processing with "Chinese-editor." *Journal of Chinese Linguistics, 13,* 347–349.
Becker, J. D. (1983). "User-friendly" design for Japanese typing. *OSD-T8301,* August.
Caldwell, S. H. (1959). The sinotype: A machine for the composition of Chinese from a keyboard. *Journal of Franklin Institute, 267,* 471–502.
Chang, S. K., Chiu, C. S., Yang, M. H., & Lin, B. S. (1973). PEACE- A phonetic encoding and Chinese editing system. *Proceedings of the First International Symposium on Computer and Chinese Input/Output Systems,* 29–47.
Fang, S. P., & Tzeng, O. J. L. (in press). Graphemic input systems for Chinese characters: A critical evaluation of the current state of the art. *Visible Language.*
Hu, L. R., Chang, Y. W., & Huang, J. K-T. (1978). The digitalized Chinese dictionary: Three corner coding method. *Ming Chuan Journal, 15,* 1–58.
Hung, D. L., & Tzeng, O. J. L. (1981). Orthographic variations and visual information Processing, *Psychological Bulletin, 90,* 377–414.
Johnson, N. F. (1975). On the function of letters in word identification: Some data and a preliminary model. *Journal of Verbal Learning and Verbal Behavior, 14,* 17–29.
Johnson, N. F. (1977). A pattern-unit model of word identification. In D. Laberge & S. J. Samuels (Eds.), *Basic processes in reading: Perception and comprehension* (pp. 91–125). Hillsdale, NJ: Lawrence Erlbaum Associates.

Johnson, N. F. (1981). Integration processes in word recognition. In O. Tzeng & H. Singer (Eds.), *Perception of print: Reading research in experimental psychology.* (pp. 29–63). Hillsdale, NJ: Lawrence Erlbaum Associates.

Kao, M., & Cheng, L-M. (Eds.) (1982). *The psychological studies of Chinese language. I.* Taipei, Taiwan: Wen Hun.

Kao, M. S. R., & Hoosain, R. (Eds.). (1984). *Psychological studies of Chinese language.* Hong Kong: Chinese Language Society of Hong Kong.

Li, H. C., Jen, C. L., Chou, H., Hu, S. P., Shan, S., & Chen, E. T. (1973). A system design for the input of Chinese characters through the use of phonetic and orthographical symbols. *Proceedings of the First International Symposium on Computers and Chinese Input/Output Systems,* 501–511.

Shen, J. S., & Sun, C. C. (1984). *Research on processes of learning to input Chinese characters: A psychological perspective.* Technical Report submitted for publication.

Smith, E. E. (1968). Choice-reaction time: An analysis of the major theoretical positions. *Psychological Bulletin, 69,* 77–110.

Turner, M. (1978). *On the process of letter and word identification within whole word presentation.* Unpublished master's thesis, Ohio State University.

Underwood, B. J. (1966). *Experimental psychology* (2nd ed.) New York: Appleton-Century-Crofts.

Underwood, B. J., & Postman, L. (1960). Extraexperimental sources of interference in forgetting. *Psychological Review, 67.* 73–95.

Wertheimer, M. (1958). Principles of perceptual organization. In D. C. Beardslee & M. Wertheimer (Eds.), *Readings in perception.* New York: D. Van Nostrand. An abridged translation by Michael Wertheimer of Untersuchungen zur Lehre von der Gestalt, II. Psychologische Forschung, 1923, *4,* 301–350. Translated and printed by permission of the publisher, Springer, Berlin.

Yamada, H. (1983). Certain problems associated with the design of input keyboards for Japanese writing. In W. E. Cooper (Ed.), *Cognitive aspects of skilled typewriting* (pp. 305–407). New York: Springer-Verlag.

15

WANDAH—A Computerized Writer's Aid

Morton P. Friedman
University of California, Los Angeles

ABSTRACT

WANDAH (*Writing-aid AND Author's Helper*) is an instructional system designed to assist writers in all phases of writing—planning and organizing ideas, transcribing ideas into print, and editing and revising. The design of WANDAH draws on three areas of research: (1) the analysis of writing as a cognitive problem-solving activity; (2) modern composition theory and research; (3) research on the human-computer interface.

WANDAH has three major components:

1. A word processor designed expressly for on-line composing. The word processor includes such features as split screen, extensive on-line "help" information, easy-to-follow menus, and special, labeled function keys.

2. A set of prewriting aids incorporating principles on modern composition theory to help writers generate ideas and plan their work.

3. A set of aids helping writers review and revise their work grammatically, stylistically, and thematically. These aids include spelling, word usage and punctuation checkers, a style analyzer, a commenting facility, plus aids that create an ex post facto outline of the work and that examine a text for coherence by looking at transition phrases and pronouns.

WANDAH is written in UCSD Pascal and runs on the IBM-PC and similar machines. The evaluation and future of WANDAH are also discussed in this paper.

INTRODUCTION

WANDAH (Writing-aid *AND* *A*uthor's *H*elpher) is the product of a research effort at the University of California, Los Angeles, aimed at studying the use of word processors in the teaching of writing. The research was funded mainly by a grant from the Exxon Education Foundation.

The project grew from two observations: First, writing—especially revising—is, for many people, easier on a word processor than on a typewriter. Second, there is the intriguing suggestion that the writing process itself may be different on a word processor.

For example, Patricia Greenfield (1984), in her recently published book, *Mind and Media,* notes the following about word processors and the writing process: "I was impressed by the changes it made in my thought processes and productive ability: I felt that I could write more quickly and more easily; revision becomes a pleasure rather than a chore" (p. 137).

As the project developed, WANDAH became much more than a word processor. WANDAH[1] became an integrated system of aids to help the writer in all phases of writing—planning and organizing ideas, transcribing ideas into print, and editing and revising. The development team for WANDAH was an inter-disciplinary group representing psychology, instructional technology, computer programming, composition instruction, and English as a second language.

THEORETICAL BASES FOR WANDAH

We believe that WANDAH is one of the first of a new generation of educational software. WANDAH has at least a modicum of intelligence, and in her we see the beginnings of an "expert system" to aid the writer (Walker & Hess, 1984).

WANDAH is based on research in three overlapping areas: First, the overall design philosophy of WANDAH is based on a cognitive model of the writing process proposed by Hayes and Flower (1980). This model views writing as a dynamic process with many constraints. The writer is trying to get ideas into words, use correct grammar, be attentive to the intended audience, write with correct spelling and punctuation, present an organized argument, and so forth. Writing is difficult because the writer has to deal simultaneously with all of these constraints. The essence of WANDAH is this: a design philosophy and a "tool kit" of *heuristic devices* to help the writer to deal with the above constraints and

This program has been published in a commercial version by Harcourt Brace Jovanovich, 1250 6th Ave., San Diego, California, 92101, under the title "HBJ Writer."

avoid cognitive overload. The "tool kit" approach also means that WANDAH is designed to handle wide individual differences in writing ability and style.

Second, the actual implementation of WANDAH on the computer is based on recent *human factors* research on the human-computer interface (Card, Moran, & Newell, 1983). WANDAH is thus based on the user's representation of the problem, not the programmer's view. WANDAH's design involves a minimum of computer jargon, good screen and keyboard design, excellent error correction, and an extensive on-line "help" facility.

Third, WANDAH uses many of the heuristics and teaching methods of modern composition pedagogy. Indeed, many of the ideas for WANDAH came directly from composition teachers who told the design team what they wanted in a computerized writer's aid designed for teaching.

THE WANDAH SYSTEM

The WANDAH sytem is outlined in Fig. 15.1. It is a hierarchical, completely integrated system that permits the writer free and easy flow among its various parts via an extensive menu system.

WANDAH
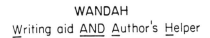

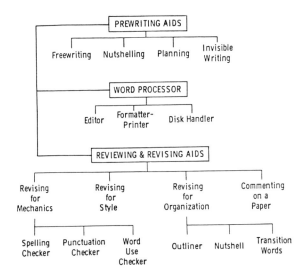

FIG. 5.1.   The WANDAH System.

The Word Processor

A "user-friendly" word processor especially designed to facilitate composing (as contrasted with producing final copy) is the heart of the WANDAH system. The complexities of learning to use a commercial word processing system can introduce a computer overload that will reduce the benefits of composing on the machine. Much care was taken in designing WANDAH's word processor to create a system that is easy to learn and to use. WANDAH has an on-line tutorial, an extensive menu system, an on-line help system and special labeled function keys. It uses the common expressions of English composition rather than computer jargon. The word processor itself is a full screen editor with one or two "windows" onto the text. This allows students, for example, to have an outline on one window and their paper on the other. Or they may have two parts of the same paper or two different papers on the screen at one time.

Prewriting Programs

WANDAH presents a variety of prewriting aids to suit different writing and teaching styles. Writers can use the aids at any time and in any combination.

Nutshelling.   This prompts the writer to type the purpose and audience of the paper, and to compose a brief summary of its main ideas.

Invisible Writing.   Many writers have trouble overcoming the urge to edit each line as it is composed. This program turns off the screen so that writers cannot see the text. The purpose is to "unblock" the writing process: because they cannot see the actual words, they must keep their work's ideas and structures constantly in mind.

Freewriting.   The program urges writers to keep typing without pause; the screen blinks if the writer stops typing for more than a few seconds. Writers may not correct errors or edit while they are freewriting.

Planning.   This asks the writer for the title and main idea (thesis) of the paper, and then for arguments supporting it and possible counter arguments. Once the writer has supplied these, the program allows the writer to select and organize the arguments into a coherent outline.

For all of these prewriting exercises, the work may be saved and later edited or expanded with the word processor.

Reviewing and Revising Aids

Once the writer has created some text—whether a complete draft or only a portion—he or she can subject it to one of the four sets of reviewing and revising aids.

Revising for Mechanics.   This goes over the text and highlights the following common problems:

1. Punctuation—points out unpaired parentheses, quotation marks, and brackets, as well as possibly improper placement of punctuation (e.g., periods, commas) within quotation marks and parentheses.
2. Word Usage—highlights words that inexperienced writers often confuse or misuse. The writer may request on-line explanation of the possible difficulty.
3. Spelling Checker—checks all the words in the text against a stored dictionary and informs the writer that unrecognized words may be misspelled.

Revising for Style.   This program helps writers see certain stylistic features of their texts: abstract words, prepositional phrases, selected gender-specific (and possibly sexist) nouns, "be" verbs, and possible nominalizations. It also provides an analysis of sentence length and paragraph length. The analyses may be printed out.

Revising for Organization.   These aids help writers to analyze the organization of their work. The writer may get printouts from each aid.

1. Nutshelling—similar to the prewriting Nutshelling routine, this tells the writer to compose a nutshell without viewing the draft.
2. Summary Outline—WANDAH presents two outline choices. The writer may receive an outline made up of the first sentence in each paragraph, or the writer may pick the *one* sentence out of each paragraph that best presents the paragraph's main idea.
3. Transition words—This highlights more than 200 selected transition words and phrases, and asks the writer to consider whether or not the paper contains smooth transitions between ideas and points. Too few transitions may mean that the individual ideas are not sufficiently developed. This aid will also highlight nearly 50 pronouns, either alone or together with the transition words and phrases. Inexperienced writers often use pronouns ambiguously and without a clear reference to previously mentioned ideas.

Commenting Facility.   Writers need readers, and knowing how readers react to a written piece can help writers improve their writing. Commenting allows student writers to read each other's work and make comments. Writing teachers or other reviewers may also use this aid to insert comments into papers.

College, junior college, and high school composition students are this program's primary audience. WANDAH will also prove useful to students in advanced college classes, and writers in academic and nonacademic settings.

WANDAH runs on the IBM Personal Computer. All of the programs in the WANDAH system are written in UCSD Pascal to make them transportable to a number of different microcomputers.

EVALUATING WANDAH

WANDAH is currently being tested at the University of California, Los Angeles, and other institutions. Our initial informal evaluations are very positive. High school and college composition students learn to use WANDAH without difficulty. Both students and teachers are enthusiastic about WANDAH and teachers report that its use improves students' writing. A more complete evaluation of WANDAH is now underway in several composition classes at the University of California, Los Angeles.

These initial positive results are encouraging but should be viewed with caution. The novelty of the computer and the enthusiasm of interested teachers are powerful variables that might account for our initial positive results.

Indeed, a fair evaluation of WANDAH is extremely difficult to set up because of the novelty effect and the further difficulty of controlling other relevant variables such as time spent on the writing task and the nature of the curriculum.

A recent review of research on learning from media by Richard Clark (1983) speaks directly to the issue of *evaluation*. Clark's conclusion is that "Media (including computer-aided instruction) do not influence learning under any conditions. . . . The best current evidence is that media are merely vehicles that deliver instruction but do not influence student achievement any more than the truck that delivers our groceries causes changes in our nutrition" (p. 445).

Put very simply, the argument is that the *method* of instruction, and not the *medium* of instruction, affects learning. In the case of WANDAH, this means first, that any simple WANDAH/non-WANDAH comparison wouldn't be sufficient because the method of instruction such as the various prewriting and revising heuristics has not been controlled. Experimental comparisons could be set up with some groups using different heuristics available on WANDAH versus paper and pencil, but these experiments are too contrived and of questionable relevance to the use of WANDAH in real writing situations.

So what are we left with for an evaluation? Our current thinking is that our best investment of effort at this time is in research on understanding and improving WANDAH rather than comparing it with contrived alternatives. This approach may be called "formative evaluation," but it leans toward a suspicion if not outright rejection of summative evaluation in favor of a view called by Malcolm Parlett (1970) "illuminative evaluation." Our interest is not in evaluating the idea of WANDAH, but rather the use of the WANDAH in actual writing situations. We are particularly interested in understanding how WANDAH is used by different teachers and different students.

THE FUTURE OF WANDAH

We have just argued that one reason WANDAH may be effective is because it employs the methods that good teachers use. And, of course, there is probably a sizable novelty effect. But what about the future? Will the computer bring fundamental changes in the way we write and do research?

We conjecture as follows: We might be seeing in WANDAH the beginnings of a more generally useful problem-solving tool for writing and doing research— a cognitive amplifier in the sense that the industrial age produced machines that amplified human physical abilities. The next generation, more intelligent *SUPER-WANDAH* will have a better knowledge of language and will be able to offer more accurate advice on style and grammar. She will have a variety of templates and outlines to prompt the user in organizing ideas. SUPER-WAN-DAH will also allow the user to interact through an intelligent, expert tutor with various data bases of knowledge. The user could thus take notes, try out different structures, search for relationships, and test hypotheses. The user will further be able to direct SUPER-WANDAH to synopsize or abstract relevant information.

This SUPER-WANDAH of the future would certainly do a better job of allowing us to deal with our cognitive load—the constraints on our organizing ideas and writing. But it just might also be a quantum leap in amplifying our problem-solving skills. This is the true promise of WANDAH. It is a research question for the future whether in such a SUPER-WANDAH the argument given earlier about the confusion of medium of communication and method of instruction is no longer valid. If so, then a SUPER-WANDAH, the medium becomes the method (or vice-versa).

ACKNOWLEDGMENT

WANDAH was developed at the University of California, Los Angeles, by the Word Processing Writing Project under a grant from the Exxon Education Foundation: Morton Friedman and Earl Rand, Principal Investigators; Ruth Von Blum, Project Director; Michael Cohen, Principal Programmer; Lisa Gerrard, Design Consultant; Andrew Magpantay and Susan Cheng, Assistant Programmers.

REFERENCES

Card, S., Moran, T., & Newell, A. (1983). *The psychology of human-computer interaction.* Hillsdale, NJ: Lawrence Erlbaum Associates.

Clark, R. (1983). Reconsidering research on learning from media. *Review of Educational Research, 53,* 445–459.

Greenfield, P. (1984). *Mind and media.* Cambridge, MA: Harvard.

Hayes, J. & Flower, L. (1980). Identifying the organization of writing processes. In L. Gregg & E. Steinberg (Eds.), *Cognitive processes in writing* (pp. 3–30). Hillsdale, NJ: Lawrence Erlbaum Associates.

Parlett, M. (1970). Evaluating innovations in teaching. In H. Butcher & E. Rudd (Eds.), *Contemporary problems in higher education* (pp. 145–150). London: McGraw-Hill.

Walker, D., & Hess, R. (Eds.). (1984). *Instructional software.* Belmont, CA: Wadsworth.

Author Index

Numbers in *italics* indicate pages with complete bibliographic information.

A

Ackerman, Z., 48, *57*
Adi, H., 92, 93, *96*
Anderson, D. R., 11, *14*
Anderson, J. R., 101, *107*, 119, *120*, 185, 186, 197, *199*
Andrew, J. D., 29, *31*
Arons, A., 48, *57*, 88, *96*
Aronson, E., 102, *107*
Atkinson, J. W., 103, *107*

B

Baddeley, A., 4, 6, *14*
Bales, R., 49, *57*
Banerji, R., 136, *137*
Bannon, L., 146, *161, 162*
Barr, R., 64, 65, *70*
Bauer, R., 205, *216*
Bayman, P., 33, 34, 35, 38–39, *44, 45*
Beagles-Roos, J., 18, 19, 21, *31, 32*
Becker, J. D., 203, *216*
Benbasat, I., 165, *179*
Berko, J., 64, *70*
Biemiller, A. J., 64, *70*
Biondi, A. M., 85, *86*
Birkner, J., 27, *32*
Birnbaum, D. W., 9, *15*

Block, R. A., 76, *85*
Bork, A., 48, 49, *57, 58*
Bowers, C., 26, *31*
Brannock, J., 88, *97*
Briars, D. J., 116, *120*
Bridge, E., 69, *70*
Broadbent, D. E., 4, *14*
Bromage, B., 33, 37, *45*, 80, *86*
Brown, J. S., 119, *120*, 184, 185, 189, 195, 199, *199, 200*
Bruner, J., 63, *70*
Bruner, J. S., 91, *97*
Buhl, J., 69, *70*
Bundy, A., 186, *200*
Burton, R. R., 119, *120*, 185, 189, 195, *200*
Busse, T. V., 116, *120*

C

Caldwell, S. H., 204, *216*
Card, S., 144, *161*, 165, 176, *179*, 221, *225*
Carpenter, T. P., 110, *120*
Carraher, T. N., 69, *70*
Carrithers, C., 167, *180*
Carroll, J. M., 167, *180*
Case, R., 63, 69, *70*, 119, *120*
Chall, J., 60, *70*
Chang, S. K., 203, *216*
Chang, Y. W., 205, *216*

227

Hayes, J. R., 77, *86,* 114, *121*
Heller, J., 112, 115, *121*
Heller, P., 33, *45*
Herman, D. J., 79, *86*
Hertz-Lazarowitz, R., 48, *57*
Hess, R., 220, *226*
Hinsley, D., 114, *121*
Hoffman, H. R., 9, *15*
Hogarth, R. N., 95, *97*
Holyoak, K. J., 84, *85,* 134, 136, *136*
Hoosain, R., 203, *217*
Houghton, R. C., 165, *180*
Hu, L. R., 205, *216*
Hu, S. P., 213, *217*
Huang, J. K-T., 205, *216*
Hung, D. L., 203, *216*
Huston, A. C., 29, *32*

I

Inhelder, B., 87, 91, 93, *97*

J

Jacob, R. J. K., 174, *180*
Jen, C. L., 213, *217*
Jenkins, H. M., 91, 92, *97*
Johnson, D., 48, *57*
Johnson, M. B., 12, *15*
Johnson, N. F., 209, 210, *216, 217*
Johnson, R., 48, *57*
Jorg, S., 19, *32*

K

Kadane, J., 117, *121,* 124, *137*
Kao, M., 203, *217*
Kao, M. S. R., 203, *217*
Karplus, R., 92, 93, *96*
Keating, D. P., 88, *97*
Kintsch, W., 79, 80, *86,* 124, *136*
Klausmeier, H., 48, *57*
Klein, R. M., 9, 11, *15*
Kolers, P. A., 165, *180*
Kramer, A., 164, *181*
Krepelka, E. J., 116, *121*
Kruk, R. S., 164, *180*
Kuhn, D., 88, 91, *97*
Kuhn, T. S., 5, *15*
Kurtz, B., 48, *57*

L

Landauer, T. K., 165, *180*
Larkin, J. H., 116, 117, *120, 121,* 124, 125,
  133, *136, 137*
Lauber, B. A., 28, *32*
Lawson, A., 92, 93, *96*
Lawson, A. E., 88, *97*
Lehrer, A., 11, 12, 13, *15*
Lester, F. K., 124, *136*
Levin, S. R., 11, *14*
Lewis, C. H., 167, *180*
Li, H. C., 213, *217*
Lin, B. S., 203, *216*
Linn, M. C., 42, *44*
Lochhead, J., 40, 42, *44, 45,* 112, *121,* 124,
  137
London, B., 189, *200*
Long, J., 165, *180*
Lyle, J. L., 9, *15*

M

MacBride, L., 12, 13, *15*
Mack, R. L., 167, *180*
MacKenzie, L., 12, 13, *15*
MacWhinney, B., 65, *70*
Maier, N. R. F., 104, *107*
Malone, T. W., 198, *200*
Mandler, G., 80, *86*
Mansfield, R. S., 116, *121*
Marsh, G., 60, 61, 64, 69, *70,* 78, *85*
Mawer, R., 136, *137*
Mayer, R. E., 33, 34, 37, 40, *44, 45,* 80, *86,*
  109, 110, 112, 114, 116, 117, *121,* 124,
  125, 126, 128, 129, *137,* 168, *180*
McArthur, D., 191, 192, *200*
McConkie, G. W., 80, *86*
McDermott, J., 125, 133, *136*
McKay, D., 33, *45*
McKinnon, J. W., 76, *86,* 88, *97*
McLuhan, M., 22, *32*
McPeck, J. E., 89, *97*
Meline, C. W., 21, *32*
Meyer, B. J. F., 80, *86*
Miceli, L., 7, 8, *15*
Michalski, R. S., 186, *200*
Miller, R. B., 149, *161*
Miller, W., 165, *180*
Moeller, G., 165, *181*
Monk, A., 164, *180*
Monty, M. L., 146, *161, 162*

Subject Index

A

Achievement, 54
Active learning, 80, 101–102
Advanced organizer, 80
Algebra planning methods, 186, 195
Algebra transformation rules, 186, 195
Algebra word problems, 40, 110–118, 123–136
Algorithms, 100, 109–111, 118–120, 124
Alphabetical system, 202
Alphabetization approach, 202, 204–205, 212, 215
Analogies, 75–76, 79
Analogy strategy, 68
Applied cognitive psychology, 3, 6–7, 11, 13, 59–60
Arcade-game play, 24
Arithmetic, 109–111, 118–119
Artificial intelligence, 185
Associative learning, 214
Attitudes, 99–101, 104–107

B

Background knowledge, 167–168, 173–174, 178, 179
Basal reading approach, 65–66
Base (known) domain, 80
BASIC, 34–37, 40–43

B

Behaviorism, 59–60
Benchmark task, 167, 173–174, 177–178
"Bottom-up" strategy, 66, 125
Bugs, 119

C

Cangjie system, 204–205
Causal relationships, 92–95
Chunked knowledge, 197
Coding collision, 205, 215
Cognitive applied psychology, 3, 6–7, 11, 14
Cognitive behavior, 50, 51
Cognitive development, 8, 17, 20, 42, 59, 62–64, 69, 78, 87
Cognitive engineering, 163, 179
Cognitive skills, 183–199
Combinatorial reasoning, 89
Command languages, 141, 156–159
Communications control module (CCM), 169–178
Communication control system (CCS), 164, 168–179
Communication network, 168–169, 176–178
Competitive behavior, 55
Composition, 198
Computer programming, 26, 33–44
Computers, 17, 19–20, 22, 26, 29, 33–44, 47–51, 54–57, 61, 141–161, 163–179, 183–199, 201–216